EAP now!

English for Academic Purposes

students' book

KATHY COX ▪ DAVID HILL

PEARSON
Longman

Pearson Education Australia
Unit 4, Level 2
14 Aquatic Drive
Frenchs Forest NSW 2086

www.pearsoned.com.au

For further information on material adapted from Tony Buzan *Use Your Head* (1995) visit Buzan Centres Limited web site: www.buzancentres.com; email: buzan@buzancentres.com; Tel: +44-1202-674676.

Acquisitions Editor: Andrew Brock
Project Editor: Jane Roy/Rebecca Pomponio
Copy Editor: Sonnet Editorial
Proofreader: Editing Solutions
Cover and internal design by *Diℓign* Pty Ltd
Cover illustration by Getty Images
Typeset by *Diℓign* Pty Ltd

Printed in Malaysia, PP

12 13 14 15   11 10 09 08 07

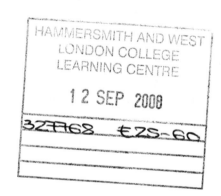

National Library of Australia
Cataloguing-in-Publication Data

Cox, Kathy, 1945-.
EAP Now! : English for academic purposes.

Bibliography.
Includes index.
ISBN 1 74091 073 7.

1. English language – Foreign speakers – Problems, exercises, etc. 2. English language – Study and teaching – Australia – Foreign speakers. I. Hill, David, 1969-.

428.2407094

PEARSON
Longman

An imprint of Pearson Education Australia (a division of Pearson Australia Group Pty Ltd)

preface— students' book

English for Academic Purposes Now! has been created for you as a course book in English for Academic Purposes. It has been written with the intention of fulfilling a need for a single book which includes the many skills that you will require in order to be successful in English tertiary education (education after high school or post-secondary education). If you wish to attend college or university, or to study in an English speaking country where you will need to have Upper Intermediate or Advanced level skills, or if you are a native speaker of English who would like to expand your repertoire of English language skills and prepare for university, this book will assist you to achieve your goals.

As experienced English language teachers ourselves, we have brought to the writing of *EAP Now!* our own understanding of the learning difficulties and cultural challenges that you will face as you undertake study in a language other than your first. There are intellectual shifts which may be required of you as you learn new ways to present your ideas and arguments in writing and speaking contexts; you will learn to question texts rather than accept them as absolutely always correct; you will make decisions as to the importance of the World Wide Web for your study; you will increase your ability to become independent learners and you will strive for cross-cultural understanding and critical cultural consciousness as a result of your studies within this course.

Learning the academic skills necessary to succeed in a tertiary environment can be an arduous, difficult and complex process. You, the student, and your teacher will set out together on a journey that this course book provides. You will work together in order to attain these skills. They are the skills and thinking modes that you will need in all the various academic environments (universities and other institutions) into which you are heading.

We believe this course book breaks new ground for EAP and we sincerely hope you enjoy using it.

Kathy Cox
David Hill

to the student

Aims and focus of *EAP Now!*

English for Academic Purposes Now! is designed to help any student who wishes to succeed in a further or higher education course which is taught in English, in particular at university or college.

The aims of this students' book are to assist you to comprehend, question, evaluate and produce a range of discourses which are relevant to academic contexts.

We hope to have anticipated some of the problems you may face and to help you overcome them as you begin your preparation in English.

Each unit contains eight skills which are thematically linked. These are:

1 Writing
2 Grammar
3 Speaking
4 Listening
5 Reading
6 Critical thinking
7 English for the Internet Age
8 Learner independence and study skills.

1 Writing

In *writing*, a great deal of work is done around essay construction and the types of essays you will be required to produce. You will learn to differentiate an explanation from an exposition, and description from argument. Answering exam questions is covered and there are tasks teaching you how to avoid plagiarism and how to reference your essays properly. Many models of varying text types are included.

2 Grammar

Grammar is taught as being a part of whole texts, that is, it is within readings, discussions and lectures rather than separate from them. You will be asked to examine the social and cultural situations (or contexts) as well as the texts themselves. Some traditional grammar points (such as articles) have been included in case you need to work in those areas.

3 Speaking

Speaking sections assist you to solve problems that you may face on campus. You will learn how to make academic requests to individual lecturers and to consider what an appropriate request comprises. You will also practise tutorial participation skills such as learning how to participate actively. Units cover research, preparation and presentation of various oral tasks required at university—these are called oral presentation skills.

4 Listening

When *listening*, you will hear many varieties of spoken English (some nine different accents are used in the recordings).

There are two lengthy lectures of over a quarter of an hour, and, although a 'real' university lecture may go on for as long as three hours, the principles, the vocabulary, the format and the content of the recording are academic and will give you authentic practice in listening to a lecture and taking notes.

5 Reading

The *reading* texts are designed to reflect the real world and are placed in real world social contexts. Each time you read, it is hoped you will ask the following: Where is this text from? When was it written? Who wrote it or might have written it? What could be their purpose for writing it? Who is the audience it is written for? What possible slant or bias is communicated within the text?

You will learn about study reading and reading to interpret essay questions.

6 Critical thinking

Critical thinking is meant to introduce you to ways of thinking and of approaching texts that will be expected of you in further and higher education courses.

You will think about power relationships and should keep in mind that even as you learn the language of academia in English, you are learning the language of powerful institutions.

We want you to respect and admire your own academic culture and add to it your knowledge of the one you are learning. You bring to the classroom and your classmates a rich knowledge of your own.

7 English for the Internet Age

We believe the Internet has a great future and you will see its importance grow. It is included here as a resource for use in academic research and as a window to the wider world outside of your classroom. Students are provided with opportunities to learn navigation around sites, and terminology that will assist you to carry out projects.

In English medium tertiary settings, a great deal of learner autonomy is expected of students—you have to carry out independent research at the library, and make judgments within your essays in addition to summarising the opinions of others. Even students who have grown up in the culture often find this a shock.

8 Learner independence and study skills

Learner independence and study skills is designed to help you to find out how you learn best and to assist you to learn to work independently.

Students like to know how they are going in terms of their own progress. Your teacher can assist you by providing answers to the activities. Additionally, peer-group evaluation and self-evaluation is included. You will learn how to keep records of your own progress and note what you do outside of the class to help your English.

The tasks are varied and relevant to EAP purposes. We sincerely hope you find that some are fun as well as a challenge.

A note about terminology

We have used the expression 'English-medium tertiary education' to cover post-high school education in countries such as Australia, Canada, Ireland, New Zealand, the UK and the USA where English is the main medium of instruction and that have many academic traditions in common. These academic traditions include such things as ways of writing and speaking (rhetorical style), methods of assessment (eg assignments, presentations or essay exams) and the concept of plagiarism.

Having said this, there are variations between the academic culture of each of the native English speaker countries and also between different disciplines within the same country. Furthermore, if you are from a country with a European academic tradition, by working through this book you may be surprised at what you notice about the differences between your own academic culture and the cultures within English-medium tertiary education.

Kathy Cox   David Hill

About the authors

Kathy Cox

traces her teaching back through her maternal ancestors. Originally from and educated in the USA, she graduated from the University of Hawaii and taught first in Pago Pago, Samoa, before travelling to New Zealand, Thailand, Malaysia and Singapore, finally settling in Australia. She has taught English for Academic Purposes to many students over the years, and their learning and social experiences form the basis for this book.

Kathy's research interests in Australia have focused on students' listening skills; drama and the part it plays in enhancing language learning; academic writing; and identity. She has a keen interest in teacher professional development and, as a Director of Studies for a decade, implemented successful programs.

David Hill

grew up in the north west of England. After studying at the University of Durham, his interest in other cultures took him around the world and eventually inspired him to become a teacher of English to speakers of other languages.

After teaching English to adults in the UK, Turkey and Japan, David settled in Australia where he now teaches and coordinates EAP and exam preparation for Australian Pacific College.

Acknowledgements

Kathy would like to acknowledge the numerous and memorable students and colleagues from whom she has learned so much, particularly those from academic preparation programs at University of Wollongong and APC. Special appreciation goes to Murray for his ongoing love and support during the years this project took to complete.

David would also like to express his appreciation to the students, friends and colleagues with whom he has had the pleasure of working over the years, most recently at APC. He extends his special thanks to Chie, whose help, encouragement and support has been immensely valuable.

table of contents

Unit 4 — Literature   77

Unit 5 — The news   107

Unit 6 — A global connection: the environment   135

Unit 7 — On campus   155

Unit 8 — A global connection: economics   177

Unit 9 — Language   201

Unit 10 — A global connection: cross-cultural communication   225

HWLC LEARNING CENTRE

Contents map

Unit Number and Theme	Speaking	Writing	Grammar	Listening	Reading (skills, texts)	Critical Thinking	English for the Internet age	Learner Independence & Study Skills
5 *The News*	Oral presentation skills and oral discourse markers 108 Oral presentation assignment 110	Compiling bibliographies and avoiding plagiarism 111	Pronominal referencing and participant tracking 112 Tense review: perfect tense 117 Register revisited 121	Distinguishing fact and opinion: Talkback radio program about fast food 122	Newspaper editorial 124 Purpose or intention of writer: identifying bias 127	Language as power: becoming a critical reader 129	Internet research project: refugees 102	Assignment research skills 134 Vocabulary for tertiary purposes: university word lists 134
6 *A Global Connection: The Environment*	Environmental issues 136 Tutorial Participation Skills 2: asking questions 143 Using visual aids in presentations 145	Research Reports 136 Mini research project 140	Reporting verbs in citation and paraphrasing 151 Future predictions 154	Tutorial participation skills 2: listening for main purpose 142 Tutorial questions: business and the environment 142	Skimming and scanning 152	Distinguishing between fact and opinion 148	Using library catalogues on the Internet 142	Reading outside class 141
7 *On Campus*	Academic requests and replies 2 156 Further oral presentation skills 159 Constructive criticism 168 Giving an oral presentation 169 Tutorial participation skills 3: discussion techniques 171	Extended essay assignment 175 Issues in education 176	Hypothesising and speculating 172 Conditionals 173	Academic requests and replies 2 156 Critical listening and peer marking of oral presentations 169	Examining texts from different points of view 162 Using a text to assist in making and supporting judgments 166	What is the purpose of education? 170	Referencing from electronic sources 161	Speaking outside class 175
8 *A Global Connection: Economics*	Effects of global trade 189	Compare and contrast essays 178 Cause and effect 181 Exposition schema (argument and discussion) 183	Nominalisation 186	Predicting main focus: university lecture on deregulated global trade 190	Vocabulary and scanning 192 Skimming for main ideas 199	Issues around globalisation 189	Internet research project 198	Faculty requirements within different disciplines 200
9 *Language*	Languages quiz and discussion 202 Persuasion 204 Explaining grammar features of your own language 221	Dissecting essay questions for meaning 209 Exposition – revisited and expanded 212 Answering short answer questions 222	Articles 207 Language of persuasion 204	Language of persuasion 204 Interview with a student about listening skills 217	Finding implied meaning 216	Reflecting on cultural aspects of persuasion 206	Internet directories 208	Listening outside class 219 Language learning experiences: Poster session 220
10 *A Global Connection: Cross-Cultural Communication*	Cross-cultural discussion of common beliefs and practices 232	Genre overview 226 Precis, abstracts and introductions 234 Extended introductions 237 Conclusions and summaries 237 Describing charts and graphs 240	Review: register 227 nominalisation 229 referencing 230 Modality 231	Note-taking from a lecture: cross-cultural communication 233	Peer review of extended essays 234 Precis and abstract 234 Interpreting information from charts and graphs 240	Critical Cultural Consciousness: political protest 232	How does and will the Internet affect you, as a student? 244	End of course friendship compliments! 246

u n i t

1

education

Education sows
not seeds in you,
but makes your
seeds grow.

KAHLIL GIBRAN

Skills focus: In this Unit, you will learn and use the following skills:

Speaking

✓ *Discussion*
✓ *Academic requests 1*

Discussion

Task A: Exploration of previous education system

Will (or Has) learning in my new educational setting be (or been) the same as learning in my home country?

Discuss in your group the following questions. Ask and tell each other the answers.

1 What do you expect learning at *tertiary level* to be like.

2 How many *hours per week* did you study when you were studying in your own country?

3 What *skills* did you concentrate on when studying English in your own country?

4 How important was *speaking and listening* in your study of English?

5 Are you going to study an *undergraduate* or *postgraduate* course?

6 What is your *field* of study?, eg will you study in the Humanities, Applied Science or Engineering, or Business?

What were your conclusions about learning and studying at home?

Briefly write your conclusions:

_____

_____

_____

_____

_____

Academic requests 1

Task A: Thinking about academic requests

Work in your group on the following. In any educational setting, you may need to speak to a supervisor, a lecturer or someone else in authority.

Can you think of any questions you might wish to ask any of these people?

Make a list of possible questions:

1 _____

2 _____

3 _____

4 _____

5 _____

- Most information is given to you in your course outlines. However, if you find yourself unable to complete an assignment on time, you must ask (request) your lecturer to allow you more time to complete it. Do this early! Don't ask for time extensions on the day it is due!

- Think about the relationship between yourself and your lecturer, tutor or supervisor. Are you equals or are they more important and powerful than you are?

- Your requests need to be polite and must include all the information needed by your supervisor.

Task B: Creating a model

Use the fields below for a request for an extension of time to complete an assignment. The model could be used for both spoken and written requests.

- Student name: (Your name) _____

- Subject studied: _____

- Name of lecturer: _____

- Name of department: _____

- Title of essay or assignment: _____

- Date due: _____

- Reason for needing extra time: _____

- Date you can hand it in: _____

- Number of days you wish the extension to be: _____

 LEARNING tip

You may ask this directly if you can get an appointment or email your lecturer at least two weeks before the due date saying that you do not think you can complete the assignment on time and may you please have an extension of time.

Task C: Role play

In pairs, play a student and the supervisor. Ask your supervisor for an extension of time based on what you wrote in the previous task.

Critical thinking

How do you like to learn language?

Task A: Quiz

Take the following quiz by circling the letter that is your answer and that is closest to your feeling.

1 *In my English class:*

   A. I would rather write most things down that I hear.

   B. I would rather practise with a partner out loud.

   C. I would rather sit quietly until I know the answer.

   D. I would rather get the chance to speak than to be quiet.

2 *When working in pairs in class:*

   A. I like to write what is going on.

   B. I like to be the leader.

   C. I like to be quiet and let the other person speak.

   D. I like to speak.

3 *When speaking in class:*

   A. I always want to be corrected.

   B. I like the teacher to allow me to finish without corrections in the middle.

   C. I feel embarrassed and know I am making mistakes.

   D. I want mistakes corrected immediately.

4 *When in class:*

   A. I wish I were outside walking or swimming or enjoying myself.

   B. I enjoy working and learning English.

   C. I don't enjoy it, but I know I must study hard.

   D. I like my classmates and know my English will improve if I complete my work.

5 *When it comes to grammar:*

   A. I like to memorise the rules by heart.

   B. I seem to use grammar correctly most of the time without memorising.

   C. I like to keep practising until the rule is not in my mind.

   D. I don't need rules, because I can hear changes in speech and see them in writing.

6 *When it comes to vocabulary:*

   A. I like to memorise all vocabulary.

   B. I like to try to use new words as soon as I have heard them.

C. I like to write down new words before I use them.

D. I like to practise new words outside of class.

7 *Outside of class:*

A. I hate making mistakes when talking.

B. I like to try to talk to people as much as I can.

C. I always worry and feel embarrassed to speak because I will make mistakes.

D. I don't care too much about mistakes, I just enjoy talking with someone.

8 *When I'm listening:*

A. I can't hear well because I'm nearly always nervous.

B. I don't hear every word, but can usually follow the **gist** of what's being said.

C. I want to hear every word so I know I understand the conversation.

D. I try to follow even when I don't know all the words.

gist
substance;
main points

On the next page, check your score to determine the 'type' of learner you are.

If your score is between 8 and 10 inclusive, look at box X.

If your score is between 11 and 13, look at box Y.

If your score is between 14 and 16, look at box Z.

Box X

Your learning style is accuracy driven. You like to be sure you are right before speaking and writing. You may be a little shy when it comes to communicating, particularly in unfamiliar situations.

You are probably an analytical person and are neat and tidy with your notes and personal dictionary.

Box Y

Your learning style is communicative. You like to make friends easily and want to talk to everyone.

Your style is relaxed and you are fairly comfortable in new situations. You will try to talk, even if you make mistakes.

You may need to work harder towards accuracy in your writing when it comes to academic English.

Box Z

Like many people, you have a combination of learning styles and ways in which you like to learn. You are relaxed and confident in some situations but like to be accurate and speak correctly in others.

Your task will be to work on study patterns that make the most of your talents, which consist of both these qualities.

How to calculate
your score

As = 2

Bs = 1

Cs = 2

Ds = 1

Add all your answers together.

SCORE _____

1 Find a person in your class who is the opposite type of learner to you and discuss with them what you think are the strengths and weaknesses of each learning type.

2 Make a list for yourself of suggestions that you think you might try after discussion with that person. Can you think of ways to **diversify** your learning style? Could you experiment with a new idea after speaking to someone different from yourself?

diversify
add to; broaden

Listening 1

Register: the new student

Register involves the particular situation of a social activity with its particular participants (where, with whom, about what, how). Register occurs in all discourse (both talking and writing are discourses). Register must be appropriate. If you write to your mother, it will be a different register than if you write to an important politician in your country to complain about an injustice. (I'm assuming here, that your mother does not happen to be an important politician, but of course she could be!

Task A: Listening for register-appropriate speech or writing in appropriate situations

Listen to (and follow along with) the extract titled: *The New Student* (Recording number 1)

You will hear the following vocabulary on the recording:

> stunned mullet: slow person who does not understand
>
> tool: useless person, stupid
>
> vegies: shortened word for vegetables
>
> bloody: swear word
>
> you'll know what for: you will be punished in some way
>
> cut it out: stop doing something

Recording script

 ① **RECORDING NUMBER 1 (10 MINUTES, 20 SECONDS)**

TITLE: **The new student**

Answer the questions that follow the recording script

1   ... the taxi cab dropped me off in front of a huge building on a busy city street. I was excited because this was my first day as a student of English and an English speaking country. It was even my first day in the country because my plane had only arrived last night.

2   So, I walked into the reception area and looked up at the sign. It said Oxcam English School, floor number 7. I got into the elevator and up I went. Ah, I was so excited. When the doors opened, I could smell a wonderful smell, like cooking of some sort. *A little strange*, I thought to myself, but checked myself because I knew this was a different country and things would all be different here. So I told the receptionist my name was Jim Park and she looked it up on a long list. *Ah, here you are, Jim. Listen, your details need inputting but right now go to room 10, the class has already started and we can sort out the money and things like that later, chef hates anyone being late!*   5   10

3   This seemed a little bit strange to me because I had already paid all my fees, but I was happy enough to obey and felt quite glad to think that I would be learning English right from the first minute I arrived. So I said to her in the best English I could, *I thank you very deeply and regretfully request you regarding my lateness due to the taxi having encountered much of traffic and in travelling other obstacles.* The receptionist looked up briefly, smiled at me and waved her hand in the direction of the hallway.   15   20

4   So, I found Room 10 and walked through two huge, swinging doors. A person at the back of the room came quickly over to me and put this garment thing over my head and then tied it around my waist, and handed me a long, sharp knife and then pointed to a bench where I was to stand. She did all this holding her finger to her mouth and gesturing for silence while glancing nervously up to the front of the room where the male teacher was standing.   25

5   Now, I just did as I was told but thought, what are these strange costumes every student is wearing? Now, it seemed we would learn English and protect our clothing at the same time. I was staring around the room at everybody and I was so surprised to see students cutting something with knives. And while I was standing there, the teacher left the front of the room, came up to me and actually yelled very close to my face! He said, *Get shoppin' and stop standin' there like a bloody stunned mullet.* This was certainly no greeting I had ever studied, and I also did not know why I should go shopping, but I knew the vocabulary word mullet and I knew that it was a fish so I looked around for a fish but saw none. So I said to him, *I am sorry, I am not able to locate the fish mullet and also may not locate any in the nearby area of my sight.* He said, *Yeah, right ... ya' smart arse' what didja say?* So I repeated, more simply this time, *I have no fish.* He seemed to understand this time but he was even more angry, and answered me with, *Of course there's no bloody fish, we're on vegies today.* Now, in any language, I always have trouble with   30   35   40

prepositions and while I was thinking about *on* as opposed to *in* or *of* as well as wondering what *vegies* meant, he continued even more loudly, *Get on with it, ya' tool, cut it out! Sort the vegies and chop the sh'llots or you'll know what for quick bloody enough!* Although I understood many of these words individually, there was nothing at all I could make sense of, except maybe *tool* which I thought must mean the knife because I was still holding it in my right hand. Ahhh, perhaps I was to cut something up? So, I considered him for a moment, but then I rejected the idea. He was embarrassing me in front of the whole class. 45

6 Now, I had been warned that methodology for learning English was very different in other countries and I was being as patient as I could, but still, how was this helping my English and why was my English teacher so very mean and aggressive to me? I had also heard that teachers were very kind. So, I began to think to myself I had made a big mistake to come to this school when he said, *You know whatcha' need son, ya' need English.* Well, *need English* I understood very clearly because it was true and it was also why I came to this school, although I was definitely not his *son. Yes, I need English,* I said to him. But then he looked even angrier and he said, *Well then, why dontcha' go to bloody English school? There's one in the buildin'!* Now I was very confused, and so I asked him, *You mean this is not then my English school, yes? I am informed with the receptionist administrator of the location of my English instruction room and my instructor whom is Mr Chef.* He screwed up his face again which became redder in colour now, and he said to me, *Say again, mate?* So, I said it again, because I know *say again* is the imperative in English, so I repeated what I said before, but even more slowly, as it appeared my English teacher did not understand my English and I had been working very hard on it. I thought maybe he was a very bad communicator, especially for an English teacher. He looked at me with a puzzled look for a moment and then said loudly, *Of course this is not yr bloody English class, this is the cooking school—errrr, wait a minute—yr on the wrong floor!* 50 55 60 65

7 So, he actually said sorry to me then I went back to the elevator and realised I had simply stepped out onto the wrong floor. When I found my real English class, things were much, much better. 70

1 Did you think anything about the text was amusing?

_____

_____

2 What was amusing?

_____

_____

3 Why do you think it was amusing?

_____

_____

4 What was the actual misunderstanding between the two participants in the story?

_____

_____

5 How does the language make it funny?

_____

_____

6 What words did you notice the student used that were very formal or very high **lexis**?

_____

_____

7 What do you think makes the student's speech inappropriate?

_____

_____

8 What words did you notice the chef using that were colloquial or simple?

_____

_____

9 When people are talking at 'cross purposes', ie they don't understand one another and are not communicating, is it always funny?

_____

_____

10 Provide examples. In your group, tell one another about any incident that has occurred where you did not understand someone or where they did not understand you. Tell about any incident where you could not communicate or where a misunderstanding led to you not understanding someone else or not being understood yourself.

> ### Task B: Listening—differences between spoken and written register

You have heard, in Task A, a person speaking who was using the wrong register. He was too formal and used a lot of nouns which were rather high vocabulary (or lexis). In academic writing, a lot of nouns and noun groups appear, whereas in speaking, a lot of verbs and verb groups appear.

1 Complete the table on the following page, using the two texts provided. They are both about survey sampling.

2 How many words are there in each text? How many in each sentence? Count the words.

Text 1

I used survey sampling when I did my first research project. It was about how many people lived in my neighbourhood and who those people were. I needed statistics in order to discover the demographics around where I lived. You can use survey sampling in a lot of disciplines and I used it because I knew it was an accepted method.

Text 2

Survey sampling is a quantitative method of research which is a 20th century phenomenon with most of its growth since the 1930s. Today, it is a widely accepted method for providing statistical data on an extensive range of subjects. Disciplines such as sociology, social psychology, demography, political science, economics, education and public health all rely on sample surveys.

Task C: Analysing evidence between spoken and written register

1 Fill in the grid below by locating the nouns and noun groups and the verbs and verb groups from the two texts concerned with survey sampling.

	Nouns/noun groups	Verbs/verb groups
Text 1		
Text 2		

2 What are your observations about the differences between these two texts?

_____

_____

_____

_____

Writing

✓ Planning essays
✓ Explanations
✓ Paragraph formatting 1

Planning essays

Task A: Discussion

With a partner discuss the questions that follow, asking each other questions relevant to your own country of origin. For example:

1 How would you explain what an essay is in your country? Does it exist?

_____

_____

2 What do you have to do in your own language to explain something, for example, how to feed a baby?

_____

3 What structure do you use in your language to explain?

_____

Task B: Definition of an essay

Choose, and circle from the possible definitions below, a definition for the English word, *essay*.

1 *n.* 1. A story of events, experiences, or the like, the act or process of narrating, (*Macquarie Dictionary* 1183).

2 *adj.* 1. Pertaining to or of the nature of books and writings, esp. those classed as literature: literary history (*Macquarie Dictionary* 1035).

3 *n.* 1. a short literary composition on a particular subject (*Macquarie Dictionary* 595).

You should not have been tempted by the answer 2, as it displays the abbreviation for adjective at the front of the definition. This definition defines *literary*. Answer 1 limits you to narration, and essays can be of differing types. This definition defines *narrative*. Number 3 is the correct answer.

Thus, if you must write 'a short literary composition on a particular subject', how will you begin? The first strategy is to understand the question you are being asked to write about. (There will be more about this in Unit 9, page 209.)

■ Planning your answer using your understanding of the question/s is the first step.

■ The second strategy is to learn the structures of various essays in English.

Task C: Three different types of essay questions

Read the following three essay questions.

1 Explain the life cycle of a butterfly.

2 One very important issue surrounding families today is the issue of the working mother. Women should not be allowed to work until their children are at least 12 years old. Discuss.

3 China in the 21st century is committed to strengthening exchange and cooperation with countries around the world. What are the historical and political factors which have led to this policy shift and what will be the possible economic consequences?

In order to analyse an essay **question** on any topic, students working in an English medium in tertiary education are expected to make judgments.

What is judgment? According to the *Macquarie Dictionary* definition 4, it is 'the forming of an opinion, estimate, notion, or conclusion, as from circumstances presented to the mind'.

In other words, based upon the reading you have done when researching your essay topic, you must make a decision and form an opinion.

Task D: Understanding key phrases

What are key phrases? How do you find them? Read the three essay questions a second time and locate and circle the following words:

- explain
- what are
- what will
- discuss

What words or phrases are located before or after the above words?

Now examine the sentences below and write a brief explanation of what you think you must answer in each question:

1 Explain the life cycle of a butterfly.

_____

_____

2 One very important issue surrounding families today is the issue of the working mother. Women should not be allowed to work until their children are at least 12 years old. Discuss.

_____

_____

_____

3 China in the 21st century is committed to strengthening exchange and cooperation with countries around the world. What are the historical and political factors which have led to this policy shift and what will be the possible economic consequences?

_____

_____

_____

Look at these types of essay plans/outlines:

1. Map type essay plan

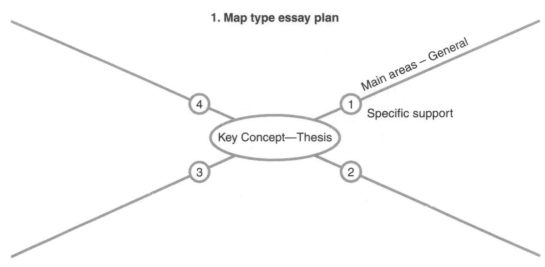

Main areas – General

Specific support

Key Concept—Thesis

2. Sequenced and numbered outlines

```
I
   A
      1
      2
      3
         a]
         b]
II                        or
   B
      1
      2
      3
III
   C
      1
      2
      3
         a]
         b]
IV
   D
      1
         a]
      2
         b]
V
   E Conclusion:
      1  Summary
      2  Recommendation
```

```
Main idea
1   support
2   variation
3   support
    a]  further support

Next main idea
1
2

Next main idea
1
2
3
```

3. Circles connected with arrows

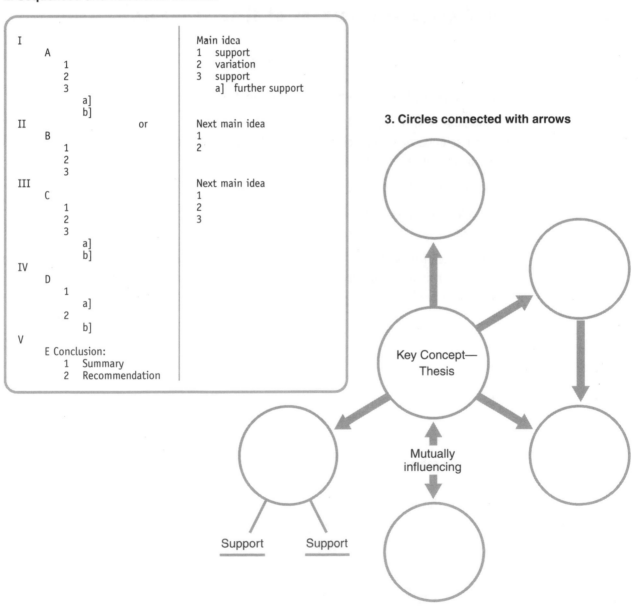

Key Concept—
Thesis

Mutually
influencing

Support   Support

Using the key phrases, make an outline following the model that you like best:

1   Map type essay plans with lines from key ideas to subsequent ideas;

2   Sequenced and numbered outlines;

3   Circles connected with arrows.

Before beginning, decide which type of essay you are being asked to write.

1   Will you explain something—as in an explanation essay—in this case, life cycle of a butterfly?

2   Will you have to argue and prove a point? This is an argument essay about working mothers. Even though the word *'discuss'* is the direction, you must actually argue a case and form an opinion one way or the other in this essay.

3   Will you write an exposition which includes explanation, discussion and argument (an exposition essay), in this case China in the 21st century?

Each of the above types of essays has methods of development. Each has characteristics that you can learn. Begin with an explanation!

Explanations and discourse markers of time sequence

Task A: Structure of an explanation

What is an explanation? What is an explanation essay?

All language is situational. It has a social function. Explanations in writing are usually found in science or social science. They often use the simple present tense and explain things or processes in an order or sequence.

The structure for the *explanation essay* titled *What is a tutorial?* is as follows:

1   Introductory statement which lets the reader know something general about the subject.

2   A sequenced explanation. Sequencing can be temporal (time markers are used = time sequence) or participatory (the same participant is used as the theme). The steps are linear a → b → c → d

And/or

A
↓
B
↓
C
↓

schema
diagram, plan

Examine the **schema** on the following page to see the structure of an *explanation essay*.

The text on the following page is an explanation of a tutorial at a Western tertiary institution. The *explanation* applies to undergraduate students.

Introductory
statement which
lets the reader
know something
general about
the subject

A definition
of terms

1 Tutorials occur in all Western university systems. The term *tutorial* derives from *tutor* which means instructor. A tutorial comprises an instructor and a group of students. It used to mean a small group of students, but today, there may be as many as 60 or 70 in a group or as few as eight or ten. So, what is a tutorial and what does it have to do with you, the student? 5

2 First, students attend lectures within their chosen fields of study. These lectures take place in large halls with seating for up to 300 or even 1000 students. Students must listen carefully and take notes while the lecturer is speaking. Students do not usually interrupt the lecturer in order to clarify something they do not understand or did not hear. 10

3 After the lecture, students should review their notes and prepare for their tutorial. The tutorial will be held in the same week as the lecture, but with fewer students. The tutor or instructor will not usually be the same person who gave the lecture in the hall.

A sequential
explanation

4 While students attend their tutorials, the tutor will point out important, relevant issues or points that were made at the lecture. They may also ask for students' input in the form of a discussion or prepared paper. 15

5 During the tutorial, a student is allowed to ask questions, to speak and indeed, at times, they are required to speak whether they are prepared or unprepared.

6 Following the tutorial, students will have time to prepare assignments that may have to be submitted to their lecturer and/or their tutor. You will learn more about this later in this book. 20

Task B: Staging in introductions

1 <u>Underline</u> the *introductory* general statement.

2 <u><u>Double</u></u> underline the *definition* found in the introduction.

3 <u><u><u>Triple</u></u></u> underline the sentence which reveals the *purpose* of the writer's explanation.

Task C: Time discourse markers

Name as many time markers as you can think of.

For example, *secondly* or *next*.

_____   _____   _____

_____   _____   _____

Write each time marker from the text, *What is a tutorial?*

_____   _____   _____

Examine three structures of explanation essays again. Match the titles below to the possible structures of explanation essays listed beneath them by placing the numbers next to the correct letters:

1 Explain the life cycle of a butterfly.

2 One very important issue surrounding families today is the issue of the working mother. Women should not be allowed to work until their children are at least 12 years old. Discuss.

3 China in the 21st century is committed to strengthening exchange and cooperation with countries around the world. What are the historical and political factors which have led to this policy shift and what will be the possible economic consequences?

4 Explain the causes of youth unemployment and the effect it has upon young people.

5 Explain the four seasons which occur in many parts of the world.

6 It wasn't until the 1960s that the rights of minorities became a focused issue for many Western countries. Trace the history of the policies in Australia which led to the end of the 'White Australia' policy in 1974.

Possible structures

A. Steps in a linear process _____

B. Steps in a cyclical process _____

C. Explanation of something that has factors and conditions, reasons and effects
_____

Task E: Writing an explanation

Write a brief explanation of something that you know about in relation to education in your own country. Use the model above (*What is a tutorial?*) and use temporal sequencers, ie *time markers* (words that signal time connection).

_____

_____

_____

_____

Paragraph formatting 1

Task A: Understanding what makes a paragraph

Read the following:

A paragraph in English is like a little essay all on its own. It has an introduction, a body and a conclusion. The introduction is the topic or initial sentence, the body is made up of sentences which provide concrete, supporting evidence of the topic or about the topic and the conclusion is the last sentence of the paragraph. Other terminology that may be clearer is **theme** for sentence 1, **support** for other sentences and **rheme** for the last. The theme is all the information up to the first verb, the support is just what it says— support (props up, verifies, holds up, gives meaning to the first sentence), and the rheme is where new information is allowed to be introduced.

So:

1 Theme/topic sentence

2 Support sentences

3 Rheme/concluding sentence.

Here's a model paragraph which is at the <u>beginning</u> of an essay (thus it is the <u>*introductory paragraph*</u>) where a student who is studying to become an English teacher has been asked the following essay question:

ESSAY QUESTION: Consider and evaluate Rubin and Thompson's description of the 'good language learner'.

In the past ten or fifteen years a great deal of research has been carried out in the field of **Linguistics**. A significant portion of this research has held as its focus the learner and how learners actually acquire or set about to acquire language. More specifically, much of the research has been concerned with learning strategies and **cognitive** styles and in particular with the '... identification of learning strategy preferences with a view to **isolating** those characteristics of the 'good language learner' (Nunan, 1991:78).

Linguistics
the study of language

cognitive
thinking

isolating
discovering

Examine the following table:

THEME or TOPIC SENTENCE	In the past ten or fifteen years a great deal of research has been carried out in the field of Linguistics.
Sentence 1 Also: STAGE 1—A general statement (Linguistics is general)	
CONCRETE SUPPORTING EVIDENCE Sentence 2 Also: STAGE 2—More information, sometimes a definition	A significant portion of this research has held as its focus the learner and how learners actually acquire or set about to acquire language.
RHEME or CONCLUDING SENTENCE Sentence 3 Also: STAGE 3—Scope and focus of the entire essay signalling what will come next	More specifically, much of the research has been concerned with learning strategies and cognitive styles and in particular with the '... identification of learning strategy preferences with a view to isolating those characteristics of the 'good language learner' (Nunan, 1991:78).

This paragraph follows certain other rules because it is the *first or introductory paragraph* of the essay. It has stages. All introductions in English have stages. There are at least three stages to an introduction. Look at the stages outlined in the table on the previous page.

Task B: Identifying paragraph requirements

In the following three paragraphs, underline and identify:

1 the topic sentence;

2 concrete supporting sentence/s;

3 concluding sentence;

4 find stages 1, 2, and 3 if you think the paragraph is an ***introduction***;

5 if a paragraph is not an introduction, then do not identify the 3 stages outlined above.

Paragraph 1

ESSAY QUESTION: Define survey research and discuss the method.

Survey sampling is a quantitative method of research which is a 20th century phenomenon with most of its growth since the 1930s. Today, it is a widely accepted method for providing statistical data on an **extensive range** of subjects. **Disciplines** such as sociology, social psychology, demography, political science, economics, education and public health all rely on sample surveys.   5

extensive range
many

disciplines
subject areas

Paragraph 2

Guling, with its curious English-style villas, has a number of beauty spots. Perhaps the best known is the Cave of the Immortal, where the Daoist monk Lu Dongbin is said to have mastered the secret of everlasting life. The Botanical Garden is the only sub-alpine one of its kind in China. Visitors can also see the former residence of Generalissimo Chiang Kai-shek.   10

Paragraph Three

ESSAY QUESTION: Refugees seeking safe havens around the world are becoming a global issue. Discuss.

Some twenty years ago, this writer read that in the new millennium, the biggest problem on earth would be homeless people seeking refuge. These people, it was said, would sail from port to port because their own countries were ruined as a result of pollution, war or famine. Other homeless peoples would be living in their own countries, but would have to live on the streets without shelter or   15 employment. Sadly, it appears that this prophecy has begun to come true as countries that are United Nations members seek solutions to the growing number of refugees from a growing number of countries.

1 Write at least one paragraph based on the models above. The paragraph topic should be a subject you know about; for example, the subject you are studying or are going to study at university or business college, or any other English medium tertiary institution.

2 Exchange your paragraphs with another student and check them using the checklist your teacher will provide.

Reading

✓ *Personal learning styles*
✓ *Identifying theme/skimming*
✓ *English-medium tertiary education*

Personal learning styles

There are two reading tasks.

1 Skim the text below without reading every word.

2 Note each topic sentence at the beginning of the four paragraphs. Topic sentences are bolded for you. You have *two minutes* for this task.

TITLE: **Personal learning styles and learning strategies**

1 **The 5th century Greek philosopher, reformer and teacher, Socrates, used a method of questioning students as a method of teaching.** Socrates believed that 'no one is wiser than you' (Apololgy 21A). The main idea was that learners should be active participants in their learning and not trust that knowledge is learned by being a passive recipient. 5

2 **This ties into current theories of language learning and studies of language.** These theories maintain that users construct reality through the use of the language. Language learning is characterised by certain strategies and research has analysed the strategies of good language learners over the years.

10

3 **Good language learners are known to carry out a number of tasks.** They are supposed to be willing to make guesses, take risks, have a strong desire to communicate, listen to themselves speaking and monitor it, transfer one thing they have learned to new situations, and work cooperatively with teachers and other students in order to develop their language learning.

15

4 **One researcher, Howard Gardner (1983), suggests that individuals have at least seven different intelligences.**

Identifying theme/skimming

Task A: Ask a partner

1 Was two minutes enough to read anything?

2 Did the topic sentences give you some understanding of what you were going to read?

3 What were two themes that the topic sentences told you about? *(Theme comes at the beginning of the sentence and includes all the words up to the first verb.)*

Task B: Write

1 Make a list of the four topic sentences.

_____

_____

_____

_____

2 In each bolded sentence, underline the words up to the first VERB. That is the *theme.*

3 Write the four themes of the four paragraphs from the text.

Task C: Understand what you have read

Answer the following questions concerning the text *Personal learning styles and learning strategies.*

A: True or False

1 Socrates believed that learners should be active participants in their own learning.

_____

2 Good language learners do one special thing. _____

3 There are more intelligences than one. _____

4 One thing that a good language learner does is to make guesses. _____

B: Now list all the tasks that good language learners are known to carry out:

a] _____

b] _____

c] _____

d] _____

e] _____

f] _____

English-medium tertiary education

Task A: Orientation to the field using prediction and skimming

Below is a text discussing some aspects of (some things about) English medium academic traditions. Before you read:

1 Write three points you think the text will discuss.

_____

_____

2 Discuss academic traditions in your own countries. For example, what is the structure of your education system (ie kindergarten begins at 6 years old, next, we go to primary school, etc)? Also write what traditions apply concerning higher education. Who goes and how expensive is it?

3 Skim the text first. When you skim, read only the first and last sentences of each paragraph. Three minutes is the time limit.

TITLE: Western education systems

1 Mainstream education systems in most English-speaking countries are broadly similar to each other. Education in general refers to a result and is produced by instruction, training or study. It is also the process involved to obtain this result. This essay will explain some of the common features of typical systems in the United Kingdom, Australia and the United States and give a brief overview of the 5 organisation of education in these countries. However, it should be borne in mind that variations on these systems are not just possible but common, due to the fact that in these countries, the responsibility for organising many aspects of education is at the state (USA and Australia) or county (UK) level. Other English-speaking countries, such as New Zealand, Canada and the Republic of Ireland, 10 have similar systems, but discussion of those is beyond the scope of this essay.

2 Before looking at the organisation of these education systems, it is important to take an overview of what they value and what their overall aims are. These values and aims have changed considerably over the last five decades or so under the influence of the results of educational research and thinking as well as through 15 political influence. As a result, the previous emphasis on memorisation of facts and theoretical knowledge has shifted towards analysis and interpretation. For example, a history essay may include dates and events, but a student would gain higher marks for showing why the events happened, or why they were important.

3 Creativity has also been emphasised, especially in subjects such as English, 20 where for many years such things as grammar and spelling were removed from the school curriculum, and students were expected to write their own stories and other texts, without instruction about how to do it. The result was judged on the impression it made. However, a return is now being made to more traditional

areas of learning such as grammar. Learning by doing is also encouraged—in 30
science lessons, instead of being told what happens when one chemical is
combined with another, students would first mix the chemicals and observe what
happened, then compare the results with what was expected. In most subjects,
knowledge is seen as a means to an end, that is, something that can be used in
some way, and is usually not learnt for its own sake. In languages for example, 35
grammar is taught as a way to make communication clear, and communicative
ability is tested more often than grammatical knowledge, but a student who can't
use grammar well will not achieve high scores on a communicative test. To
reflect these aims, exams usually focus on the application of knowledge rather
than just repeating it. Therefore, for example, essays that give facts as reasons 40
for an opinion are valued more than essays that simply describe.

4 Methods of instruction fit in with the aims of education. Active learning, that
is, learning by doing, is often encouraged over passive learning strategies such
as memorisation (Commonwealth of Australia, 2002). If the teacher simply gives
facts which the students then learn, this is seen as a bad teaching strategy and 45
is referred to in a disparaging way as 'spoon-feeding', as when a mother gives
food directly to a baby. Instead, good teaching is seen as setting up situations
in which students find things out for themselves, preferably in a varied,
interesting and motivating way which caters for the wide range of different
personalities and learning styles that exist in any class. 50

curricula
study plans
trend pattern,
fashion

5 Exams remain an important part of **curricula** in Australia, the UK and the USA,
although the **trend** is very much towards forms of continuous assessment, such
as essays and other assignments contributing to the overall score for the course,
or practical sessions (especially in the sciences) or larger projects that involve
research or writing a report based on the students' own reading of the subject. 55
The amount of continuous assessment generally increases at the higher levels—
it is rare to find an undergraduate university course which is assessed only by
exams, and at the master's level, most courses have no exams.

culminates
ends

6 The main source of funds for most schools in each of these countries is the
government. The proportion of private schools varies. Education normally 60
culminates in major public exams, whether at private or public schools. Therefore,
both public and private schools generally teach, especially in later years, to the
same curriculum.

non-compulsory
not required
compulsory
required

7 As for the way in which education is organised, it usually begins with a period
of **non-compulsory** pre-school or kindergarten education. For example, in 65
Australia, parents are encouraged to send their children to pre-school for two
years before **compulsory** education (DETYA, 2000). Compulsory education begins
at different times in different countries: usually just before the 5th birthday in
the UK (BBC, 2001), and at age 6 in North America (Fulbright Commission,
2001) and most parts of Australia (DETYA, 2000). 70

socialisation
mixing with
others

8 Primary or elementary school lasts for around six years, and focuses on basic
literacy and numeracy skills, creative skills such as art, as well as **socialisation**
and with a varying element of sport and physical education. Children spend

most of their time in the same class with the same teacher, although occasionally subject specialists are brought in, or students are timetabled to spend a lesson or so each week with a teacher who has a strength in a particular area such as science or art. A large part of lessons is spent with children working together in groups, and as a consequence, lessons can be quite noisy. Children sitting in **regimented** lines of desks, working individually on text book exercises in silence is regarded as a thing of the past in these countries. Schools are commonly decorated with paintings and posters produced by the children themselves, and considerable efforts are made to ensure that the study environment is bright, cheerful and friendly. In the USA, elementary school is often referred to as grade school: each year is called a 'grade', follows a set syllabus, and students have to pass an exam to move to the next grade the following year.

regimented
military style

75

80

85

9 After primary or elementary school, the next phase of students' education (usually at age 11 or 12, depending on the country) is rather different in **character**. Instead of having the same teacher most of the day, pupils move from classroom to classroom to study different subjects, each taught by a different, subject-specialist teacher. The actual organisation of this period varies between countries and sometimes from area to area (eg, the UK), with sometimes all students from the beginning of this period to 18 years old being at the same school, usually known as a high school (or sometimes secondary school or grammar school in the UK), or this period being divided between two schools, middle school and high school (some parts of the UK), or junior high and high school (most of the USA). Work gets more advanced as the student gets older, culminating in major public exams at age 16 and/or 18. However, it is often just before this point that compulsory schooling comes to an end: students are allowed to stop attending school after their 15th or 16th birthday in each of these countries (BBC, 2001; DETYA, 2000; Fulbright Commission, 2001), though in practice this isn't common. By this time, students have specialised to some extent, in that they choose many of their subjects. In the UK, this is quite extreme—after 16, students are, until quite recently, expected to choose only three subjects, which could be as narrow as 'double maths' and physics, and very soon the content they are studying is at a similar level to the first year at university in the USA (Fulbright Commission, 2001), where the education system favours breadth of knowledge, with, for example, university science students being required to study subjects from the arts or language departments.

character
type

90

95

100

105

110

10 Most countries have a wide range of options at the next ('tertiary') stage of education, but basically this **boils down** to two main alternatives. For the more academically inclined, there are universities and junior colleges (USA), while for those wishing for a more practical course, or a trade qualification, colleges of further education (UK) or technical and further education colleges (Australia). After the first (or 'bachelor') degree, it is possible to progress to master's degrees, then to PhD programs, by which time the **focus** is almost entirely on the student's own original research (except in some North American cases). The first degree is known as 'undergraduate' study, and any course that requires a first degree as condition of entry is a 'postgraduate' degree.

boils down
results in/
comes to

focus
emphasis

115

120

Thus, western education systems have many common features, especially in terms of their aims and methodology, but under the surface there are a significant number of differences, which anyone visiting any of these countries for educational reasons would do well to become informed about.

References

BBC (2001) *Secondary Schools*, BBC News
http://news.bbc.co.uk/hi/english/education/uk_systems/newsid_115000/115872.stm (6 May 2002).

Commonwealth of Australia (2002) Australian way of studyng, *Study in Australia*
http://studyinaustralia.gov.au/Contents/WhatToStudy/AustStudy.html (21 April 2002)

DETYA (2000) Australia Country Education profile, 3rd Edition On-line. Canberra:
DETYA. http://www.detya.gov.au/noosr/cep/australia/index.htm (21 April 2002)

Fullbright Commission (2001) *School Education in the USA*.
http://www.fulbright/co.uk/eas/school/school/htm (12 May 2002)

The structure of the explanation essay above is as follows:

There is an introductory statement which lets the reader know something general about the subject. There is a sequenced explanation. Sequencing can be temporal (time markers are used = time sequence) or participatory (the same participant is used as the theme and constitutes evidence.

Task B: Writing, recognising stages

1 Underline the introductory general statement.

2 Underline the definition found in the introduction.

3 Underline the sentence that reveals the purpose of the writer's explanation.

4 Highlight or underline markers of time—temporal sequencers. These are words like next, after that, finally.

Discussion

5 You may have noticed that there are several brackets with a name and a date, for example: (Detya, 2001). These correspond to lines ('entries') in the bibliography at the end. Speculate or tell other people in your group about the purpose of these.

6 Explain the similarities between your education system and what you have just read.

7 Explain the differences between your education system and what you have just read.

Task C: Writing an explanation essay using your own knowledge

Write a text/essay outlining the education system in your own country using the text above as a model.

Grammar

Cohesion and avoiding sentence fragments

You need cohesion in your writing so that the writing makes sense to the reader.

What is cohesion?

1 Cohesion comes first from knowing what you want to say—ie **meaning.**

overall structure
whole plan

2 You need to understand the **overall structure** of the type of writing, reading or speaking you are engaged in and have an understanding of the **context.**

context
background, situation

3 You must use whole sentences and use correct **discourse markers/sentence connectors/links** between and within sentences and paragraphs.

> **Task A:** Examining cohesion in texts—sense or no sense?

■ Read the text below and see if it makes sense to you. Is it sensible or non-sensible?

Tim's story and a couple of TV shows I have watched recently got me thinking about just what we ate. More importantly, just what are all these chemicals going to do to us? Piperohal—extensively used as a substitute for vanilla. Benzyl acetate—used to give ice cream its strawberry flavour. It is used as a nitrate solvent. Chemical additives are much less expensive than the real thing.

You might almost have been fooled into thinking this paragraph makes sense because it is about the same thing which is something to do with chemicals in foods. However, it is *nonsense* because:

1 Who is Tim? A writer cannot simply begin with such a specific idea (Tim's story), because the reader does not know who Tim is, nor what the story is.

2 What is Tim's story?

3 The next sentence begins with the sentence connector, *More importantly*—more importantly than what? Than Tim's story that the reader knows nothing about? What is the reference to something important? The first important thing needs to be stated **previously** for the words *more importantly* to be used.

4 Sentence 2 begins *more importantly* and then goes on to use *these*. What does *these* refer to? It must **refer back** and there is nothing earlier in the writing to which *these* may refer.

5 Piperohal—extensively *used as a substitute for vanilla* is not a sentence. It needs the verb 'is' after the theme or main idea which is the chemical name, Piperohal.

6 *Benzyl acetate* ... is not a sentence. It needs the verb 'is' after the chemical name.

7 The last sentence—*chemical additives are much less expensive than the real thing* is a statement of fact but it does not relate to the information above. It has nothing to do with Tim, and it does not explain.

Read the re-written paragraph below.

I recently read a story about a 13-year-old boy, named Tim, who committed suicide. Some doctors believed it was due to chemical imbalances brought about by food additives that Tim could have been allergic to.

Tim's story and a couple of TV shows I have watched recently got me thinking about just what we ate. Many foods, particularly ice cream, use chemicals. Piperohal is used extensively as a substitute for vanilla and benzyl acetate is used to give ice cream its strawberry flavour (it is used as a nitrate solvent). We eat these foods and enjoy them, but, more importantly just what are all these chemicals going to do to us? Chemical additives are much less expensive than the real thing, so I think companies are tempted to use them and will continue to do so, perhaps at the expense of our health.

1 Underline all differences you find in the re-written text.

2 Make a list of the additional information that was needed to make it make sense.

_____

_____

_____

3 What is the topic of the paragraph now?

_____

_____

_____

4 What is Tim's story?

_____

_____

_____

Listening 2

Markers which indicate main ideas: library orientation talk

Listen to the following *University Library Orientation Talk*.

When speakers speak, they 'signal' you as to what may come next. In this listening, try to listen for the order, main ideas, definitions and when the conclusion will occur. Listening for signals will help you.

Task A: Listening for signals or cues (discourse markers) which signal (point to) important ideas and features of a listening

(2) As you listen to Recording number 2 tick how many times you hear the following using the grid below.

Lecturer signals order/using the following phrases		Lecturer signals importance (main ideas)		Lecturer signals definitions		Lecturer signals conclusion or end of part or whole	
I'm here to tell you ...	☐	The most important thing ...	☐	What I mean by that is ...	☐	Finally...	☐
First ...	☐	You also need to know ...	☐	There are several ways to look at ...	☐	To sum up ...	☐
Next ...	☐	It's essential that ...	☐	For example ...	☐	In conclusion ...	☐
		You certainly need to know	☐				
Now ...	☐	There is/ there are a couple of important ...	☐			So ...	☐

Task B: Listening for specific information

Listen to the *University Library Orientation Talk* again and answer the following questions as you listen.

1 How much does it cost to get an inter-library loan?

_____

2 What does she say is the 'most important thing to remember'?

_____

3 Why is it 'essential that' you bring your student card to the library?

_____

4 How much is a library fine for a day?

_____

5 For how long can you borrow popular books?

_____

6 For how long can you borrow books from the reserve collection?

_____

7 What happens to you at the end of the year if you have library fines which are outstanding?

_____

8 What is one of 'several things' that can help you find information?

_____

9 What are the names of the two libraries discussed in her talk?

_____

10 May anyone request an inter-library book loan?

_____

English for the Internet Age

In this section we cover reading—more practice with explanation; identifying definitions; and writing—register.

> ### Task A: Identifying stages in an explanation essay and skimming—further practice

Using the text below (from a book for new computer users, titled _A Mug's Guide to Using Computers_),

1 Read the introduction and mark the stages.

2 Skim the rest of the text and for each topic below write the number(s) of the paragraph(s) to which it most closely corresponds:

  i using websites

  ii speeding things up

  iii web addresses

  iv starting

  v organisation of home pages

  vi domain names

Chapter 3: Using the Internet

1   The Internet is wonderful research tool, and using it can really help you find the information you want. But first, you should get to grips with the basics.

2   The first thing to do is to start your web browser, which is a program that lets you view Internet pages (also called web pages). These are not like pages in a book—they are all different sizes and don't have numbers—really they are   5 documents on the Internet. The most popular browsers are called Navigator and Explorer. Find the icon (remember what that is—a little picture) on the screen which has one of these names next to it and double click. Then the program opens! If you get a strange error message, don't worry. It probably means you're not connected to the Internet. Just ask someone who knows about computers,   10 or jump to Chapter 16 of this book. But if not, that's great! Now, find a box labelled 'Location' or 'Address'. Inside the box, you'll find some strange gibberish starting with 'www'. This stands for the World Wide Web, one of the most common ways of using the Internet. It is usually just called 'the web' because computer people hate using long words. It is a vast collection of information   15 on millions of computers all around the world, most of which can be accessed from your computer, right now! Sounds fantastic, doesn't it!

3   So, smarty-pants, how do we access all this information, I hear you ask? Well, I'll show you. In the box, type a web address (for example, www.bbc.co.uk) and press the enter key on your keyboard. And, hey presto, before long, you'll see   20 the home page of guess what? The BBC from the UK, of course! So, how could you guess the organisation so easily? Because the web address usually gives us lots of information about what the website is. Working from right to left, that is, backwards for English speakers, the first thing we see is 'uk'. This of course, indicates the country. Most countries have a two letter code, for example,   25 Australia is 'au' and China is 'cn'. But be careful—this doesn't always truthfully show you the country of origin. For example, a little group of islands in the South Pacific has made bags of money recently because its code is 'tv'—so of course TV companies have paid millions to use the code. And you'll find many websites which don't have these letters ... mostly from the USA. I wonder why   30 that happened??! By the way, if you want to impress your friends, you can tell them that web addresses are technically known as URLs, which stands for 'Uniform Resource Locaters'. Sounds like something to help a soldier who's lost his clothes!

4   Going further backwards, the next letters show (or at least pretend to show)   35 the kind of organisation which 'owns' the site. You can see what these mean in table 1.

Table 1: **Meanings of some common top level domain names**

Meaning	Abbreviations in countries which like longer words	Abbreviations in countries which like shorter words
Educational/academic	.edu	.ac
Organisations (usually non-profit organisations)	.org	.org
Network service providers (the companies through which you connect to the internet)	.net	.ne
Companies	.com	.co
Government, including local government	.gov	.gov

5   After that are some letters for the name of the organisation, or whatever the
owner chooses—for example, www.doggiecatcher.com—try it—it really exists!!
By the way, this name, in this case 'doggiecatcher', is often called a 'domain   40
name', though technically '.com' and the country codes are also domain names.
Anything after a slash ('/') refers to file names and folder names of pages of the
website, a little bit like the way you save word processing files.

6   So, now that we know what web addresses mean, let's move on to how to use
the site. Look again at the screen. What you can see is the 'home page', that   45
is, main document, of the website. From here you should be able to get to every
section of the website.

7   How? Well, there should be lots of underlined words on this page. It means that
if you click on one of these, you'll be transported to another page, that is,
another document. Do it! The website is really just a collection of pages like   50
this one, connected together with hyperlinks, which are the underlined words
like the one you just clicked on. Again, computer people dislike long words so
they shorten this to 'link'. Clicking on a link is called 'following a link', and
doing this several times means you're 'navigating' the web, or, if you have no
particular purpose, 'surfing the net'. Congratulations on your new skill!   55

8   So, how are home pages organised? Well, they vary but usually the main links
are down the left hand side or along the top. These take you directly to the
different sections of the site. Sometimes there will be a separate side panel, or
a frame, with these main links. When you go to another page, often this panel
stays the same. This will help you find the information you want quickly.   60

9   A very useful trick is to use the right mouse button. Doing this is known as
'right clicking' and when you do it, you'll see a little menu of items appear like
a genie from a magic lantern. Without touching the mouse buttons, move the
mouse up slowly until you come to something saying 'Open in New Window',

then click on this. A new window will open, and you can move between windows   65
in the normal way as mentioned in the previous chapter. This is great if you
have a slow Internet connection, because instead of waiting for a page to open,
you can be reading one while another is opening. Saves a lot of time!

Task B: Reading—scanning; identifying methods of defining; Internet vocabulary

▨ You need pens or highlighters of two different colours for this task.

1 This is a race!! Using one colour each, who in the class will be first to circle or
   highlight all the following words in the text you read titled *A Mug's Guide to Using
   Computers*?

web browser/browser	internet pages/web pages	icon
www/World Wide Web	web	web address
domain name	slash	home page
site	hyperlink	link
following a link	navigating the web	surfing the net
frame	right clicking	

2 Look at this example from the text (lines 3–4):

   '... *your web browser, which is a program that lets you view Internet pages*, ...'

   i Which word is being defined?

   _____

   ii What is the word's meaning?

   _____

   _____

   In the same sentence, 'which' is a relative pronoun. So, one way to give a definition
   is to follow the pattern:

   word + relative pronoun + meaning

   where **word** is the word being defined.

3 Now, for each of the words in step 1, circle or highlight their meaning in a different
   colour from the one you used before, on the text.

4 Write the highlighted examples in the table on the following page, next to its pattern.

   After checking the answers, the table will be a useful reference for your future
   writing and reading.

Pattern	Example from the text
word + relative pronoun + meaning	... your web browser, which is a program that lets you view Internet pages ....
word ... ... they are meaning	... Internet pages ... basically they are documents on the Internet
word (meaning)	icon (... it's a little picture)
abbreviation. This/which/that stands for full expression	
word ... ... It is meaning	
for example	
meaning ... is/are ... called (a) word	
meaning ... is/are ... known as word	
word, that is, meaning	
full expression ... shorten(ed) to abbreviation	
meaning means ... word	
meaning, or (a) word,	

5 The words you highlighted in Task B are all useful later in this book and in your future studies. Check that their meanings are clear to you, and ask your teacher if they aren't.

> ### Task C: Language features of informal writing

■ You've probably noticed that this is an informal text. But what makes it informal?

1 Find and mark on the text (where possible) in a new colour examples of the following language features of informal texts.

- 'And' and 'But' at the beginning of sentences.

- Informal vocabulary, such as _____ and _____.

- Relatively short, simple sentences.

- Use of imperatives (verb with no subject to give instructions).

- Informal punctuation, eg exclamation mark (!).

- Extensive use of pronouns like 'you', 'your' and 'we', which include the reader or writer directly.

- Idioms, such as _____.

- Redundancy, that is, saying something more times than is necessary. For example, _____.

2 Think of some other examples of informal written texts that might have these features.

_____

_____

_____

_____

Task D: Writing—giving meanings

Choose a topic that you know something about. Write an explanation of it (academic style or an informal, humorous 'Mug's Guide' style). Try to use a variety of techniques for explaining meaning.

Learner independence & study skills

How to use this book in and out of the classroom

Task A: What's in this book?

1 Look at the Table of Contents, starting on page vii at the front of this book.

a] What sections come before Unit 1?

_____

_____

b] Skim these sections. How do you think they can help you? Many books have similar sections, so it's useful to know their purpose.

_____

_____

2 Look at the Contents map on pages x and xi at the front of this book. Where will you look:

   a] if you're going to write an argument essay, and aren't sure you remember all the features of one?   Unit ___ page ___

   b] if you've heard that Internet directories are useful, but aren't sure how exactly to use them or how to find them?   Unit ___ page ___

   c] if you want to listen to some tutorials to find out more about them?   Unit ___ page ___

   d] In this Unit, you've already done some work on academic requests. In which unit will you find further practice on this?   Unit ___ page ___

 LEARNING t i p

> This book was designed to help you in two ways:
> - to prepare for tertiary studies in English
> - as a reference for you to keep and use throughout your tertiary studies (yes, even after your EAP course has finished!)

Task B: Using the cross-references

Cross-references are given to help you find where the skill you are working on has previously appeared in the book, or where you can find more practice later in the book.

To practise using cross-references, answer the following questions:

a] Look at Unit 3, page 61. A cross-reference appears which says 'See Unit 2, page 43'. How can this help you?

_____

b] Look at Unit 4, page 78. The cross-reference says 'See Unit 1, page 16'. How can this help you?

_____

c] Look at Unit 4, page 86. The cross-reference says 'See Unit 1, page 15; Unit 2, page 48; Unit 3, page 66'. How can this help you?

_____

Other helpful features in this book are:
- margin notes next to essays to explain vocabulary;
- paragraph numbers beside texts;
- line numbers beside texts;
- headings to each task which tell you why you are doing the task;
- a summary page at the beginning of each Unit which shows what you will study in the Unit; and
- an index for quick reference.

unit 2
clan and kinship

Show me your
mother's face;
I will tell you who
you are.

KAHLIL GIBRAN

Skills focus: In this Unit, you will learn and use the following skills:

Speaking

Discussion: orientation to this Unit's topic

> ### Task A: Orientation discussion

1 In groups, look at the family-related words below and explain to the group the ones you know. If there are some words that no one knows, check their meaning in a learner's dictionary.

br<u>i</u>ng (children) up (vb)	<u>e</u>lderly (adj)	s<u>o</u>cial ... (n)
c<u>a</u>rer (n)	gener<u>a</u>tion(s) (n)	(the child's) <u>u</u>pbringing (n)
ch<u>i</u>ld rearing (n)	r<u>ai</u>se (vb) (children)	w<u>e</u>lfare (n)

2 Discuss the following questions a] to h], to share knowledge and vocabulary around the topic of this unit. **Your answers should be from your own culture.** Try to use the vocabulary from the box above, ticking it off as you do so.

In some countries, families live together in large groups, with several generations together, and maybe with uncles and aunts under the same roof. This is called an extended family. However, in other countries, families live in much smaller groups with only parents and their children in the same **household**.

household
group of people living together in the same house

a] Describe your family. Does it fit into any of the above patterns?

b] What kind of family arrangement is 'typical' for your country? How close is your family to the typical pattern?

c] Until what age do children usually continue to live with their parents? For example, do they leave home when they start university? When they get married? Is it the same for males and females?

d] Is the age at which people get married increasing, decreasing or staying the same? What reasons are commonly given for this? What is your opinion?

e] Did people use to have more children than nowadays? If so, what are the reasons?

f] Do grandparents generally live with their children and grandchildren? Or do they generally prefer to live separately?

g] How much influence (or power) do parents have over their young adult children (eg helping them to decide which subjects to study at university, which career, when and with whom to get married, etc)?

h] In some countries, because society has changed radically in the last few years, there is a 'generation gap', that is, parents and children find it difficult to relate to each other. Does this happen in your society? Is it a significant problem?

Reading

✓ *Scanning*
✓ *Finding meaning from context*
✓ *Collocation*

Scanning

> ### Task A: What is scanning and when is it useful?

▮ Can you remember from Unit 1 how to skim?

Another technique for quickly getting information from a text is scanning. In scanning, you look only for specific information, for example, times, dates and specific ideas. You know the kind of thing you're looking for before you start. You don't read every word!

When you scan, it's often useful to skim first to find which paragraphs the information is most likely to be in.

1 Choose the most likely answers in the table below to help you distinguish between skimming and scanning.

	skimming	scanning
Aim to read quickly	yes/no	yes/no
Know the particular word or idea you're looking for before you begin reading	yes/no	yes/no
Read every word of the text	yes/no	yes/no
Look for main ideas	yes/no	yes/no
Look for specific information, such as numbers, dates or specific facts	yes/no	yes/no
Focus on topic sentences, summary sentences, introductions, abstracts and conclusions	yes/no	yes/no

2 In the following situations, which is more useful, scanning or skimming?

a] Reading the TV times pages of a newspaper to find when a particular program is on.

b] Reading the contents page of a book to decide whether it covers the area you're looking for.

c] Reading a book review to decide whether it's generally good, OK or bad.

d] Reading a journal article to find the percentage of people who said that they believe TV violence affects children negatively.

e] Reading an index to find the pages on which something called Heisenberg's uncertainty principle is mentioned.

f] Reading a chapter of a book to find out whether it mentions M A K Halliday.

g] Reading an article to decide whether it might contain information useful to your research project.

h] Reading the **blurb** on the back cover of a book to find out whether it is useful for beginning students in a particular field.

blurb a short description of a product, written for sales purposes. Often on the back cover of a book.

To become more familiar with your course book, find the answers to these questions. Who will be the first to answer all of them?

1 If you want to focus on skills for dealing with vocabulary, which section of this Unit will be particularly relevant?

2 Imagine your teacher has just given you back some homework with symbols written on it. He tells the class that these are correction codes. In which section of this Unit is a correction marking code explained?

3 Where in the book (near the back) is this code given?

4 If you enjoy fiction, which Unit of this book will be especially interesting for you?

5 In which Unit is Tutorial Participation Skills I covered?

6 Which other units also cover tutorial participation skills?

7 In Unit 3, what kind of essays are covered?

8 In Unit 3, which essay is about genetically modified food?

9 In the essay starting on page 39, which paragraph mentions the proportion of older people in the population?

10 Which paragraph of the same essay mentions social interaction?

Finding meaning from context

Task A: Scanning race

This will prepare you for the next task. Who in the class will be first to circle or highlight all the boxed words in the following student essay?

albeit	demography/-ic	numerous	supplemented
attuned to	gain	prevent	sustained
a burden	mutual	rather than	trend

Question: 'It is to the benefit of society for family units, living together, to include the older generation.'

What is your view on this matter?

1 A major social trend in many countries has been for elderly people to live increasingly by themselves rather than with their children. Often they have pride in remaining independent and don't want to feel a burden on their families. However, there would be considerable advantages for society if more elderly people lived with their adult children rather than alone or in nursing homes. 5 Clearly this wouldn't work in every case, but reasons include mutual benefit for all members of the family, and the fact that this can help society cope with the massive demographic changes predicted for the future.

2 All generations gain benefit from living in extended families. Most grandparents and great-grandparents enjoy spending time with their grandchildren—it is 10 common to hear them say that having children around makes them feel younger. In addition, for parents, it is cheaper when children are looked after by their older relatives than in child care centres.

3 Benefits for the children are numerous, and clearly what is good for them is good for the whole family. Family care is likely to be of higher quality than at a child care 15 centre for many reasons. It will be better attuned to the children's needs because the family members know them better and because there are fewer children to look after in a family home than in a child care centre. Further, families generally have greater emotional involvement in the child's development than people looking after the child as a job. It's also an advantage that this kind of care can strengthen family 20 bonds due to the increased contact that family members have with each other. The experience that grandparents and great-grandparents bring to child-rearing, from the years of raising their own children, is an additional reason. However, it must be remembered that care centres have staff with professional training which family members rarely get the opportunity to gain, and they also provide opportunities for 25 social interaction with other children beyond those available in the family home. Child care facilities thus do have a place in children's upbringing, but their use must be balanced against the advantages of home care.

4 A further benefit to society results from expected changes in the demography of almost every country. As health care improves, people are living longer lives. Also, 30 in most developed countries, birth rates are decreasing. Both these trends serve to increase the proportion of older people in the population, and decrease the future proportion of working age people. The result is that government services, such as subsidised health care and nursing homes, cannot be sustained at the same level into the future. Therefore, other ways of looking after the elderly must 35 be considered, for example, families looking after their own elderly parents. This must be supplemented, however, with some government support, albeit reduced from the present level, to prevent people having to leave jobs or reduce their working hours to look after elderly relatives.

5 In summary, the benefits of encouraging more elderly people to live with their 40 children or grandchildren are considerable and, overall, provide advantages for all members of the family and offer a way to deal with demographic shifts. However, some level of support services would still be necessary in many cases. Therefore, the elderly should be encouraged, where reasonable, to move in with their children while welfare services should be tailored to support this. 45

Task B: Finding meaning from context

1 Look at the following sentence:

It was a cold, snowy day so I put on my putongsway. As I left the house, I pulled it tightly down over my ears.

Without looking in your dictionaries, what does 'putongsway' mean?

 LEARNING t i p

> Noticing meanings from context may feel uncomfortable at first, but if you practise it enough, it will help you because:
>
> ■ it can be quicker than using a dictionary;
>
> ■ it is a natural way to learn vocabulary—it's how you learnt words in your first language;
>
> ■ it can be done without breaking the fluency of your reading;
>
> ■ although it sometimes gives you only a vague impression of the meaning, this is often enough. You can refine (make better) your understanding of the meaning later.

2 In pairs, mark the words **from the table on page 38** that you already know. Explain their meanings to your partner if he or she doesn't already know them.

3 Using the context of the passage, match the words from **Task A** with the meanings below, writing them in the gaps.

Example:

1 *albeit*   though (introduces an opposite idea)

2 _____   a general change in a number over time—up or down

3 _____   a problem, hard work

4 _____   added

5 _____   sizes of populations of different age groups etc

6 _____   familiar with

7 _____   get, obtain, receive

8 _____   instead of (separates two alternative ideas)

9 _____   kept over time

10 _____   a large number of; many

11 _____   shared, affecting both

12 _____   stop

4 Find a new partner. Compare answers. Explain how you found your answers. For example, which words could you find from the immediate context? For which words did you have to read large parts of the text to find their meaning?

Collocation

From the above, you will have noticed that 'attuned' in this context can be replaced with 'familiar'. But if this happens, the words around it also have to change. In fact, we would have to change 'better attuned to' to 'more familiar with'. But, why? Why can't we say 'more attuned with'?

To answer this, one useful explanation is that 'well' and 'better' are used naturally with 'attuned', whereas 'more' fits naturally with 'familiar'. These word sets are called collocations. We can say that 'well' collocates with 'attuned'.

 LEARNING tip

> Noticing collocations is one of the best things you can do to make your English sound natural.

In the following examples, cross out the ones that don't collocate. For each set, there are some examples in the text, but you will also have to use your experience of English.

1 considerable advantages
considerable good points
considerable benefits

2 members of the family
members of the company
members of the group

3 high quality
top quality
large quality

4 have contact with
do contact with
make contact with

5 birth rates
marriage rates
divorce rates

6 friend support
government support
family support

Discuss these questions with a partner to help you learn some of the language from the *Social benefits of extended families* essay on page 39.

1 'Social trend' (line 1) refers to a change in society. Mention some social trends you have observed in your country. What other kinds of trends have you heard of?

2 'Birth rates' (line 33). Is the birth rate in your country falling or rising? Why? What other rates can you think of? Check that they collocate by asking your teacher. In your out of class study, how can you check if something collocates?

3 Is 'subsidised health care' (line 34) available in your country?

4 What is your experience of the ideas mentioned in the essay? Which parts (if any) do you agree with? Which parts (if any) do you disagree with? Give reasons for your answers.

English for the Internet Age

Scanning for required information and choosing appropriate links

> **Task A: Choosing links by scanning**

Web pages contain lots of information that you have to deal with quickly. So scanning and skimming are very useful. To practise, we'll do an Internet treasure hunt. Form pairs, and race the other pairs to find answers to the following questions:

1 How much is the cheapest one-way air ticket, economy class, from London to Bangkok with Qantas, on 31 December this year? (www.qantas.com.au)

2 Is it possible to study for a Master's degree in physics at the University of Durham in the UK? (www.durham.ac.uk)

3 Does the main library at University of Technology, Sydney, hold a copy of a book called *The Songlines* by Bruce Chatwin? (www.uts.edu.au)

4 On what day do classes start at the beginning of the next semester at Pennsylvania State University in the USA? (www.psu.edu)

5 What is the first step in applying for accommodation at the University of Manchester, UK? (www.man.ac.uk)

6 Is there a club for students who like drinking wine at the University of Canterbury at Christchurch, New Zealand? (www.canterbury.ac.nz)

Writing and Reading

✓ *Argument essays and staging introductions and conclusions*
✓ *Essay plans*
✓ *Cohesion through discourse markers: addition and contrast*
✓ *Differentiating between main and supporting ideas*

Argument essays and staging introductions and conclusions

> **Task A: Prediction to help comprehension**

1 Read the essay entitled *Social benefits of extended families* again, this time focusing on the ideas given.

2 In Task B you will read an essay which answers the same question as the one you read in the previous section. However, it expresses the opposite opinion. Before you read it predict some of the ideas that might be in it, and some of the evidence that might be used.

Task B: Stages of an argument essay

An argument essay gives an opinion and supports it with evidence. Its purpose is to persuade the reader to agree with the opinion, or to show reasons for a particular opinion.

See Unit 1, *Paragraph formatting 1*, page 16.

1 Examine and study the stages and purposes of argument essays, given below.

Stages of argument essays (parts)		Purpose of stage
Introduction Gives an overall view of the essay	General statement	To introduce the reader to the subject of the essay.
	Definition(s) (optional)	To explain any important technical words to the reader.
	Thesis	To give the opinion of the writer.
	Preview/scope or essay map	To tell the reader what parts of the topic will be included in the essay.
Body The main part of the essay, where evidence is presented, with support.	Arguments	To explain to the reader the evidence that supports the thesis. The most important ideas usually come first.
Conclusion To relate the argument to real-world action	Summary	To give the reader a brief reminder of the main ideas, while restating the thesis.
(No new evidence is given in the conclusion)	Recommendation	To tell the reader what the writer believes is the best action to take, considering the evidence in the essay.

2 On the next page, you are going to read an essay that answers the same question as the one you read on page 39 (*Social benefits of extended families*). However, this new essay expresses the opposite view. It's another example of an argument essay and was written by another person. As you read, notice how the purpose of each stage is fulfilled.

 LEARNING tip

It is a good idea to keep this model of an argument essay. Every time you write an argument essay, either here or at university or college, use it to check that you have included all the stages.

Question: 'It is to the benefit of society for family units, living together, to include the older generation.'

What is your view on this matter?

TITLE: **Family responsibility: A dangerous policy?**

General statement → There has been talk in some political circles that some responsibility for social welfare should be shifted from governments to families. This would involve a reversal of the current trend towards increasingly smaller families and would encourage several generations to live together in extended families. However, this is a 5

Thesis statement → dangerous policy that could lead to a variety of social problems, not

Preview/ scope → only for the elderly people themselves, but also for the families that would have to look after them.

Argument 1's topic statement → Often, it is the elderly people themselves who are reluctant to live with their children. Several main reasons are commonly given for 10 this. The first is that many want to retain their independence. They want be able to come and go as they please, and to be able to live their lives in their own way and not have to fit in with other people, even if they are family. When with their family, they often feel they have lost some control over their lives, even if the alternative is to 15 rely on support services such as visits from nurses or people to cook their meals.

Further concrete supporting evidence for Argument 1 → their meals. Secondly, many elderly people are proud of being able to look after themselves, and would feel deep shame to be looked after by anyone, even close family members. In other cases, the children may have had to move to a distant city for work or other 20 reasons, and their parents might not want to leave the house and the place they knew well, and leave all their friends and neighbours, to join their children in a city or town where they have no roots.

Concrete supporting evidence for Argument 1

Argument 2's topic statement → A further problem is that people in the family, usually women, are likely to have to spend time as carers. The inevitable consequence of 25 this is that the person or people have to take time out from their jobs and their working lives, and not only do they lose the income and self-respect that a job provides, but also the ensuing gap in their career may mean that when they eventually return to work, they have lost the opportunity to develop work skills that could have 30 led to promotion. This is clearly not to the benefit of society.

Concrete supporting evidence for Argument 2

Concluding sentence

Argument 3's topic statement → Extended families also reduce the independence of younger family members. A family, especially an extended one, can be a stifling environment, in that young people can be made to feel it is their duty to carry out the wishes of their elders, which may not always 35 be in their best interests. This is also against nature – it is a natural tendency for young people to want to leave the parental influence and make decisions by themselves. Indeed, many argue, it is only by doing this that a young person can learn valuable lessons in life

Concrete supporting evidence for Argument 3

through making their own decisions and being directly affected by their consequences. Though many of these young people may benefit to some extent from the greater experience and knowledge of their family elders, overall the scope for personal growth of young adult family members is reduced in extended families.

40

Optional demonstration that opposite viewpoint to Argument 3 has also been considered

body

Argument 4's topic statement →

Promoting the extended family model will also be likely to disadvantage those who, through no fault of their own, cannot live in an extended family. For example, if their children live overseas, if there is a family argument which still prevents them from living together, or if there simply are no children, then for the individuals concerned, this policy fails. No matter what happens, it is essential that government support is available to people such as these.

45

50

Concrete supporting evidence for Argument 4 →

Summary →

In conclusion, it is clear that severe social problems will result if a return to living in extended families is encouraged. Individuals should be able to choose how they organise their living arrangements, and everyone should have the chance to enjoy the benefits of independent living.

55

conclusion

Recommendation →

 LEARNING tip

You may have noticed that the essay question doesn't ask for support or evidence. However, it's essential!

It's important to get used to providing support and evidence for everything, even when you aren't asked for it.

3 Look back at the essay you read beginning on page 39. Draw boxes around (or colour) the stages in the essay. Use the example you just looked at to help you do this.

Task C: Useful expressions for preview/scope (in introductions) and summary stages of essays

Your teacher will give you some journals. In pairs, choose one, and for each article, identify the preview/scope and the beginning of the conclusion. Record useful expressions that you find in the table below.

Preview/scope expressions	Expressions to begin conclusions
eg ... will be examined ...	eg In conclusion, ...

Task D: Speaking—brainstorming as preparation for writing

LEARNING t i p

Before writing, discussing ideas often helps to make them clear in your mind. Also, sharing ideas will help if it's difficult to think about the topic.

1 Look at the questions below and decide your opinion for each.

2 Explain the reasons for your opinion to other students. Feel free to agree with, disagree with, and question the other students.

Argument essay questions

1 Which is a better living arrangement, nuclear or extended families?

2 Women are better at looking after children than men.

3 Men are just as good/better at looking after children than women.

4 Divorce is always bad for children.

5 Increasing ease of divorce threatens to destroy the traditional family unit.

6 Family members are more important than friends.

Task E: Writing an argument essay

Choose a question you talked about in Task D and write an essay in response. Remember to include all the stages, and focus especially on the introduction and conclusion.

Essay plans

Task A: Writing essay plans

There are many ways to write an essay plan, but the one we are going to use here is in the following format.

Essay plan diagram

See Unit 1, page 13.

- Thesis
  - 1st main idea
    - 1st concrete supporting evidence for 1st main idea
    - 2nd concrete supporting evidence for 1st main idea
      - concrete supporting evidence for 2nd concrete supporting evidence
    - 3rd concrete supporting evidence for 1st main idea
  - 2nd main idea
    - 1st concrete supporting evidence for 2nd main idea
  -
  - ... etc ...
  -

> **WRITING:** An essay plan shows how the ideas in the essay are organised. Making an essay plan before you start to write will help you to:
> - organise your essay and your thoughts;
> - write your essay quickly.

1 Below is an essay plan for the *Social benefits of extended families* essay from page 39. Complete it with the notes below it, and using the essay as a guide.

Note: ↑ = increasing or higher, ↓ = decreasing or lower, ⟹ = therefore, advs = advantages. Most essay plans would have more abbreviations than this, but abbreviations are covered later in this Unit.

Essay plan

- extended families—beneficial
  - benefits all generations
    - _____
    - cheaper child care for parents
    - children benefit: ↑ quality care
      - _____
        - family knows child well
        - fewer children
      - _____
    - strengthen family bonds
      - _____
    - but advs of care centres
    - professional training
      - _____
    - ⟹ use them sometimes
  - demographic change
    - longer lives + birth rate ↓ : _____ & working age people ↓
      - _____
      - _____
    - but: some government support: keep people employed

Notes to go in essay plan above

- → proportion of old people ↑
- g/parents enjoy g/kids
- ⟹ extended families: solve this problem
- social interaction
- better attuned:
- ↑ emotional involvement
- ⟹ services for old people: future problems
- experience of g/parents

2 This essay plan now clearly shows the relationship of the ideas in the essay. In this essay what kind of words separate the main and supporting ideas?

Cohesion through discourse markers: addition and contrast

Task A: Cohesion through discourse markers

In writing and speaking, discourse markers often separate ideas. Discourse markers also show the relationships (types of connection) between ideas.

See also
Unit 1, page 15;
Unit 3, page 66;
Unit 4, page 86.

There are many types of discourse markers. In Unit 1, you looked at discourse markers of time sequence and you will look at more discourse markers in later units. Here, you'll look at discourse markers of addition (which connect similar ideas) and discourse markers of contrast (which connect different or opposite ideas).

1 Look at the *Family responsibilities: A dangerous policy* essay. The discourse signals of addition and contrast are underlined on it. Add them to the correct column of the table below. Use their context and your previous knowledge to help.

2 Look at the *Social benefits of extended families* essay. Find the discourse markers of addition and contrast, and also add them to the correct column of the table.

3 Add any other discourse markers of addition or contrast that you know.

Addition	Contrast

Differentiating between main and supporting ideas

Task A: Differentiating between main and supporting ideas

Write a plan for the essay entitled *Family responsibility: A dangerous policy* on page 44. In doing this, use the discourse markers to identify the main ideas and supporting ideas.

Critical thinking and Writing

✓ *Differentiating between weak and strong evidence*
✓ *Providing concrete supporting evidence*

Differentiating between weak and strong evidence

> **Task A: Critical thinking—what constitutes strong/weak evidence?**
>
> Look at the following extracts from texts and then:
>
> - Underline the evidence in each.
>
> - Decide which evidence is strong and which is weak. Think about your reasons.
>
> - With other students, compare your answers and discuss your reasons.

1 Another reason that women are better than men at raising children is that they are kinder. My mother was a good example. She did many kind things not only for me but also for many other people she met, including strangers.

2 Living costs are also increasing in the area of housing affordability. In a recent survey, 68% of people said that they found it more difficult to pay their rent or housing loan than last year.

3 The decline in the fertility rate is a further reason that immigration will become more and more important. According to Weston (2001), the fertility rate in this country has fallen from 3.5 live births per woman in 1961 to its lowest level ever, 1.8 babies per woman, in 1999 and 2000. This trend looks set to continue into the future. Weston (Ibid.) also states that the minimum fertility rate necessary to sustain a population at a constant level is 2.1 births per female. Therefore, unless this trend reverses, immigration is necessary to sustain the population.

4 No evidence has yet been found of a direct link between this particular product and heart disease or other illnesses. Therefore, we would conclude that it is perfectly safe for people of all ages to take it.

5 It appears for the moment that there is unlikely to be a connection between eating this product and ability to concentrate. Despite extensive research focused on investigating this link, such as Crumlin (1996), Detford (2000) and Gandiger-Hertzog (2002), no evidence has yet been found.

6 People from Govindia can no longer be trusted. This conclusion stems from the fact that two tourists from that country were recently convicted of murder while visiting this country. Also, the Prime Minister of Govindia has declared that he will search any fishing boats from our country if his police suspect them of carrying illegal drugs, which is obviously a ridiculous accusation. Any country that does that clearly does not respect our national sovereignty.

7 Despite popular myths, chocolate contains little that is bad for the skin. The Confederation of Chocolate Product Manufacturers report of 2002 states that 'Our research demonstrates there is no direct link between chocolate consumption and teenage acne' (page 35).

- In conclusion, what traps should you avoid when giving evidence for your own opinions?

Providing concrete supporting evidence

> ### Task A: Writing body paragraphs

Look back at the essay you wrote in Task E on page 46.

1 Look at the body paragraphs. Try to improve them in the light of what you have learned in this section. Writing a plan for your essay, like the one on page 47, will help to clarify ideas.

2 Feel free to adjust the introduction and conclusion to make it fit with the revised body. Writers do this all the time!

Listening

✓ *Note taking*
✓ *Predicting focus and listening for supporting ideas*

Note taking

> ### Task A: Note taking

1 When you listen to lectures and read for assignments, you will need to take notes. Ask your partner to show you how they take notes from speakers, then show them how you take notes. How are they organised—linearly, in a table, or as a spider diagram (see following)? What interesting techniques can you learn from them?

Organising notes

1 Linear

14.2.03
Dr Bernhard

Marriage in Ancient Greece

Age – girls: ~14 (young — greater chance -virgin)
men: ~30 -after military service

girls – no choice of husband
– husband chosen by kyrios: male guardian

look up!

families chose according to – money
– politics
– for the family
not individual.

2 Spider diagram

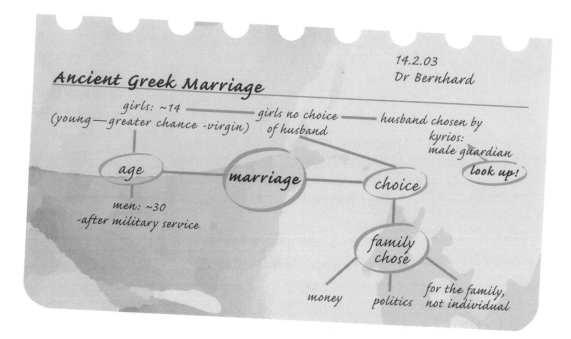

14.2.03
Dr Bernhard

Ancient Greek Marriage

girls: ~14
(young — greater chance -virgin)

girls no choice of husband

husband chosen by kyrios: male guardian

look up!

age — **marriage** — **choice**

men: ~30
-after military service

family chose

money   politics   for the family, not individual

3 Table

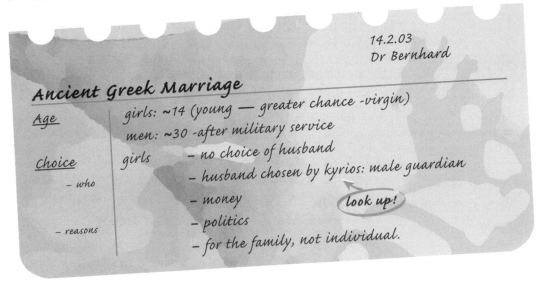

14.2.03
Dr Bernhard

Ancient Greek Marriage

Age	girls: ~14 (young — greater chance -virgin) men: ~30 -after military service
Choice	girls — no choice of husband
— who	— husband chosen by kyrios: male guardian *look up!*
	— money
	— politics
— reasons	— for the family, not individual.

2 Discuss with your partner why taking notes is useful. Write down as many reasons as you can.

3 Do you ⊙circle and <u>underline</u>? Do you use highlighter pens of differing colours to mark similar ideas? Do you use abbreviations (abrv) that you can later recognise?

4 Over the page are some common abbreviations. You might see them in many places. For example, lecturers often use them when writing on the board. In pairs, one person choose an abbreviation and say the meaning. The other should write it down. Repeat a few times, then swap.

Common symbols for abbreviation	Latin symbols for abbreviation
> greater than	eg for example
< less than	ie that is ..., used to explain what the previous idea means (not for examples)
= equals, is the same as, means	
+ and	cf to compare with or compared with
/ or	NB important note
∧ insert	viz someone or something just referred to—a previous reference, namely, ...
→ previous idea influences or leads to the next one	
↔ mutually influencing ideas	et al and others, or all of us
∴ thus, therefore, so	Ibid. same reference as the previous one
⇒ therefore,	
* very important point	etc and so on, and so on
≠ is not equal, is not the same as	

Predicting focus and listening for supporting ideas

Task A: Predicting the focus of a lecture; stages in introductions of lectures

You are going to listen to a lecture about families, given by a sociology department of a university (Recording number 3).

1 Listen to the beginning of the lecture and mark the quotation below which best shows the focus or main idea of the lecture:

a] 'The family has been found to be a major institutional component in every known social system.'

b] 'A family may be defined as a group, related by marriage, blood or adoption residing in a common household, communicating with each other according to their respective roles and maintaining a common culture.'

c] 'For example, what is a "normal" family? And, is there such a thing as a "normal" family?'

d] '... whatever any family does within its own structure is considered "normal" by that family and pretty much what anyone else does is considered not normal' (Garfinkel, 1967).

2 Why did you choose your answer to Instruction 1?

Lectures and academic talks are often organised in a similar way to essays: the stages are similar and have similar functions.

3 Write the letter of the other sentences against the appropriate function below. You may want to look again at the section on argument essays on page 43 to remind yourself of the stages of introductions. One of these fuctions has no example.

Thesis [ ]   Part of the general statement [ ]

A supporting idea [ ]   Definition [ ]

1   Read the methods of support below.

   a] logical argument

   b] examples

   c] research—described and referenced

   d] quotes from the literature, with references

   e] the lecturer's own personal experiences

   f] asking the audience to reflect on their own personal experiences.

   Listen to the rest of the lecture and tick which of the above the lecturer uses to support his thesis. (More than one answer is possible.)

2   Tables like the ones below are often helpful for taking notes from lectures or written articles. Two possible ways of expressing the main ideas are given in the two tables below. Both are very different ways of looking at the same lecture, but both are OK.

   Listen and fill in both tables. Each gap may contain one or more words.

Perspective 1

Main idea	Supporting idea
research procedure	■ US students, _____ backgrounds ■ swapped _____ ■ weren't allowed to _____ ■ tried to participate naturally at _____ ■ _____ and _____ about the experience afterwards
results	■ their new family did everything _____ from their own family ■ they didn't know _____ ■ they considered their new family's habits to be _____ ■ they considered their own family's practices to be the _____ ones
conclusions	■ even families in the same _____ have different ideas of normal family behaviour

Perspective 2

Main idea	Supporting idea
Each family has a different view of what is 'normal' behaviour	Students who swapped families found: ■ their new family did everything _____ from their own family ■ they didn't know _____ ■ they considered their new family's habits to be _____ ■ they considered their own family's practices to be the _____ ones ■ this was despite the students having the same _____

You will hear the introductions to two further lectures. The first is about how life developed in the universe. It is from the physics department of a science faculty at a university.

 1 Listen to this introduction and mark the statement below which is closest to the *focus or main idea* of the lecture.

a] cosmological constants

b] the importance of cosmological constants

c] applications of the anthropic cosmological principle

d] why life exists.

LEARNING tip

Lecturers will often refer to a previous lecture, or review key points, by asking audience members to explain certain aspects to him/her. This is a way of actively involving the audience and it helps them to remember these points.

 2 Listen to the introduction to the next lecture, which is from a department of art history within an arts faculty, and is about Korean art in particular. Take notes of the main idea.

3 Compare your answers in pairs. If there are differences, discuss the good and bad points about the two answers.

Grammar

Definite articles

Task A: What does 'the' actually mean?

Let's develop a hypothesis by looking at some examples of what someone might say to start a new topic in a conversation.

For example, if someone starts a new topic in a conversation by saying:

> You know the girl we were talking about the other day? Well, I saw her last night ...

'the' is chosen before 'girl' because both speaker and listener know which girl is being talked about.

However, if the same person says:

> I saw something really strange last night. There was a girl ...

'a' is chosen before 'girl' because the listener doesn't know which girl (yet!).

From this it appears that:

> 'the ...X...' shows that we know which ...X...

Let's test this hypothesis. For the underlined noun groups in sentences 1–5 and those numbered 6–9 in the paragraph, choose from the list of possible reasons why speaker and listener, or reader and writer, might know which one.

1 <u>The moon's</u> looking beautiful tonight.

2 <u>The dangers of overeating</u> shouldn't be ignored.

3 <u>The first prize</u> went to Simona.

4 I hope I can meet <u>the girl we spoke to in the restaurant</u> again—she's stunning!

5 That's <u>the best restaurant I've eaten at since I came here</u>!

6–9 (taken from Recording number 5)

Last week, if you remember, we looked at representations of people in pre-modern Korean art. This week, we'll look at [6] <u>the difference between the art of the higher classes and art painted and used by more ordinary people</u>. In particular, we'll look at Korean folk art and [7] <u>the various theories about who actually painted it</u>. Was it really ordinary people, or could it have been court painters doing work during periods when they couldn't work for [8] <u>the upper classes</u>? And if so, could this mean that, after all, even [9] <u>the folk art</u> was actually painted by the upper class?

Possible reasons

a] Only one exists in the context.

b] The idea has already been introduced in the text/conversation.

c] The noun is defined or made more specific by the phrase that follows it.

d] Using a superlative automatically specifies which one(s) you mean.

e] It is referring to all that exist in the context.

Task B: Using articles

Practise choosing when to use 'the' by filling in the gaps in the passage with either 'the' or Ø to indicate no article.

Marriages in ancient Greece involved young brides. Girls were thought more likely to be [1]_____ virgins if they got married early, and 14 appears to be [2]_____ most common age (Powers, 1997). However, for [3]_____ men, it was a completely different story. Due to [4]_____ fact that they had to perform military service, [5]_____ age at which they got married was around twice that for women.

Choice of 6_____ husband was something that women had no control over. Instead, their *kyrios* (male guardian) chose for them. Factors involved were 7_____ money and 8_____ family politics. 9_____ Alliances between 10_____ families were more important than 11_____ feelings of 12_____ people who were actually getting married (ibid). It seems that it was only in 13_____ myths of 14_____ period that 15_____ love marriages occurred.

Learner independence & study skills

Self-correction marking code

Task A: How to use the code

Do you remember better how to do something if:

- someone does it for you?

- you do it yourself?

The two-stage self-correction marking code is a way to help you correct your own writing after your teacher has examined it. The teacher writes codes near any mistakes. These codes tell you what kind of mistakes you have made and this makes it easier to correct them yourself and remember them! If you can't work out how to correct something, you should ask your teacher.

There is a correction code key in Appendix A. Use it to self-correct your writing. Focus on use of 'the'.

 LEARNING tip

One of the best ways to improve your grammar and word choice is to self-correct.

Speaking and Writing

Discussion and essay questions

Here are some extra issues for you to talk and/or write about.

- What types of family exist? What is the typical or traditional family arrangement in your culture?

- How has family organisation changed in your country? Think of such things as changes in work patterns and increased tolerance of non-traditional views.

- What are some of the effects that divorce has on children?

- Families of the future are likely to take more diverse forms than in the present. Discuss.

science and technology

There is no convenience in our present day civilisation that does not cause discomfort.

KAHLIL GIBRAN

Skills focus: In this Unit, you will learn and use the following skills:

Speaking 1

Orientation: some issues in science and technology

Task A: Discussion

Look at the statements below and decide what your opinions are about them. Then, explain your opinions to your partner, giving your reasons. Feel free to agree, disagree or question your partner.

> We should be grateful to scientists—the technology provided by their insights and discoveries is the reason for the high standard of living that we have now.

> New developments in science often cause more problems than they solve

> We don't need to worry too much about things like environmental problems … if the need to solve a problem is great enough, scientists will manage to solve it.

> There are some areas that should be off-limits to scientific research.

> It's better to spend money on solving major problems like shortage of food than on useless things like space travel.

Task B: Vocabulary for this Unit

Match the words to their meanings. Use your learner's dictionary for words you can't match. Underlined syllables are stressed.

Words		
assert (vb)	genetically modified (GM)	resistant to ~ (adj)
breed (vb, trans)	legislation (n)	reproduce (vb)
consumers (n)	mechanisation (n)	rural (adj)
determine (vb)	pests (n)	the environment (n)
diesel (n)	processed food	the (general) public (n)
environmentalist (n)	produce (n)	yield (n, vb)
gene (n)	radically (adj)	urban (adj)
genetic (adj)/genetically (adv)		

Words	Meanings
	a kind of fuel, usually for heavy vehicles
	ordinary people
	countryside where farmers work
	surprisingly big, or dramatic
	laws
	find out
	people who buy and use things
	natural things around us (air, plants, etc)
	replacing older ways of doing things with machines
	person opposed to damage to natural things around us
	food that has been highly cooked and packaged
	to choose carefully which animals or plants to allow to reproduce, in order to produce a better version. This commonly happens, for instance, with race horses.
	insects or other animals that damage crops or property
	produce more of the same kind (usually for animals and plants)
	part of animal and plant cells which controls the characteristics of the whole animal or plant—it's made up of DNA
	living things with altered genes
	amounts produced—in this text, crops
	not damaged or affected by something
	the food grown on a farm
	associated with the genes
	say strongly
	related to cities

Listening

Listening for reasons: interview with a scientist

Task A: Orientation discussion

In groups, discuss the following questions:

- What do you know about genetically modified (GM) food?
- How do you know if something you buy at the supermarket has GM ingredients?
- Do you know of any reasons that are given for and against GM food?

Task B: Listening for markers that indicate reasons

Listen to an interview between Dr Reynolds, an expert on genetically modified food, and Simon Bennet, a television reporter. As you listen, each time you hear one of the words or phrases below, place a tick in the box.

in order to	☐	because	☐	so	☐
reasons	☐	mean(s)	☐	why?	☐
infinitive with 'to'	☐	thus	☐	as a consequence	☐

6

Task C: Listening for reasons

The words in Task B above indicate that there is a reason given either before or after the word. Listen again, and give reasons as answers to the following questions.

1 Why have humans been breeding plants? (2 reasons)

_____

2 Why is it impossible to quickly make big changes in a species by breeding?

_____

3 Why is genetic engineering considered a good thing by some people? (2 reasons)

_____

4 Why are some consumers concerned about GM foods?

_____

5 Why are environmentalists concerned about GM foods?

_____

6 Why are the food companies publicising the testing they have done on GM foods?

_____

Writing 1

Discussion essays

 LEARNING tip

Discussion essays consider different points of view around an opinion. For example, there could be advantages and disadvantages of a choice of action, or evidence for and against a particular opinion.

See Unit 2, page 43.

Task A: Stages in a discussion essay

Examine and study the stages and purposes of each part below. What are the differences between discussion essays and argument essays (introduced in Unit 2)?

Stages of discussion essays (parts)		Purpose of stage
Introduction Gives an overall view of the essay	General statement	To introduce the reader to the subject of the essay.
	Position (sometimes not possible)	To give the opinion of the writer.
	Definition(s) (optional)	To explain any important technical words to the reader.
	Preview/scope or essay map	To tell the reader what parts of the topic will be included in the essay.
Body The main part of the essay, where evidence is presented, with support.	Arguments for	To explain to the reader the evidence for the positive side of the issue, with support. The most important ideas usually come first.
	Arguments against	To explain to the reader the evidence for the negative side of the issue, with support. The most important ideas usually come first.
Conclusion To relate the points to real-world action (No new evidence is given in the conclusion)	Summary	To give the reader a brief reminder of the main ideas, while restating the issue. Sometimes also says which ideas the writer believes have the strongest evidence.
	Recommendation	To tell the reader what the writer believes is the best action to take, considering the evidence in the essay.

Note: Sometimes there may be more than two points of view to an issue. In that case, the body paragraphs will describe as many points of view as necessary.

Task B: Reading—example discussion essay

Read the example of a discussion essay below. It has been divided into the stages given above as an example to illustrate staging.

> It is a good idea to keep this model of a discussion. Every time you write a discussion essay, either here or at college or at university, use it to make sure you have included all stages.

TITLE: Genetically modified foods

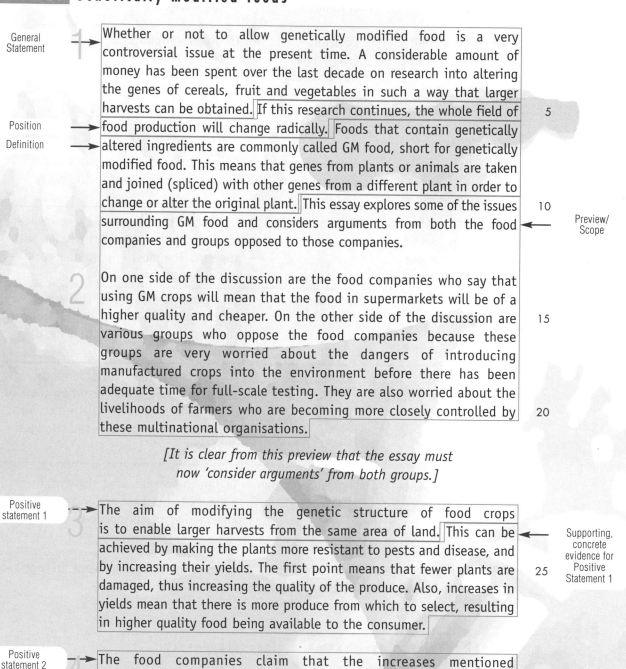

General Statement

Whether or not to allow genetically modified food is a very controversial issue at the present time. A considerable amount of money has been spent over the last decade on research into altering the genes of cereals, fruit and vegetables in such a way that larger harvests can be obtained. If this research continues, the whole field of food production will change radically. Foods that contain genetically altered ingredients are commonly called GM food, short for genetically modified food. This means that genes from plants or animals are taken and joined (spliced) with other genes from a different plant in order to change or alter the original plant. This essay explores some of the issues surrounding GM food and considers arguments from both the food companies and groups opposed to those companies.

Position

Definition

5

10

Preview/ Scope

On one side of the discussion are the food companies who say that using GM crops will mean that the food in supermarkets will be of a higher quality and cheaper. On the other side of the discussion are various groups who oppose the food companies because these groups are very worried about the dangers of introducing manufactured crops into the environment before there has been adequate time for full-scale testing. They are also worried about the livelihoods of farmers who are becoming more closely controlled by these multinational organisations.

15

20

[It is clear from this preview that the essay must now 'consider arguments' from both groups.]

Positive statement 1

The aim of modifying the genetic structure of food crops is to enable larger harvests from the same area of land. This can be achieved by making the plants more resistant to pests and disease, and by increasing their yields. The first point means that fewer plants are damaged, thus increasing the quality of the produce. Also, increases in yields mean that there is more produce from which to select, resulting in higher quality food being available to the consumer.

25

Supporting, concrete evidence for Positive Statement 1

Positive statement 2

The food companies claim that the increases mentioned above will lead to food prices falling. This applies not only to produce that is sold unprocessed, but also to the ingredients in a wide variety of food on sale in the supermarket. If the ingredients can be produced more cheaply, this will result in a fall in the price of the foods that contain them.

30

Supporting, concrete evidence for Positive Statement 2

introduction

body

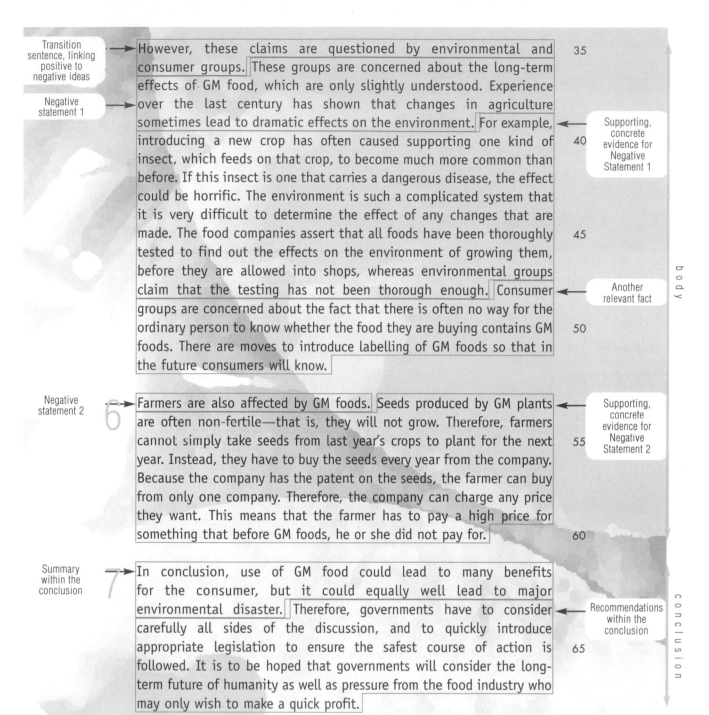

Transition sentence, linking positive to negative ideas → However, these claims are questioned by environmental and consumer groups. These groups are concerned about the long-term effects of GM food, which are only slightly understood. **Negative statement 1** → Experience over the last century has shown that changes in agriculture sometimes lead to dramatic effects on the environment. **Supporting, concrete evidence for Negative Statement 1** → For example, introducing a new crop has often caused supporting one kind of insect, which feeds on that crop, to become much more common than before. If this insect is one that carries a dangerous disease, the effect could be horrific. The environment is such a complicated system that it is very difficult to determine the effect of any changes that are made. The food companies assert that all foods have been thoroughly tested to find out the effects on the environment of growing them, before they are allowed into shops, whereas environmental groups claim that the testing has not been thorough enough. **Another relevant fact** → Consumer groups are concerned about the fact that there is often no way for the ordinary person to know whether the food they are buying contains GM foods. There are moves to introduce labelling of GM foods so that in the future consumers will know.

Negative statement 2 → Farmers are also affected by GM foods. **Supporting, concrete evidence for Negative Statement 2** → Seeds produced by GM plants are often non-fertile—that is, they will not grow. Therefore, farmers cannot simply take seeds from last year's crops to plant for the next year. Instead, they have to buy the seeds every year from the company. Because the company has the patent on the seeds, the farmer can buy from only one company. Therefore, the company can charge any price they want. This means that the farmer has to pay a high price for something that before GM foods, he or she did not pay for.

Summary within the conclusion → In conclusion, use of GM food could lead to many benefits for the consumer, but it could equally well lead to major environmental disaster. **Recommendations within the conclusion** → Therefore, governments have to consider carefully all sides of the discussion, and to quickly introduce appropriate legislation to ensure the safest course of action is followed. It is to be hoped that governments will consider the long-term future of humanity as well as pressure from the food industry who may only wish to make a quick profit.

35

40

45

50

55

60

65

body

conclusion

Task C: Recognising stages in a discussion essay

Draw a box around (or colour) the stages of the Introduction, Body and Conclusion within the discussion essay below titled, *The mechanisation of agriculture and its effect on quality of life*. Use the model from the essay titled *Genetically modified foods* above. The general statement from the introduction has been done for you.

General statement

1

extensive
used a lot

Major developments have taken place in the field of agriculture during the last century, one of the most important of which has been the introduction and **extensive** use of machinery. This has had great effects on the environment and on the lives of millions of people around the world. For the purposes of this essay, we will take the mechanisation of agriculture to mean the use of any device that is powered by anything other than humans or animals, on a farm. Careful consideration of some of the effects of agricultural mechanisation, both positive and negative, is essential for any country currently experiencing an increase in the use of such machines.

5

2

output
the things that
are made

phenomenal
surprisingly
more than
expected,
impressive

contribute
assist or help

The vast increase in **output** that has been made possible by more use of mechanisation is probably the most important positive effect of this process. The speed of planting crops, spreading fertilisers and pesticides, and harvesting, is **phenomenal**. All three of these processes **contribute** to equally enormous increases in production. Mechanisation has improved food production during this century and has helped to feed the larger world population.

10

3

Increased use of farm machinery has also generally led to a decrease in costs. This may seem surprising when the considerable cost of initial purchase of equipment is considered (this may be tens of thousands of dollars for a tractor, or hundreds of thousands of dollars for a large piece of equipment like a combine harvester). However, a tractor enables one person to perform so much more work that the extra profit, made from having more crop to sell, more than covers the purchase and running costs of the tractor. Through similar savings using other pieces of equipment, costs per hectare of food production have fallen significantly.

15

20

4

proponents
people who
support the idea
mentioned (in
this case,
agricultural
mechanisation)

inevitably
this always
happens

Despite these highly positive results of mechanisation, there are also several negative factors that aren't always considered by the **proponents** of this process. One of the most important of these is employment. As in all other fields of life, the increasing use of machines **inevitably** results in the same job being done by fewer people. It can be argued that some jobs are created in designing and maintaining the machines, but almost always more jobs are lost than created, and in addition the people whose jobs are lost often do not have the skills to undertake the newly created jobs. Therefore many jobs have to go, leading to a variety of social problems in rural communities.

25

30

5

slums
city areas of
very low quality
housing, without
normal services
such as a
reliable water
supply

One of these problems is that the unemployed of the countryside have to go elsewhere to find work—the obvious places to look are the larger cities, where further problems occur. Thus the increasing use of machinery leads to an explosion in urban population. Because the people moving to the cities are usually poor, this causes problems of sub-standard housing (resulting in **slums**), transport problems and urban poverty, as there are not necessarily more jobs available in the city than there were in the countryside. Also, the movement of people to the cities often means that families are spilt up, and villages which were once strong communities become too small to support essential services such as post offices and public transport. This leads to the irreversible break-up of these communities as people move to the cities.

35

40

6 In addition, the use of machinery on farms contributes to environmental destruction. Machines allow larger areas to be cultivated, thus leading to loss of the **habitat** in which wildlife lives. For example, in England, the increasing use   45
of machines has made it easy for farmers to remove the hedges that used to separate fields. Thus many species of butterfly are now **facing extinction** because they have nowhere to live and breed. In Australia, over-use of the land by machines has resulted in many farms becoming like deserts.

7 Furthermore, the energy that agricultural machines use is mostly produced from   50
the burning of diesel, which causes pollution as well as adding to global warming. Electricity that is sometimes used to power farm machinery is also usually produced in environmentally **unsound** ways.

8 In summary, there are many disadvantages to the mechanisation of agriculture as well as advantages. With the increasing population of the world, most   55
governments consider that expanding mechanisation is the only way to feed the additional hungry mouths. However, it would be sensible for governments to take steps to minimise the disadvantages of this process.

9 Developed countries experienced these disadvantages some time ago, and while many of them have been overcome, a significant number of mistakes were made.   60
It would be wise for countries currently undergoing mechanisation to study these mistakes carefully and to avoid making the same ones themselves.

habitat
the trees, plants, rivers etc where that animal usually lives

facing extinction
there are very few of those animals still living, and soon there might be none of them

unsound
bad or negative

Reading and Writing

Avoiding the repetition of words

Repeated words in essays make an essay boring to read. To produce a good style in writing, it is important to repeat as few words as possible. To do this, you need to use synonyms. Synonyms are words that have the same meaning.

You can use a thesaurus to find synonyms.

 LEARNING tip

> It is useful to use a thesaurus when writing an essay. Using one will also help you learn new lexis (words)!

Task A: Identifying synonyms; vocabulary development; understanding lexical cohesion

Look at the essay *The mechanisation of agriculture* on the previous page. Use the paragraph numbers given in the table below to find in the essay the synonyms of the words given. The first one has been done for you. Each answer may consist of more than one word.

Word	Paragraph number	Synonym
large	1	great
	3	*
	9	*
very big	2	*
	2	*
	2	*
agricultural mechanisation	1	
	3	

* means that the word that goes in this space belongs in front of other words.

 LEARNING t i p

> Using synonyms in this way helps to connect ideas in a text—it is called lexical cohesion. Try to use this next time you write.

Grammar

Cohesion through discourse markers: contrast, deduction, example, addition and summation

Cohesion within a text means that the text makes sense. A text with good cohesion is sensible, not nonsense. Cohesion comes about in a text through lexis (words) or grammar. One way of providing cohesion is to refer to the same idea using different words (see previous section). Another way is to use discourse markers. We looked at time sequence discourse markers in Unit 1, page 15 and discourse markers of addition and contrast in Unit 2, page 48. You'll look at cause and effect discourse markers on page 86 and at another way of providing cohesion, using pronouns, in Unit 4, page 87.

Task A: Discourse markers and their function

In the table below, place the words (discourse markers) from the next page under their correct function. The first line has been done for you.

Add information	Contrast	Summarise/ conclude	Reason/ result/ cause/effect	Give examples
and	but	to summarise	therefore	for example

Discourse markers

in summary	whereas	therefore
on the other hand	however	on the contrary
thus	in addition	additionally
such as	...not only...but also	in conclusion
though	to summarise	moreover
but		

Task B: Identifying discourse markers

1   Return to the essays *The mechanisation of agriculture and its effect on the quality of life* and *Genetically modified food* and mark every discourse signal you can find. Add them to the table in Task A.

2   Look also at other texts that you have read. Add discourse markers from those to the table.

Task C: Grammar of discourse markers

1   Look at the following examples. What is the difference between them?

- Some companies are enthusiastic about GM food. However, many people are very worried about its dangers.

- Some companies are enthusiastic about GM food, but many people are very worried about its dangers.

The meaning is almost exactly the same, but the grammar is different. 'However' contrasts ideas in different sentences, compared with 'but' which contrasts ideas in the same sentence.

Therefore, in formal written English, the following sentences would be considered incorrect (though they are OK in informal situations).

- Some companies are very enthusiastic about GM food, however, many people are very worried about its dangers

- Some companies are very enthusiastic about GM food. But, many people are very worried about its dangers.

This rule also applies to other discourse markers. In addition, some discourse markers can only be used with noun groups.

2   Fill in the table, on the following page to show how these discourse markers are used in the texts in which you found them in Task B. The same word can go in more than one column.

 LEARNING tip

> This table will be very useful to you in the future! Keep it as a reference!!

Connect ideas in different sentences (followed by a clause)	Connect ideas in the same sentence (followed by a clause)	Connect ideas in the same sentence (followed by a noun group)
addition In addition, ...	... and ...	..., as well as ...
contrast		
summary		
reason/result/cause/effect		
example		

ENGLISH FOR ACADEMIC PURPOSES s t u d e n t s ' b o o k

Put appropriate discourse markers in the gaps below.

1 There are two reasons for supporting pure scientific research. Firstly, it satisfies humans' natural curiosity about the universe in which they live. .... Secondly, technological advances that followed on from pure scientific research have led to improvements in our lives. _____, the non-stick coating on saucepans has made washing the dishes so much easier. _____, improved aeroplane materials have made flying faster, quieter and cheaper. _____, we should be grateful for pure scientific research.

2 Exploration of space has resulted in improved understanding about weather systems on other planets and moons in our solar system. _____, we have an improved understanding of the Earth's weather systems _____ the consequences of future changes such as global warming.

3 It is so easy for scientific advances to cause problems. _____, nuclear energy sounded wonderful when it was first developed, _____ of its expected low cost _____ lack of pollution. Safety was a concern and was taken seriously _____ careful precautions were usually taken, and in most cases these did actually result in a low chance of an accident. _____, nothing is perfect, including safety systems, and when problems do happen, the consequences are extremely serious. _____, although actual operation of a nuclear reactor produces little visible pollution, disposal of the radioactive materials that are produced is extremely difficult and expensive, _____ consequently nuclear power is now considered too expensive in many countries. _____, many governments have stopped planning to build more nuclear reactors. This example clearly shows that the miracle of yesterday may become the disaster of tomorrow. Not every scientific advance has the expected result.

English for the Internet Age

Searching the World Wide Web

A search engine is an Internet tool which you can use to find a list of sites that are related to a key word or words.

Follow these instructions on a computer that is already connected to the Internet.

1 Start the Internet browser.

2 On the toolbar of the browser (near the top of the screen), click on the button labelled 'Search'.

3 When the page appears, you will see an empty box. Click in this box.

4 Type in the key word you want to search for. When you have done this, press the button marked 'Search'.

5 A new page will appear. This will give 10 or so sites in which your key word or phrase appears, with a small amount of information about each site.

6 The number of sites which the search program found is usually displayed near the top of the list.

7 Quickly read the details given about each site to decide which might contain the most useful or interesting information. Don't try to understand everything—it will take too long, and most of it won't be relevant. The reading skill used here is skimming. (See Unit 1, page 20.)

8 Right-click on the link for a page that you have chosen, and select 'Open link in new window'.

9 You can click on the boxes at the bottom of the screen, or use the window menu, to return to the search results—then you will be able to repeat step 8 in order to see as many pages as necessary.

10 To see more search results, there is usually a link near the bottom of the page which takes you to the next ones.

> ## Task B: Looking at the effect of key words on searches

To search for sites containing two separate words (not a phrase), type + (plus sign) before each word. For example, to search for sites containing information about tourism by aeroplane, you could type

> +air +tourism

This will give sites containing the word 'air' and also the word 'tourism', and these words may not be next to each other on the page. However, if you search for

> air tourism

you would only get a list of sites that contained the phrase 'air tourism', that is, with the word 'aeroplane' immediately before the word 'tourism' (on some sites, you would have to put quotes around the phrase, ie 'air tourism').

If you want to search for a mixture of words and phrases, then it's best to put the phrase in quotation marks. For example, if you want to search for information about transportation of nuclear waste, you could type:

> transportation +'nuclear waste'

The list of results will include pages with the words 'nuclear' and 'waste' together, and the word 'transportation' somewhere else on the page.

1 Imagine you have been asked to write an essay about the advantages and disadvantages of television for children. Which of the following would you expect to be the most useful key words to use for this search? Why?

- +television +advantages
- +television +problems
- +television +children +advantages
- +television +'effect on children'

2 Try the searches in Question 1 and decide which one is the most effective.

 LEARNING t i p

> The more specific the search words are; the more likely you are to find useful sites.

3 For the following subjects, with a partner, write some search words that you may use to find information about the subject.

- the effects of video games on children
- the advantages of information technology
- recent developments in rocket science
- recent discoveries about our solar system
- the effects of mobile phones on the brain.

4 Now try some of the searches in the previous step. How effective are they?

> **Task C: Internet research**

Later you are going to speak and write about a technological issue of your choice. You may want to look ahead to the table on page 73. Choose one issue now, and search the Internet for information about your issue. Use what you have learned in this section to help you.

Speaking 2

Interrupting, suggesting, accepting and rejecting ideas

To express your views in a discussion, you may use some of the phrases below.

> **Task A: Expressions for interrupting, suggesting, accepting and rejecting ideas**

Copy the phrases into the correct column of the table. Add any others you or someone else in your group knows.

Phrases

Yes, but on the other hand ...	That's what you've read, but I've read ...
Could I just say ...	Hang on ...
I'm afraid I disagree with that idea ...	My view is that ...
What about the fact that ...?	I think ...
I agree with you to some extent, but ...	That may be so, but ...
No, I don't agree ...	Well yes, however ...
Well, you may have a point, but ...	

Interrupting to make a relevant point	Suggesting an idea	Rejecting an idea	Accepting an idea, but putting your own view forward

Task B: Discussion

1 Make a list of scientific or technological issues that recently have been in the news. Include the issue you researched in the task on Internet research.

2 Write down your opinion about each issue.

3 In small groups, discuss these issues, trying to use as many of these expressions as possible. To encourage you to use the new expressions, do this as a game. In this, one person should be an observer, counting how many times each person uses one of the expressions. Whoever uses the largest number is the winner. Change observer every time you move to a new issue.

Critical thinking

Analysis of positive and negative aspects of technology

As we noted in Unit 2, it's often easier to write if you discuss your ideas first. Your lecturers at university will usually be happy for you to do this as long as your assignment doesn't become too similar to someone else's!

Task A: Discussion about technological advances

Opposite is a table that lists advantages and disadvantages of various forms of technology, including the ideas used in the two essays you have read in this Unit. In small groups, choose three or four of these developments and discuss them, adding to the ideas given. Use the expressions on this page.

Advantages	Development	Disadvantages
■ Increases in production ■ ■ Decreased costs of production	Agricultural mechanisation	■ Reduced employment in agriculture ■ shift of population from countryside to cities ■ loss of habitat for wild animals and other environmental problems
■ ■ ■ tourism	Airborne transport	■ ■ ■ war
■ higher agricultural yields ■ lower prices	Genetically Modified Food	■ unknown effect on environment ■ farmers tied more tightly to food companies
■ ■ ■	Information technology	■ ■ ■ Access to advantages of technology depends on wealth
■ ■ ■	Mass production	■ Workers have lower range of skills ■ Lower personal involvement of workers leads to less pride in the work done. ■
■ ■ ■	Motor vehicles	■ ■ ■
■ ■ ■	Nuclear power	■ ■ ■
■ ■ ■	Television	■ ■ ■

Writing 2

Writing a discussion essay

Task A: Writing a discussion essay

Now that you have completed this unit's work on discussion essays, choose one of the above subjects for which you have plenty of ideas. Write a discussion essay about this subject using ideas from your discussion in the previous section. Remember to first write a plan. Follow the format of a discussion essay that you studied earlier on page 61. Also, use synonyms to avoid repetition of words, as you learned on page 65. In addition, use some of the discourse markers we discussed on page 66.

Learner independence & study skills

How to remember for longer

Task A: How good is your memory?

1 When you learn something new, either on your EAP course or any other course, how much do you remember later? Draw a curved line on this graph to show how much you <u>think</u> you remember:

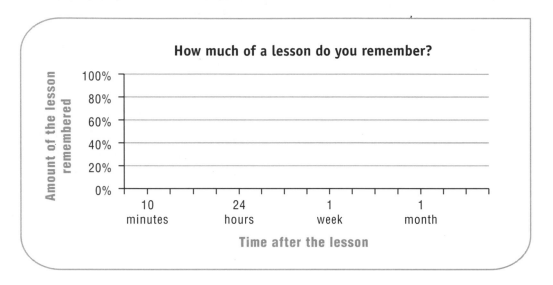

How much of a lesson do you remember?

Amount of the lesson remembered: 100%, 80%, 60%, 40%, 20%, 0%

Time after the lesson: 10 minutes, 24 hours, 1 week, 1 month

2 Next, compare with the other people in the class. Are other people's graphs similar or different?

3 Now, look at page 249 in Appendix B. This graph (Graph I) shows how most people's memory works. It is adapted from psychologist Tony Buzan's book *Use Your Head* (BBC, 1995), which is a very useful book for anyone wanting to learn how to study more effectively, and is easy to read. Discuss with your partner:

- Is there anything that surprises you about this graph?
- How similar is it to the one that you drew?

Task B: Discussion—how important is review?

1 How do you think that reviewing what you have read changes the graph? Draw a new line on the graph to show what you think will happen if you review at the intervals given on the bottom axis (10 minutes, 24 hours, 1 week and 1 month)?

2 Now, look at the graph on page 250 in Appendix B. Discuss with a partner:

- Does this graph surprise you?
- Is it different from the graph you drew?
- Can you think of any ways of overcoming the problem of forgetting what was learnt?
- How important do you think review is?

1 Find a diary for this year. A small, pocket-sized one is OK. (If you are near the end of the year, you will need one for next year, too!)

2 What were the main points, vocabulary etc that you learnt today? Write a reference to them on your year planner or diary for tomorrow, one week from now and one month from now. Do this every day that you have lessons, learn or study anything.

3 Every time that you study, look at your diary or planner for the things you should review on the days since you last studied. If you do this regularly, you will find that it becomes much easier, and you will be amazed by how much you remember!

Writing 3

Issues in science and technology

Task A: Analysing questions—which genre?

Look at the essay questions in the box below. Next to each, write 'explanation', 'argument', 'discussion' or 'argument or discussion'.

Questions

1 It is too early to know the long-term effects of growing genetically modified (GM) food. Therefore, GM food should not be grown outside well protected laboratories. To what extent do you agree with this point of view?

2 Mobile phones have brought new rules of etiquette to society. What are the rules about the use of mobile phones in your society? For example, should you switch off mobile phones before going into a cinema? What is the **rationale** behind these rules?

3 Explain your opinion about the following statement: 'The use of animals in scientific research should be restricted to the areas of medical research which could **potentially** result in human life being saved.'

4 Money spent on sending people into space should be diverted to other more **worthwhile** causes such as reducing world hunger. Discuss.

5 Scientific research is an expression of humanity's natural curiosity about the universe around us. Give your reasons for your point of view about this statement.

rationale
reasons/logical
explanation

potentially
if something
could potentially
happen, it's
possible that it
will happen

worthwhile
useful, not a
waste

Task B: Speaking and writing—discussion

Choose one of the essay titles above. Use the following steps to write your answer (that is, the essay):

1 Decide whether the answer should be an explanation essay (see Unit 1, page 14), argument essay (see Unit 2, page 43) or a discussion essay (see this Unit, page 61).

2 Discuss the question with a partner. This will help you to get ideas for your answer.

3 Write a plan for your essay (see Unit 1, page 13).

4 Show and explain your plan to the partner you spoke with in Step 2.

5 Write a first draft of your essay, paying attention to the organisation of ideas, discourse markers and style of writing. A first draft is a first writing. It is written with the intention of changing it later, as part of the process of writing.

6 Show your first draft to your partner, who should try to find weak points in your argument; for example, weakly supported ideas (see Unit 2, page 49). Then read it yourself and try to make improvements.

7 Write a second draft, which should include the suggestions from Step 6. Also, make sure that the style is appropriate for academic writing.

8 Write as many further drafts as you like.

9 Hand it in and celebrate a job well done!

 LEARNING t i p

> **WRITING:** It's useful to follow these stages when writing any essay, no matter what course you're studying. Keep referring to this list in your future studies.

literature

The pen is a
sceptre, but how
scarce kings are
among the writers!

KAHLIL GIBRAN

Skills focus: In this Unit, you will learn and use the following skills:

Writing

✓ *Paragraph formatting 2: topic sentences*
✓ *Methods of development: providing concrete supporting evidence*
✓ *Creative writing*

Paragraph formatting 2: topic sentences

See Unit 1,
page 16.

When expressing ideas in English, the main thought or important point generally comes first. For example, if I want to tell you *what I did last night* (and what I did was go to a movie) … and, in the context of the conversation, the words *last night* indicate the **time** of the action, and the **time** of the action is the most important point …

I **don't** say:

1 *The movie I went to last night was very good.*

I **don't** say:

2 *I saw a very good movie last night.*

I **do** say:

3 *Last night, I went to a very good movie.*

Why don't I say (1) or (2)? What is wrong with those sentences? Nothing is grammatically wrong with them in terms of clause construction. But the answer is the *order* is wrong. Number (3) is the only way to express the importance of 'last night, I'. Remember I said I wanted to tell you **what I did last night**, *therefore,* **Last night, I** becomes the theme of the sentence—**Last night, I** … is most important and it comes first in the sentence. It is the theme; it is the main idea; it is the beginning of the topic sentence; and it is the topic of the conversation until the conversation shifts (probably to discuss the movie seen last night). 'It' (the topic, the theme, the main idea) consists of all the words up to the first verb.

The end of the sentence—*very good movie*—is the rheme or the other important idea/participant in the sentence.

> ### Task A: Theme/topic in English

Using the instructions, write possible topic sentences for the following main ideas:

1 You wish to *describe the kitchen* in your house or apartment.

_____

_____

2 You wish to *argue by giving reasons, that the blue shirt is better* than the black one for a party.

_____

_____

3 You wish to state that *synonyms for words can be found in a thesaurus.*

_____

_____

Write three more 'topic sentences' based upon subjects that you think up yourself. Write your idea first, then write the sentence based upon that idea. Remember to place your **main purpose first** in each sentence.

1 _____

_____

2 _____

_____

3 _____

_____

How can you make certain your paragraphs are cohesive? In other words, how can you make sure your paragraph makes sense to the reader?

Some common problems in student writing:

- too many ideas are introduced in one paragraph;
- sentences are not related closely enough to each other;
- methods of development are not clear.

Methods of paragraph development: providing concrete supporting evidence

Task A: Developing paragraphs using different methods

Using the first three topic sentences you have created in Task A above, expand each sentence and provide further information. You will be writing a paragraph. Here are the three previous topic sentences and three methods of developing those sentences into paragraphs. In the first sentence about the kitchen, you should go on to *describe* everything you can. Think of shape, colour and furniture. Use adjectives. Write the topic sentence again and then continue.

DESCRIPTION

1 The kitchen in my apartment is _____ the walls are painted.

_____

_____

_____

_____

_____

_____

_____

GIVING REASONS

2 The blue shirt will look better for Aaron's party than the yellow one. I know it will! The blue one is _____

_____

_____

_____

_____

_____

GIVING DEFINITIONS AND EXAMPLES

3 If you need to find a word that is better than the one you are thinking of, use a thesaurus _____

_____

_____

_____

_____

_____

_____

Task B: Methods of development of paragraphs, *continued*

Examine the following models on pages 82–83, A through to D, beginning with cause and effect. These are further examples of methods to use to develop ideas and information after you have organised and planned what you will write.

1 Study the examples, *noting the methods outlined for you in bold type*. Write the methods of development which are listed A to D. The first one (A) is cause and effect.

A *cause and effect*

B _____

C _____

D _____

2 Locate the exact language that shows you that the method named is the method used and write that language below each model.

3 Write four more paragraphs of your own, using the methods of development from the models A through to D.

A _____

B _____

C _____

D _____

Models A–D

A. CAUSE AND EFFECT

There needs to be a correct relationship between humans and the earth which is our environment, that is to say ... the land and all its resources. This is because humans depend upon the earth's resources for survival. Therefore, if a balance is not maintained between our use of the earth and our desire for progress (which has tended to over-use resources to the point of destruction), the inevitable result could be the destruction of the land and the people upon it. Thus, due to the dependency of humans upon their natural environment, the destruction of ourselves will follow the destruction of our environment.

_____

_____

_____

_____

_____

B. LISTING OF DETAILS

Tofu is an excellent food source which is light on the stomach, full of protein, versatile to prepare, and derived from soybeans, a sustainable crop. It costs less than meat-based protein too. That's why it is used in so many countries as an important and healthy food.

_____

_____

_____

_____

_____

C. ANALOGY

A human is very much like a machine—a car—for example. Fuel is required to sustain movement and to operate the body. The heart pumps like an engine and there are interconnecting moveable parts.

_____

_____

_____

_____

_____

D. COMPARISON AND CONTRAST

Writing stories or writing a book is like composing songs. The writer has to have an initial idea, as does a songwriter. They both have to find an audience. The writer needs a publisher and a distributor for their stories or books and a songwriter needs a recording producer and a distributor for their music. They differ in that a writer rarely reads their work aloud but a songwriter expects their song to be performed aloud (sung).

_____

_____

_____

_____

_____

_____

_____

(*Source*: Adapted by the authors from an original concept of seven methods of development from 'The Process of Writing' in *The World Book of Word Power*, Chicago, USA: Field Enterprises Educational Corporation 1991, p. 197.)

Creative writing

When writers write, they always have something to say. They write for a purpose, for an audience, and with a method—even if they are not aware of it. In this section, you, as author, are to write some pieces based upon your own thoughts. The writing could be fictional but based on your experience and feelings. It does not have to be fiction.

(**Task A:** Learning some conventions of poetry and writing your own poems)

First, examine the poems and follow the instructions beneath each one.

Love's Emblems
by John Fletcher 1579–1625

Now the lusty spring is seen;
Golden yellow, gaudy blue,
Daintily invite the view:
Everywhere on every green
Roses blushing as they blow,
    And enticing men to pull
Lilies whiter than the snow,
Woodbines of sweet honey full:
    All love's emblems, and all cry
    'Ladies, if not pluck'd, we die.'

1 a] What is the theme of the poem? _____

b] Is there more than one theme? What other theme besides *Spring* is mentioned?

_____

c] Count the syllables in each line of the poem. How many are there? _____

d] Write the last word of every line in a vertical row.

    1 _____

    2 _____

    3 _____

    4 _____

    5 _____

    6 _____

    7 _____

    8 _____

    9 _____

  10 _____

e] Find the words that rhyme from the words above and note which lines rhyme with each other. _____

_____

f] Are there any patterns that you can see? _____

_____

g] What conclusions can you draw about typical sixteenth century poetry? _____

_____

h] Write your own sixteenth century poem in English.

2 Select words from the circle in order to compose poetry of your own. You are not bound by convention or rules. Write as you wish, you do not need to rhyme or have a certain number of syllables per line.

leaving verse
clan love beauty song content unto as a the I thee
sing lonely feed eyes deep drown upon anguish soul pale kissed
temple none now gone among cloudy day or of on be to go my thy your
when her can his in of against fine turning shaded touch voice however
taught soft sweet and birds roses lilies dark banish see when rest quiet all
are know hours dream laid face passion here sweet earth silent
covers cold lift to up but with your alone all beyond
cove core heart fire true grace

- First, examine the model that describes a holiday taken by the author.
- Write your own description of a beautiful place that you love.

A holiday ...

What a surprise! All our careful plans were not realised in this holiday adventure, but what occurred was far more exciting and fun. First, our flight was delayed by six hours so that we arrived late at night and not in the day time. Our bed and breakfast hosts were fast asleep and we were forced to wake them to provide our key. They were very kind and invited us in for coffee to chat late into the night about our country. There was such heavy rain that at times we could barely hear them speaking. Our hosts' kindness and the terrible rain was the first surprise.

Next, our morning bus which was scheduled to pick us up and drive us to the markets did not arrive because the same rain which had delayed our flight had closed the roads and the bus could not get through. Instead of the tour we were going to take, our hosts contacted some friends with a boat who came over the flooded road and took us around what used to be streets but had suddenly become waterways. The only transport was by boat. This was a real natural disaster (thankfully no people were drowned nor injured, only property) and yet we were still having fun looking at the sights from our little boat. We cruised from our bed and breakfast into a *klong* or canal and from there were negotiated around the city.

The shops were open, even though there was a foot or so of water on their floors. We shopped amid smiles and children laughing all round their familiar street landscape which was now changed to a slow moving stream. They hopped and waded with their waist cloths lifted above their knees, black-brown eyes and white teeth sparkling with joy at such unusualness. The bargains were the same, the people wished to barter and argue prices, just as usual. It was strange that even though there was such disruption, people stayed cheerful and optimistic about the future. But that's Thailand all over, isn't it?

My holiday (or description of somewhere you love):

_____

_____

_____

_____

_____

_____

_____

_____

_____

Grammar

✓ *Cause and effect: discourse markers or signals*
✓ *Ellipsis and substitution*

Cause and effect: discourse markers or signals

See also
Unit 1, page 15;
Unit 2, page 48;
Unit 3, page 66.

When writing, talking or reading about cause and effect the following types of cues or signals may occur:

■ contrast and comparison;

■ condition and consequence;

■ reason.

Task A: Noticing discourse markers and how they function in texts

1 Examine the following table, then ⟨circle⟩ every discourse cue which indicates contrast, comparison, condition, consequence or reason that you find in the reading texts in this Unit titled *Writers talk about writing*, beginning on page 89.

2 Use the table below to assist you.

contrast	comparison	condition	consequence	reason
conversely	similarly	if	as a result	since
while	likewise	unless	thus	as
in comparison	correspondingly	provided that	so	so
in contrast	equally	for	therefore	because (of)
whereas	in the same way	so that	consequently	due to
instead	in the same manner	whether	it follows that	owing to
on the contrary		depending on	thereby	the reason why
but	equally important		then	
	as		in that case	
			admittedly	
			accordingly	
			hence	
			leads to	

Ellipsis and substitution

1 **Ellipsis:** Look up the word 'ellipses' in your learner's dictionary then choose a definition from the list below.

   a] circle used in a sentence in mathematics;

   b] a postmodern term used in literature;

   c] the moon when it is darkened by the earth's revolutions;

   d] the omission from a sentence of a word or words that would clarify meaning.

> *Question:* Why does English omit words that could make the meaning clearer?
> *Answer:* To avoid repetition.

Read the following.

Example 1

I enjoyed the lunch very much, but I thought the lunch was a little expensive. The lunch was special and we ordered the lunch a day in advance.

Although correct, it reads with too much repetition. Four 'lunches' in two sentences is too many!

■ Read the following using ellipsis and substitution:

            (the lunch)   **(the lunch)**
I enjoyed the lunch very much, but I thought (it) ^ a little expensive. (It) ^ was
       (the lunch)
special and we ordered ^ a day in advance.

'It' substitutes for 'lunch' in the first instance and there is an omission in the last instance. The reader must carry the information forward in their mind in texts. Substitution and ellipsis go together.

Example 2

If your friends don't want to speak English, how can you encourage your friends to speak English?

If your friends don't want to speak English, how can you encourage them to do so?

                (your friends)
If your friends don't want to speak English, how can you encourage them ^ to

(to speak English)
do *so* ^ ?

Example 3 ( ) = what is ellipsed

Life is never easy and it is difficult to be happy all the time. People seek happiness in many ways and we all need to learn how ^(...).

Life is never easy and it is difficult to be happy. People seek happiness in many ways and we all need to learn how (to be happy).

Read the following excerpt from a young adult story and find the omissions or ellipsed words, and note the substitutions:

The howling simply would not stop! I lay in my bedroom listening to the wind,
(1)   (2)
certain, however, that it ^ came from a different source ^.

(3)
I had heard it ^ before, one dark night when both my parents went to a dinner
(4)
party and left me home alone. I had insisted ^ because at thirteen, I am
(5)
certainly old enough ^ !

(6)   (7)
What was it ^ ? And why was it ^ so eerie? I decided to contact my best
(8)   (9)   (10)
friend, Sam, and ask him ^ to listen ^ over the phone. I picked it ^ up and
(11)   (12)
waited for the dial tone. There was none ^ . Strange ^ , I thought. I decided
(13)
to use my mobile phone ^ instead.

Now things got even stranger. My mobile had a message on the screen that

said 'Welcome to the Howling'! I absolutely freaked out and threw the phone
(14)
across the room before realising that answering ^ was the only way I might
(15)
ever find out what was really going on. I raced across the room, picked it ^
(16)
up, then realised that I didn't know how ^ !

1 _____	2 _____
3 _____	4 _____
5 _____	6 _____
7 _____	8 _____
9 _____	10 _____
11 _____	12 _____
13 _____	14 _____
15 _____	16 _____

Getting used to ellipses in English will help you to understand written texts.

Reading

✓ *Writers talk about writing*
✓ *Text types*
✓ *Note taking from reading*

Writers talk about writing

Use the table on page 86 and circle all the discourse markers you can find in the following statements made by famous writers.

1 *In comparison to real life, fiction frees us from ourselves and helps us revel in the muddle of life. (When writing)... fictional time is wonderfully flexible. It can be stretched so that we can look about and take in every detail of the scene, then consider every option, as we never can in reality.* (David Malouf)

2 *The only piece of advice I can give (about writing) is that if you feel passionately about something, go with it and follow your heart and tell something that moves you as best you can.* (Nicholas Evans)

3 *When (my mother) left I sat down and I thought about my own life and thought this was a story worth telling. That's how I started writing this story.* (Jung Chang)

4 *So when people ask me why I write, the answer is not to become rich and famous— because ... if you set out to do that, then you're never going to be either of those things. It's just that the bug bites you, it itches so badly and only one thing will stop it itching and that's to scratch it with a pen.* (Wilbur Smith)

5 *... because ever since I was a child if there was one thing I knew that if I could do, I would do, it was write a book. But when I was in my teenage years, it was the last thing that I would ever have the luxury of being able to do and so the other things were really just ways of keeping my head above water.* (Arundhati Roy)

6 *The reason ... (that my work is a little bit unpleasant or prickly)... is that my mind was warped when I was very young by being deprived of any knowledge of sex.* (Roald Dahl)

7 *Provided that a person had space, quiet, money and an understanding family (or no family at all), I believe anyone who really wished to become a writer, could become a writer. Admittedly, I make this claim only for those who love writing. I suppose this is depending upon whether you think that talent is everything or not. Dedication is equally important if not more so.* (Nom de Plume)

Text types

In English, as in all languages, different texts are written for different purposes and in different ways. The next tasks should assist you to learn about some of the language features that make these texts recognisable. You will try to discover what language features make a crime fiction a crime fiction, and what different language features make an informative or scientific text an informative or scientific text.

Isn't it all English? Yes, it is all English. But you use different participants (people/no people); different processes (kinds of verbs); there are different circumstances (situations) and they have different social purposes.

Task A: Recognising different text types

Read the following text types 1–8 and try to match them with the titles A–I that follow.

Text type 1

1   Atalanta was a huntress. She was renowned by both mortals and the gods for her amazing speed in running. She was beautiful to behold and many men desired her. She, however, did not wish to marry and begged her father to allow her to remain free.

2   Her father refused the swift-running huntress her request and insisted that she choose and marry one of the men who loved her. Since Atalanta would never defy her father, she agreed but convinced him to allow her to arrange a contest so that she might choose the right man.

3   Because Atalanta could run as fast as the wind, she created a contest whereby any of her suitors who was able to outrun her would be allowed to marry her. But, if she defeated them, the man would have to die.

4   Many men came to the valley where Atalanta and her father lived. They ran and ran against her, but she always beat them and each one was put to death. Her cruelty became known throughout the land and many people came just to view such a cruel maiden.

5   One day, Hippomenes came to see the contest. He thought he would despise the girl for her cruelty but once he saw her, he fell in love with her as others had before him. He sought help from Aphrodite, the goddess of love. Now, this goddess decided to help Hippomenes and she gave him three golden apples.

6   With these in his pockets, Hippomenes told Atalanta's father that he wished to race against his daughter, the girl as swift as a deer and as beautiful as a rainbow.

7   During the race, Hippomenes pretended to be tired and acted exhausted. While running, he would pant loudly and each time that Atalanta glanced at him, he tossed a golden apple in her path. Knowing how tired this suitor was and knowing that she could beat him easily, Atalanta stooped to pick up the golden fruit once and then twice. The third time she did this, Hippomenes ran with all his strength and just beat her by stretching for the winning post and touching it first. Since Aphrodite was the goddess of love, Atalanta and Hippomenes married happily and Atalanta forgave him for his trickery for she greatly admired the golden apples and thought him clever and handsome to have devised such a trick.

Text type 2

1   It was around 5 pm when I reached the front door of the empty apartment building which houses my tiny, rented office. I had had to sleep most of the day after last night's confrontation with Mick and his nasty mates. I needed to

touch base and check my answering machine before tomorrow so it didn't really matter how late it was.

When I got inside, I matched the new, black Mazda MX5 convertible parked out front with the petite, pixie-faced young woman standing impatiently outside my office door. It was obvious she was waiting to see me since my office is the only occupied room in the place. I unlocked the door, glancing at my own name—Casey O'Rourke—etched on the glass.

Before speaking, I grabbed the cigarettes off my battered desk, tapped one out of the pack and offered it to her. She smiled briefly, more of a grimace really, said her name was Stacy Beech and took one. I noticed her nails were bitten to the quick.

'How can I help you?'

Text type 3

O fairest Monticello, we bring to thee our praise;
It is with deepest rev'rence
That we our voices raise,
As on thru life we journey,
Sweet mem'ries will remain,
The years of toil and pleasure,
Replete with wisdom's gain,
Those years of riches measure
That will not come again,
May we be ever worthy,
Standing firm without a fear,
May we your ideals echo,
O Alma Mater dear,
You would join the numbers that form her glorious past,
Pledge yourselves to Monticello, Faithful to the last.

(*Source:* Monticello College's 105 Commencement, 1943)

Text type 4

She dreamed daily of home. There were so many things she missed—the soft eyes of the cattle curiously examining her when she stepped into the grassy paddocks; the early morning mist, white and silent that rested on the mountains then lifted to reveal an enormous blue sky; mute-colored valley birds hopping, dancing and flying in silhouette, landing on silver-green gums, all these were sweet visions in her mind.

2 Belle had begun to live for the time she could leave. She hated the frantic pace, the noise and dirt of this tired, greedy city and longed to return to her family and the peace of her father's simple farm.

Text type 5

The Giant Panda

1 The panda is a bear-like carnivore named *beishung* by the Chinese. It has a body about two and a half metres long (six feet) and weighs about 158 kilos (three hundred pounds). It has thick, dense fur which is white except for the black legs and ears, black round the eyes and on the shoulders. It has five toes with claws on each foot. The cheek teeth are broad and the skull is deep with prominent ridges for the attachment of strong muscles needed in chewing fibrous shoots. It lives in the cold damp bamboo forests on the hillsides of eastern Tibet and Szechwan in southwest China.

2 Pandas live mainly on the ground but can climb trees if they face danger. They are active throughout the whole year, unlike some bears, which hibernate. They are generally solitary animals except in the breeding season when they mix in order to mate and they spend 10 to 12 hours a day feeding. They eat bamboo shoots and grasses, gentians, irises and crocuses and also some animal food. They can flip small fish out of water with their paws.

3 Genus and species: *Ailuropoda melanoleuca*
Class: *Mammalia*
Order: *Carnivora*
Family: *Procyonidae*

(*Source:* Information based upon facts from *Encyclopedia of Mammals*, BBC Publishing, 1975.)

Text type 6

1 The relationship between culture and language has increasingly become a subject for exploration as has the classroom goal of modifying student (and perhaps teacher) 'monocultural awareness' (Byram, 1990). Titles such as *Cultural Awareness in the Classroom* (Dink, 1999) and statements such as '... cultural learning is ... preparing the learners for intercultural communication' (Delanoy, 1997:60) have peppered journals and teaching magazines in the last decade. Intercultural communication both inside and outside the EFL classroom is an important reality.

Text type 7

1 Last night at 11:00 pm, the driver of a Rexon oil tanker truck lost control on the Houbeen Beach Highway endangering motorists and causing massive pollution when its load was spilled into the Miami Ocean 2 kms north of Brassby.

Thousands of litres of oil were dumped and this morning were being contained in a massive clean up operation. 'It's too late for the beautiful birds dead on the beach and for many of our fish which this accident has destroyed,' said local resident, Mr Sam Tolafu. Residents of the idyllic island paradise are pitching in to save whatever wildlife they can by cleaning the birds that have survived. All beaches are closed until further notice.

Now match the number of the text type to the letter of its title (not all letters will match a text type, ie there are more names of texts than text types).

A Crime fiction _____

B Fiction _____

C Scientific text _____

D Greek myth _____

E College (university) song _____

F Biography _____

G News story _____

H Abstract for journal article _____

I Recipe _____

When you complete the above exercise, write the name of the text type, (for example, *crime fiction*) in the line next to the actual text in the space provided.

> ## Task B: Recognising the language features of differing text types

Read the following boxed *language features* of each text type and match them with the text titles A–I by writing the name of the number after the letter and name of text type. There are more text types than texts.

A Crime fiction _____

B Fiction _____

C Scientific text _____

D Greek myth _____

E College (university) song _____

F Biography _____

G News story _____

H Abstract for journal article _____

I Recipe _____

Language features 1

- first person narrative—the 'voice' of the narrator is evident and clear in the reader's mind;
  - staging—introduction with time, location, setting the scene;
  - past and past continuous tense;
  - processes (verbs) are material and mental;
  - participants are human;
  - location (place) important;
  - time important;
  - descriptive details prominent—of objects and events.

Language features 2

- third person narrative;
  - past tense;
  - participants are gods/goddesses of Roman/Greek origin;
  - processes (verbs) are material and action;
  - content of story imaginary;
  - resolution of story clear (coda);
  - sometimes a moral or lesson to be learned.

Language features 3

- explanation is statement of fact—factual text;
  - participants are non-human;
  - processes (verbs) are relational (to be: is/has, etc);
  - some technical vocabulary;
  - present simple tense.

Language features 4

- narrator—omnipresent (knows all but is not present);
  - participants are human;
  - processes (verbs) are mental—non-verbal action;
  - description is important.

Language features 5

- personal—includes reader as 'we';
  - participants—people, things and events;
  - processes (verbs)—present, present continuous, future;
  - rhetoric.

Language features 6

- authoritative address to reader;
  - participants are outside the text;
  - processes (verbs) are relational;
  - clauses are long and tend to have many nominal groups (more nouns than verbs);
  - presents an argument or proposes a thesis for an educated reader to consider.

Language features 7

- headline which signals importance;
  - newsworthy event;
  - verbs of action to retell;
  - processes (verbs) which quote;
  - circumstances of time and place;
  - specific participants.

Task C: Recognising different purposes of text types

Choose from the following **purposes** and match them to the text types you read previously in Task A.

Purpose or intention of text/author

1 _____

To provide information about natural and non-natural phenomena.

2 _____

To provide information about newsworthy events to readers.

3 _____

To persuade a reader that something is the case and to report on theory and/or research.

4 _____

To entertain a reader and to describe a particular person or persons in a particular place or places.

5 _____

To engage a group of people in one act of appreciation in a ceremony using song and to relate historical events.

6 _____

To entertain a reader and to describe persons and events around a crime.

7 _____

To entertain and enlighten a reader using ancient stories which may have a moral or warning.

Text types:

- fiction
- crime fiction
- scientific text
- Greek myth
- college song
- news story
- journal abstract

Note taking from whole books

When you read for assignments, examinations, and research for presentations, how will you take notes and organise your study materials? The following tasks will help you to:

- improve your speed;
- know what to write down and what to leave out;
- improve your ability to organise your notes;
- practise skimming and scanning for relevant material.

Task A: Getting a global view of a text

Using the text provided by your teacher or yourself:

- examine the whole book.
- tick the following when you are finished

Did you: yes   no

1 Look at the cover? ☐ ☐

2 Open the front pages and note the copyright date? ☐ ☐

3 See who the author/s are? ☐ ☐

4 Note the publisher and the city where the book was published? ☐ ☐

5 Open the book to the back and find index pages? ☐ ☐

6 Open the book to the back and find references? ☐ ☐

7 Examine the Table of Contents if there is one? ☐ ☐

8 Examine the chapter headings? ☐ ☐

9 Examine the chapter sub-headings? ☐ ☐

10 Read the back cover of the book carefully—more than once? ☐ ☐

Task B: Getting around a book—the whole book

Using the same text complete the following:

1 Write the complete title, the author/s name, the publication date, the publishing house and city of publication:

_____

_____

2 Note the pages where you found the index:

_____

3 Note the pages where you found references:

_____

4 Summarise the back cover in your own words:

_____

_____

5 Scan the index and search for one topic. Look for all the words that are similar or related to the topic. Write the page numbers here:

_____

Task C: Note taking from books

1 Choose one chapter from your book to take notes from.

2 _Very quickly_ look over the entire chapter.

3 Note down any headings that are in **bold.**

See Unit 2, pages 50–51.

4 Decide upon a method for note-taking—writing numbers 1, 2, 3, 4 etc or letters A, B, C, D etc. You can combine numbers and letters by making the main points or themes either a letter or a number and listing smaller details beneath.

Next is an example of notes taken from the short text which follows:

TITLE: Using a library

We have found over the years that many students do not actually gain the best benefit from their libraries. Our research (2000) showed that many students wander around looking in areas hoping to find what they want after searching for a particular book on a reading list which has been checked out by someone else.

Often, their attitude is that if the book they sought is gone, then they cannot complete their assignment. This article hopes to show students some ways to approach the situation differently.

First, students need to learn that the cataloguing system used is the Dewey Decimal. This is a classification system of classifying books into ten major subject classes and then further dividing ideas by tens, the divisions being represented by the numbers in a decimal system. The most useful thing a student may do is to attend their library orientation class and learn how to access this cataloguing system.

(_Source_: Connor & Wessley, 2002 'Library Systems and Students', _Using a Library_, Randoff Publishers, New York, p. 22)

Notes:

Connor & Wessley, 2002 'Library Systems and Students', _Using a Library_, Randoff Publishers, New York, p. 22

Note that the first thing to do is to be sure to write the source in its entirety and correctly! Don't forget to do this!

Now begin note taking:

1 Research (2000) Connor & Wessley.

2 Students should learn Dewey Decimal Classification system

A. Dewey Decimal—def. Classify—10 major subject classes, then divide ideas by 10s.

See Unit 2, page 52.

Notice the word 'def.' in the notes above. It stands for *definition*. It is an abbreviation for the word definition. There are some standard abbreviations but you also should devise them for yourself (just be sure you remember what you decided upon so that you can read your notes and recognise your own abv/s (that's abv/s for abbreviations).

Here are a few additional abbreviations that the authors use and that are not included in other units. Some are commonly known to writers of English.

- U = you
- R = are
- TV = television
- bk = book
- ref = reference
- ref 2 = refer to
- wman = woman
- cond. = condition
- etc = and so forth or so on.

Many of these are common sense and you can devise your own abbreviations in addition to the table which appears in this book in Unit 2, page 52.

Task D: Practise summarising information in topic sentences

No one can teach you exactly how to summarise, but you must find the themes (remember? all the words up to the first verb) and you can usually read the first and last sentences of paragraphs to find main and important concepts.

Choose three different texts. Try shortening the first and last sentences of your own texts in order to make summaries for note taking:

Text 1

- Topic sentence: _____
- Revised summary: _____

Text 2

- Topic sentence: _____
- Revised summary: _____

Text 3

- Topic sentence: _____
- Revised summary: _____

Listening

Listening for pleasure and listening for non-linguistic cues

(7)   Listen to the dramatic presentation of a hero who was really a villain in Australia in the 1800s (Recording number 7).

Vocabulary (your teacher will assist you with the meanings):

- armour
- invincible
- euroa
- wombat heads
- Big, ugly, fat-necked, wombat-headed, big-bellied, narrow-hipped, splay-footed, sons of Irish baliffs of English landlords
- fat necks
- she's in a delicate condition
- apparition.

Task A: Listening for non-linguistic cues which carry action forward

Listen a second time to the recording and listen for sounds that are not people speaking.

Make a list of everything you hear.

1 _____

2 _____

3 _____

4 _____

5 _____

6 _____

7 _____

8 _____

9 _____

Task B: Discovering—what is the point of these non-linguistic cues?

- Can you work out any reasons for the sounds?
- Examine the following reasons and try to match them to the sounds you listed previously.
  1 Present action taking place that you cannot see.
  2 Actions that have been mentioned and are now completed.
  3 Location changes.
  4 Time passing.

1   Does your country have a villain who is a hero? Discuss.

2   What is the person's name?

3   When did they live if they are no longer living now?

4   Is the person male or female?

5   Are their deeds social, political or creative?

6   What makes a hero?

7   What makes a villain?

8   What cultural qualities does your nation have that makes this person famous and popular?

Critical thinking

Considering writing styles

Task A: Comparison of text types from your own language with English

1   Make a list of as many types of writing (different text types) that you can think of from your own country. Work in groups with others of the same culture or nationality if there are any in your class.

2   Using your list, consider what features are the *same* according to your work on text types in English that you completed earlier in this Unit.

3   Using your list, consider what features are *different* according to your work on text types in English that you completed earlier in this Unit.

Speaking

Tutorial participation skills 1

See Unit 3, page 71, *Interrupting.*

Like oral presentations, tutorials are an important part of university life. You will be expected to be able to initiate, add and take part in discussions around the issues that your lecturers from various faculties have presented. You can 'get an idea on the floor' by simply recognising when another speaker is pausing or hesitating and it is appropriate for you to begin speaking. You can also begin speaking by simply agreeing or disagreeing with a speaker, thereby making it your turn to speak. This is called 'turn-taking'.

■ In groups of five, read the following paragraphs aloud:

Student 1

I think fiction is the best form of writing. I really love to get lost in the characters' lives and to just forget about the real world for a while. It really is the best.

Student 2

I don't agree, I think non-fiction leaves story-telling for dead. Don't you remember the saying 'truth is stranger than fiction?' (*Byron, Don Juan*)

Student 3

Yes, but a lot of fiction has truth in it. It has been researched and some stories have a whole lot of fact in them. Look at that book by Peter Carey about the Australian outlaw Ned Kelly. It is fiction but based on fact.

Student 4

With respect, I have read that book and there is no truth in it at all! Carey made it all up!

Student 5

I agree, about *that* book, but that doesn't mean that no fiction books have facts in them. There are heaps of so-called fiction that have facts. Look at crime novels, they often have a lot of true stuff in them!

Now, examine the table and place the turn-taking cues from the five students into the correct lines: agree or disagree

The cues are beneath the table:

Agree	Disagree

Yes, but   *I agree*

With respect   *I don't agree*

Add the following cues to the columns—will the speaker agree with the statement made by the previous speaker or disagree?

Hang on a minute ...   *What makes you think that?...*

Certainly ...   *Why not look at it like this?...*

Yes ...   *Well, you have a point there, but ...*

Speech ideas—You have one minute to:

1 Explain why you're late to class.

2 Tell about the greatest gift you have ever received.

3 Talk about the most wonderful teacher you have ever had.

4 Talk about the worst teacher you have ever had.

5 Tell us how your dream lover looks and acts.

6 Tell us your idea of the most wonderful place on earth.

7 Explain how being the richest person in the world would be wonderful.

8 Explain how being the richest person in the world would be terrible.

9 Explain how you might save the world from an alien space landing.

10 Convince us that the computer is the best invention of the 20th century.

Learner independence & study skills

Time management

Task A : Examining your use of time

Write next to the times one sentence explaining everything you did and will do today:

AM (in the morning)

6 _____

7 _____

8 _____

9 _____

10 _____

11 _____

12 _____

PM (in the afternoon)

1 _____

2 _____

3 _____

4 _____

5 _____

(in the evening)

6 _____

7 _____

8 _____

9 _____

10 _____

11 _____

12 midnight

1 _____

2 _____

- Compare this list with a partner.
- Are your lives just the same? How are they same, and how are they different?

Now fill in the following weekly timetable, noting truthfully what you do in each space of time.

	Sunday	**Monday**	**Tuesday**	**Wednesday**	**Thursday**	**Friday**	**Saturday**
6 to 9							
9 to 12							
12 to 5							
5 to 10							

- Have you organised a timetable such as this before?
- Have you ever considered examining what you do with each day, week, month?

At university and any other tertiary study you undertake, you will need to focus your life around assessment dates such as examinations, assignments due, tutorials and oral presentations, term dates (beginnings/endings).

- Begin looking at your own life now and see what you really do with your time.
- Do you watch a lot of TV? (More than two hours a day is a lot!)
- Do you study and never go out and enjoy yourself?
- Do you work 20 hours per week and spend another five getting to and from work?

- Just what does your life look like?
- Can you fit four hours a day in for studying?

Task B: Creating a personal timetable that includes 30 hours of study

Revise your timetable to include 30 hours per week of study if it is not there now.

English for the Internet Age and Critical thinking

Evaluating academic credibility of information on the Internet

Task A: Can Internet information be trusted?

Useful vocabulary: 'If something has **credibility** (n), people feel they can believe and trust it. Also **credible** (adj).

1 What's easier—getting a book published or putting a web page on the Internet? Why? Think about whether the information is checked before being published, and whether anyone is going to lose money if the project isn't successful.

2 From your answers which do you think is more likely to be true and accurate—information in a book or on a website?

3 If the website is published by a well-respected organisation, would your answer to Question 2 change? Would your answer change in other situations as well?

Task B: Critical thinking—predicting bias and accuracy

Imagine you are reading for an assignment which asks whether banning firearms (guns) is likely to reduce the number of homicides (murders). Answer the following questions 1–3 for each of the websites (a) to (f) below.

1 Would you expect a balanced or a one-sided (biased) view?

2 Would you suspect the accuracy of the information?

3 What further questions would you want to investigate before you believe the information you found? (eg in (b), does the charity have a particular opinion about gun use, eg that carrying a gun deters crime?)

Websites

pressure group an organisation which aims to influence government opinion over a particular issue

a] A firearms manufacturing company.

b] A charity that helps the families of crime victims.

c] A **pressure group** that wants to ban people from using guns.

d] Someone who has done some research in their spare time. There is no evidence that they have studied the subject carefully.

e] An investigation, at a well-respected university, into murder rates in countries where guns are banned, compared with countries where guns are allowed.

f] Police statistics about gun ownership.

Task C: Evaluating website credibility

1 After completing Tasks A and B, what would you look for in a website before using information from it in an assignment? Does your answer agree with the content of the evaluation forms below?

2 Continue researching the connection between firearm ownership and murder rates. Try the following sites. Use the evaluation forms to help you decide which sites are credible enough to investigate further. If you chose to use the information from the site in an essay, what other considerations would you take into account (eg compare the information on the site with information from other sources, or look for information biased in the opposite way)?

You can follow other links but you don't have to go outside the sites.

a] www.gunowners.org/ ➔ Fact Sheets ➔ 1999: Firearms Fact Sheet

b] www.abanet.org/gunviol/

c] www.handguncontrol.org ➔ Facts

 LEARNING t i p

> To find latest update dates, author, publisher etc of a website, look at the bottom and top of the page.

Website evaluation form 1: Looking at bias

Kind of organisation (eg government, political party, **professional association**, pressure group, none (private individual) ...?	
Author's **institutional affiliation**	
Purpose of the page (eg to advertise, entertain, give information, persuade ...?)	
Evidence of **ulterior motive** (eg make money, gain power by promoting a particular view)?	
Summary: Can expect a non-balanced viewpoint?	

professional association a group of people from a particular profession, who support other members of the profession

institutional affiliation means the organisation who the person is paid by or is a member of

ulterior motive an unsaid reason for doing something

Website evaluation form 2: Looking at accuracy of information

Author's **credentials** (eg qualifications, experience ...)	
Is there a reason to respect the organisation (eg part of government, respected NGO, etc)	
Are there references? Is it original research?	
When was the site last updated? Is it up-to-date?	
Summary: Can see a reason for lack of accuracy? (Remember that bias can also be a reason for inaccuracy.)	

credentials
a person's qualifications, experience and other qualities that show there is a reason to believe the person

LEARNING tip

The evaluation forms can be used with any information source, not just Internet sites.

Task D: Searching and evaluating

Find websites relating to an issue of your own choice. Decide whether you could use them in an assignment.

unit 5 the news

> The wolf preys
> upon the lamb in the
> dark of the night,
> but the blood stains
> remain to accuse
> him by day.
>
> **KAHLIL GIBRAN**

Skills focus: In this Unit, you will learn and use the following skills:

Speaking

✓ Oral presentation skills and oral discourse markers.
✓ Oral presentation assignment.

Oral presentation skills and oral discourse markers

At university and in business contexts, people are required to prepare material and present it orally. It is a fact that a large percentage of your mark from certain subjects is derived from the tutorial sessions where you will be asked to present oral work based upon your own research. Sometimes this makes up as much as 40% of your assessment.

> **Task A: How to prepare and present an oral presentation (or maybe how *not* to)**

1 Tick what you believe are the correct statements from the following lists based upon 'What makes a good oral presentation'.

2 Write False next to statements you think are not accurate.

3 Write what you believe are the correct sentences under the False ones.

Preparation and research

a It is important to research the topic using a number of different sources.

_____

b You should write the paper once and once only.

_____

c You should begin research and preparation as soon as you know what your topic is.

_____

d If given a choice of topics, you should wait to go to the library about one week before the presentation is due.

_____

Presentation

a You should speak very quickly so as to keep within the time limit.

_____

b You should speak slowly and clearly so as to keep your audience interested.

_____

c You should use overheads (OHTs), or a computer program such as PowerPoint or Persuasion to present your paper.

_____

d You should practise your presentation in front of a mirror.

e You should write your presentation out word for word and then read it exactly as it is written.

Delivery on the day

a You should hold your paper up proudly in front of your face and read it to the audience.

b Your OHTs should be written in very large point size.

c You should have a clear outline at the beginning of the presentation.

d Your Introduction should be the longest part of the presentation.

e You should impress your audience by using very long, complicated sentences.

Question time

a You cannot prepare for question time so wait and see what the other students/audience will ask you.

b It is best to avoid this 10 minute period (the usual time for questions) if possible, by making your presentation longer.

 Ask your teacher for the <u>Answers</u> on how to make a fool of yourself and get a low mark.

Task B: Using discourse cues to recognise stages of a presentation

1 Ask your partner to read out half of the oral discourse cues or markers:

2 Match the oral discourse markers to the correct stage of a presentation by filling out the table below. Now, change roles and you read.

Stages of a presentation

Introduction—this is the stage where you explain the title of your talk, give background information, provide definitions of terms and the scope of what you will cover.

Body—this is the stage where you show the research you have accomplished, make relevant points if you have an argument to put forward, counter other arguments and name your sources.

Conclusion—this is the stage where you summarise each main point (state again) and give a recommendation for the future.

Introduction	Body	Conclusion

Discourse cues/markers

Today, I would like to ...; In conclusion; There are three main points ...; In 2002, Barker and Johnston ...; To summarise ...; In order to define 'cactus' it is important to consider ...; This talk will cover two current theories around the topic of ...; Thus, it is obvious that the government should provide ...; It is beyond the scope of this presentation to include everything around the topic of forestry, so ...; It would appear that one solution might be to ...; Actually, there is not a great deal of research that has been carried out around this subject ...; Let me begin by ...; A great deal of research has been carried out around this aspect of the subject since 1922 ...; Next; However; It is worth considering ...

Oral presentation assignment

You will prepare and give an oral presentation to members of your class. You have had some information about oral presentations already in this Unit at page 108, and will get more help in Unit 6 at page 145 and in Unit 7 on page 159. When you come to Unit 7 (page 169), you will give your presentation. Your teacher will tell you on which day you should present.

Your teacher will give you information to complete the form below—this is information you should know before you start **any** assignment. Your teacher will also tell you where in Appendix C to look for the assessment criteria that will be used.

Topic:

Due date:

Length of presentation (minutes):

Assessment criteria: See Appendix C page:

Other requirements

- Your presentation must give an opinion and this must be supported with evidence from your reading, and with logical argument.
- You should go to a library to carry out your research.
- Your presentation should show that you have read from several books and articles.
- It should show that you have critically analysed the information you read.

 LEARNING tip

> In your tertiary course, it's important to find out as much as you can about how an assignment will be assessed before you start preparing it!

Writing

Compiling bibliographies

A bibliography includes every reference book, article, website, newspaper, or, even person from which or whom an idea came. Students often believe they only need to mention or reference when they copy words directly from the text. This is not true. You must also include in your bibliography the pages from sources that gave you an idea or understanding of the topic.

You must compile a bibliography (sometimes titled References) at the end of every researched essay you are asked to write for any subject studied.

Here is a sample of what one looks like:

Bibliography

Bassey, M (1986) 'Does action research require sophisticated research methods?' Hustler, D, Cassidy, A, & Cuff, EC (eds) *Action Research in Classrooms and Schools*, Allen & Unwin, London, p. 18.

Burns, R (1994) *Introduction to Research Methods*, Longman Cheshire, Melbourne, p. 32.

Burns, R (1993) *Research and Education in ESL*, Longman Cheshire, Melbourne.

Burns, R (1990) 'ESL learners in context', *Journal of TESOL Psychology*, Vol. 3, No. 4, pp. 8–20.

Cohen, L & Manion, L (1994) *Research Methods in Education*, Routledge, London.

Elliott, J (1994) 'Research on teachers' knowledge and action research', *Educational Action Research*, Vol. 2, No. 1, pp 23–35.

Zancor, P (2002) 'Overseas students coping and not coping', *Educational On-line OS Journal*, http//www.EdJourn.com lifeat//go.tesol/ef01.html (23 Sept 2003).

Plagiarism

Plagiarism means writing ideas from any source and not acknowledging that source. In other words, to plagiarise is to use another person's words and pretend they are your own.

You may copy work but you must show your reader that it is copied. This is part of research!

Look it up. Use it. Acknowledge it.

Task A: Understanding bibliographies

1 Which citings (references) have page numbers at the end of the reference?

2 Why are page numbers shown on some references and not others?

3 What does (eds) mean in the first citing?

4 Why does Bassey appear first and Zancor appear last?

5 Why are *italics* used at the end of some references and at the beginning of others?

6 In the first reference, is *Action Research in Classrooms and Schools* a book or a journal? How can you tell?

7 In the reference (Elliott) is *Educational Action Research* the title of a book or a journal? How can you tell?

8 Did you notice more than one reference from the same author? Name the author.

9 In what order are the dates of publication of the author from question 8 presented?

10 Some disciplines suggest from oldest to most recent publication dates for the same author. You may choose—just remember to be consistent.

A bibliography is a list of all the source materials that you used or consulted in the preparation of your assignment. Bibliographies link to the body text of your essay. A bibliography is a list and explanation of the references in the body text. Each reference in the list must match a reference in your essay.

Task B: Analysing references in body texts

1 Read the following two texts and circle every reference.

Text 1: extract from an essay

Bassey (1986:18) looks at 'change' and improvement' as the search for 'right decision', while Burns (1994:32) looks for 'a process of improvement and reform'. Both have valuable insights to assist a new student of research.

Note the last sentence, *Both have valuable insights to assist a new student of research*. This is a critical comment—ie it displays critical thinking by the writer of the essay— this will be YOU. First you quote, then you draw some conclusion about what you have just quoted. Reference the quote and you have not plagiarised!

2 You should have circled Bassey (1986:18) and Burns (1994:32). Now answer the following:

a] How many authors are there in the first reference? _____

b] What year was the text from which the quote came published?

_____

c] Who is Burns? _____

d] What page number did the quote from Burns come from? _____

e] What year did Burns publish the text from which the quote came?

_____

Text 2: extract from a newspaper

China Daily

Vol. 21, No. 6701   Friday, September 21, 2001

APEC meeting to promote regional economy

by Min Zeng, *China Daily* staff

Top leaders of the 21 member Asia Pacific Economic Cooperation (APEC) forum will gather in Shanghai from October 20–21 to look in depth at the region's economy, Foreign Ministry spokesman Zhu Bangzao said yesterday in Beijing.

Text 2 is an actual extract from a newspaper. Here is how it would be written up if you wished to quote this extract exactly:

'Top leaders of the 21 member Asia Pacific Economic Co-operation (APEC) forum will gather in Shanghai from October 20-21 to look in depth at the region's economy', Foreign Ministry spokesman Zhu Bangzao said yesterday in Beijing. (Zeng 2001:1)

Task C: Writing bibliographic references correctly

Write the bibliographic reference correctly for the reference in Text 2 as it appeared above (Zeng 2001:1).

_____

_____

Examine the bibliography below and fill in the missing spaces by referring to the bibliography on page 111.

_____ , M (1986) 'Does action research require sophisticated research methods?' in Hustler, D, Cassidy, A, & Cuff, EC _____ *Action. Research in Classrooms and Schools*, Allen & Unwin, London _____.

Burns, R _____ *Introduction to Research Methods,* Longman Cheshire, Melbourne, p. 32.

Burns, R (1993) *Research and Education in ESL,* Longman Cheshire, _____.

Burns, _____ (1990) 'ESL learners in context', *Journal of TESOL Psychology* _____ No. 4, pp 8–20.

Cohen, L & Manion, L (1994) _____ Routledge, London.

Elliott, J _____ 'Research on teachers' knowledge and action research', *Educational Action Research* Vol 2, No. 1 _____.

See Unit 7, page 161.

Task D: Referencing from the WWW (World Wide Web)

There is no worldwide accepted standard for WWW referencing, but the following will guide you.

You must always quote references when using the WWW. Quote the reference information which **should be found in the document**. If that information is not there, then use the entire web address as follows: *author's name, year of publication, title of web page, title of website/complete work, web address, date of publication or if not available—the date you visited the website.*

Li, Wei (1994) Three Generations, two languages, one family 'Language choice and language shift in a Chinese community in Britain' http://www.latrobe.edu.au/education/celia/tesl-ej/ej04/r6.html (6 June 2003)

Also see *The Columbia Guide to Online Style*. (Columbia University Press (2002) Basic CGOS Style. *The Columbia Guide to Online Style* http://www.columbia.edu/cu/cup/cgos/idx_basic.html (6 June 2003))

Grammar

✓ *Pronominal referencing and participant tracking*
✓ *Tense review: perfect tenses*
✓ *Register revisited*

Pronominal referencing and participant tracking

Task A: Identifying main participants and tracking them in a text

Read the news story below and identify the main participant. For example, in the previous sentence, the main participant is *the news story*.

> The body of a Japanese man who was a keen fisherman was found on the river bank at Wagowdgi on Friday night. The man was last seen fishing from the rocks above Wagowdgi River late Friday afternoon. He was identified by his wife as Mr John Suzuki and they were holidaying in the area. Mr Suzuki is survived by his wife and two children.

1   Name the first and main participant mentioned in the news story in the first
    sentence _____

2   Find the reference to him in the second sentence _____

3   Find the reference/s to him in the third sentence _____

4   Find the reference to him in the last sentence _____

Now examine the bolded text:

> **The body of a Japanese man who was a keen fisherman** was found on the
> river bank at Wagowdgi on Friday night. **The man** was last seen fishing from
> the rocks above Wagowdgi River late Friday afternoon. **He** was identified by
> his wife as **Mr John Suzuki** and they were holidaying in the area. **Mr Suzuki**
> is survived by his wife and two children.

Here is another way to show and keep track of the main participant.

The body of a Japanese man who was a keen fisherman

↓

The man

↓

He

↓

Mr John Suzuki

↓

Mr Suzuki

Brief explanation of substitution in English

The body of a Japanese man is the noun phrase, *the man* is the same noun, *he* is the
pronoun substituted for *man* which refers back to the man and *Mr John Suzuki* is the
proper noun in the form of the man's name.

The important point here is not the grammatical names, rather, how the grammar
works. The reader must **keep track** of the idea or person that the writer introduces.

See Unit 4,
page 87,
substitution.

> ### Task B: Tracking multiple participants

Read the next news story and track the following participants using the grid that
follows the texts:

1   London firefighters

2   the scene of a factory fire

3   five workers

4   work.

You can colour code or number them as you track them the first time. Do one at a time.

> London firefighters rushed to the scene of a factory fire, saving lives in 1
> West London on Saturday night. The firefighters fought the chemical 2
> blaze for over seven hours. The brave and tired men rescued five 3
> workers who were working overtime on the premises. 4
>
> They were overcome by smoke and were lying on the factory floor when 5
> firefighters broke the doors to enter the blazing building to check if 6
> anyone was inside. 7
>
> The premises were presumed empty, but the workers had the key and had 8
> arranged with one another to complete work there to meet a deadline. 9
> This work was crucial for a major overseas contract for the company. 10
> The men in red said they were 'just doing their job correctly' by 11
> checking the building for people. No charges are to be laid against the men. 12

Write each reference to the four participants found in the news item in the table below.

London firefighters	The scene of a factory fire	Five workers	Work
Line:	Line:	Line:	Line:
1			
2			
3			
6			
11			

Task C: Practice in locating and tracking a main participant

1 Read the beginning of the next news story and locate the main participant/s that will require tracking if you were to continue reading.

> In the USA, a shocking, recent death penalty study of 4,578 cases in a 23-year period (1973–1995) concluded that the courts found serious, reversible error in nearly 7 of every 10 capital sentence cases that were fully reviewed during the period (Moore, 2001).

List here:

a] _____ b] _____

c] _____ d] _____

2 Now track *a ... death penalty study of 4,578 cases in a 23-year period (1973–1995):*

_____

3 Now track *a 23-year period.*

a] _____ b] _____

Tense review: perfect tenses

These activities will assist you to understand the past perfect tense and revise the genre of narrative or recount. Past, past perfect and past continuous tenses are used in the following narrative, which is based upon a true story about a whaling ship called the *Essex*. The *Essex* is famous because it is the only whaling ship ever sunk by a whale. The ship was built in 1796 in Salem, Massachusetts, which is now part of the USA and her last whaling voyage in the Pacific Ocean took place in November 1819.

The account is an extract from the book Owen Chase wrote on the wreck of the *Essex*. He was first mate on the ship and was 23 years old. He later became a captain and wrote a book titled, *Narrative of the Most Extraordinary and Distressing Shipwreck of the Whaleship* Essex.

The narrative is a factual recount of the events. This is followed by the story of what happened to the crew while their ship was sinking. Both texts are true stories, and because they are recount, will contain certain grammatical features and structure:

- time and date
- place
- chronological order with temporal sequencers
- description of events, but not many feelings
- specific participants
- verbs of action.

TEXT 1: *Narrative of the Most Extraordinary and Distressing Shipwreck of the whaleship* Essex, by Captain Owen Chase, 1821

The whaleship *Essex* left Nantucket on her last whaling voyage to the Pacific on August 12, 1819, under Captain Pollard. It carried a crew of 21 men, one was a boy of only 15.

The *Essex* sailed from the Galapagos Islands. Presently a whale rose and spouted a short distance ahead of my boat. I made all speed towards him, came up with him and struck him with a harpoon. Feeling the harpoon he threw himself in an agony over towards the boat and giving a severe blow with his tail struck the boat near the edge of the water amidships and stove a hole in her. I immediately took up the boat hatchet and cut the line from the harpoon to disengage the boat from the whale which by this time was moving off with great velocity. I succeeded in getting clear of him with the loss of the harpoon and line and finding the water pouring fast into the boat, I hastily stuffed four or five of our jackets in the hole, ordering one man to

5

10

keep constantly bailing and the rest to pull immediately for the ship. We
succeeded in keeping the boat free and shortly gained (arrived at) the ship. 15

3 The boat which had been stove was immediately hoisted in, ... I was in the act
of nailing on the canvas when I observed a very large spermaceti whale, as well
as I could judge about 85 feet [26 metres] in length. He broke water about 20
rods [100 metres = 110 yards] off our weather bow and he was lying quietly,
with his head in a direction for the ship ... In less than two or three seconds, 20
he made directly for us at the rate of about three knots. I ordered the boy at
the helm to put it hard up, intending to sheer off and avoid him.

4 The words were scarcely out of my mouth before he came down upon us with
full speed and struck the ship with his head, just forward of the fore-chains. He
gave us such an appalling and tremendous jar as nearly threw us all on our faces 25
... We looked at each other with perfect amazement, deprived almost of the
power of speech. Many minutes elapsed before we were able to realize the
dreadful accident ... The whale started off in a direction to leeward (away from
the ship).

5 ... I dispatched orders ... I again discovered the whale, apparently in 30
convulsions ... He was enveloped in the foam of the sea ... and I could
distinctly see him smite his jaws together, as if distracted with rage and fury.
He remained a short time in this situation and then started off with great
velocity across the bow of the ship to windward. I was aroused with the cry of
a man at the hatchway: 'Here he is—he is making for us again'. 35

6 I turned around and saw him, about 100 rods directly ahead of us, coming down
apparently with twice his ordinary speed and, it appeared to me at that
moment, with tenfold fury and vengeance in his aspect. The surf flew in all
directions about him, and his course towards us was marked by white foam a
rod in width, which he made with the continual violent thrashing of his tail. His 40
head was about half out of water, and in that way he came upon and again
struck the ship. He struck her to windward, directly under the cathead, and
completely stove in her bow ...

7 Not a moment, however, was to be lost in endeavouring to provide for the
extremity to which it was now certain we were reduced. We were more than a 45
thousand miles from the nearest land with nothing but a light open boat as the
resource of safety for myself and companions. I ordered the men to cease
pumping and everyone to provide for himself ...

In Text 2, which follows, the writer is not giving a first hand account in the past, but
is telling the reader about known past events, and for this reason, the past perfect tense
is used a great deal.

Read the following and note the past perfect tense (expressing a past action that was
completed before another past time or event).

1

The crew were in three whale boats while their ship was sinking. They had had time to gain access to the other boats. There was plenty of time while the crew sadly watched their ship, its decks awash, slowly sinking. Before the *Essex* went down, however, members of the crew had gone aboard several times to collect food, water and other things. They had taken as much as they had room for in the boats.   5

2

They had sails and masts in all boats and were more than 1600 kilometres away from the nearest land mass. Those who were rescued eventually, were rescued three months later.

3

They told their rescuers how in great storms and in the darkness the three boats had become separated. The winds had blown them off course. They told how   10 supplies of food and water in their boat had run low and how at the time of their rescue they were living on a handful (70 grams) of bread each per day. They told how one after another their crew mates had died of starvation and thirst until there were only three survivors left out of seven. Day after day, week after week, they had looked in vain for a sail. They told how they had eaten   15 parts of the dead men's bodies in order to stay alive. They told how the huge waves in great storms had threatened to sink their boat and how they had had to keep bailing to keep afloat. Only their trust in God's goodness had saved them from the hopelessness and despair which leads to death ...

An interesting note: It was a son of Owen Chase, himself a whaler following his father's trade, whom Herman Melville spoke to and to whom the son gave a copy of his father's book (about the sinking of the *Essex* by a whale). Melville used the story in his masterpiece *Moby Dick*, which you may have heard about or read.

(*Source*: Compiled from and with the permission of G.A. Pittman (1983) *Whales and Whaling in the Pacific*: New Caledonia, SPC pp 77–88.)

Task A: Processes or verbs—choosing the correct tense

1 Underline or circle all verbs (processes) in each recount narrative.

2 Make a list of each of the verbs (processes). Include the noun so that you have a phrase, not just an isolated verb. For example, in line 1 of the first text, you would write—The *Essex* <u>sailed</u>; a whale <u>rose and spouted</u>;

3 Next to your list, note which tense is used.

4 Go back to each sentence and examine the verbs in their context. Why do you think the simple past is used in the first recount?

5 Why is the past perfect used in the second recount?

6 Can you create a paragraph of a story and then another paragraph which tells about that story and which uses these two tenses? For example, tell (or write) a story about a famous tragedy in your country. Write it as the person to whom it happened. Then, write a sequel to your story explaining further, but not in the first person.

Compare the first person account, *Narrative of the Most Extraordinary and Distressing Shipwreck of the Whaleship* Essex, to the third person narrative, *What happened to the crew of the* Essex?

Use the table below:

First person narrative		Third person narrative	
Narrative of the Most ...		What happened to the crew ...?	
Author	Owen Chase	Author	Unknown
Target audience	Present day historians; anyone interested in whaling	Target audience	The same audience
Purpose for writing (author's possible intention)	To share a very difficult experience with others. To set the record straight concerning the sinking of a whaling ship	Purpose for writing (author's possible intention)	To explain a story of the past and to let people know what the crew told their rescuers
Source	A book by Owen Chase	Source	Unknown
Time	The actual time of the event (although we know it was written after)	Time	Many months or even years after the event
Place	The Pacific Ocean, a thousand miles from the nearest land off the Galapagos islands and the whaling ship *Essex*	Place	The sinking ship; the boats where the crew lived; the country where the crew ended up after being rescued

Task C: Learning the features of a narrative

Refer to the items below, which were pointed out at the beginning of these narratives. Next to each one, write evidence of them from either of the two texts.

- time and date _____

- place _____

- chronological order with temporal sequencers _____

- description of events, but not many feelings _____

- specific participants _____

- verbs of action _____

See page 114, participant tracking.

Task D: Tracking a participant

Track the participant—the whale—in Text 1, *Narrative of the Most Extraordinary and Distressing Shipwreck of the Whaleship* Essex.

Use any format you wish—circle all, or make a list of the words—draw lines from each reference to the next.

Task E: Tense choices in context

1 Circle or underline the verbs (include the subjects) in Text 2.

2 Make a list of each and write the tense beside them.

Register revisited

Task A: Recognising the features/requirements of a news story

Read the following 'news story' and comment upon the register by answering the questions at the end of the story.

Prime Minister supports higher university fees

The Prime Minister said he was going right ahead with charging higher money costs to students who want to go to college. He reckoned that people can afford it and anyway if they can't it really doesn't matter all that much because most people who want to get an education will do something to get it. They can always borrow money must be his philosophy.

Fees are too high now according to many students that I talked to. They figure they will have to quit going and get a job instead. It's terrible and rotten, I think. It's like education will only be for the very rich really soon. It's getting like that now.

1 Does the article read like a news story?

2 What is the usual format for reporting the news? Fill in the spaces below using the story and then comment upon what is missing or different in this news item.

3 Headline _____

4 Name of reporter _____

5 Summary of the event _____

6 Time and place stated _____

7 Background to the event _____

8 Grammar—action verbs _____

9 Processes (verbs) of thinking and feeling _____

10 Higher lexis (vocabulary) written language _____

_____

11 If it is not a news story, what does it read like?

_____

_____

Listening

Distinguishing between fact and opinion

Task A: Listening for key phrases which signal opinions

Listen to the tape of a radio talk back program (Recording number 8: *Talk back radio program: Fast food around the world*) concerned with the fast food industry and fast food chains around the world. While listening, place a tick next to the following phrases each time you hear them:

a] I want to tell you

b] I think

c] I reckon

d] I know

e] In fact

f] The fact of the matter is

g] You're not suggesting

h] But believe me, the facts

i] I refer you and your listeners to

j] There's pretty indisputable evidence that

k] I mean

l] Like I say

Task B: Facts, opinions and power relationships

1 Who has the most power in the situation of a radio talk back show:

    a] the radio announcer

    b] the callers?

2 How does the announcer use his power in this situation?

3 Is he kind or abrupt?

4 Note the comments the announcer makes after each caller has finished speaking. Choose which comments you think express *the announcer's opinion* from the ones below:

    a] Ya couldn't cook it yourself for the price.

b] Well, you were lucky to have a job, aren't you?

c] Ya get all that free training and experience and ya want top dollars too.

d] You sound like a drama queen getting in some corporate bashing to me.

e] Like I say, I've been eating good ole fast food for ever and it's fine.

5 Is the announcer ever rude to the callers? _____

6 Note one statement that the announcer makes that you think is rude.

_____

_____

7 Do you think it would be difficult to speak on air if you phoned into a radio station? _____

8 Have you ever phoned a talk back show host and made a statement?

_____

9 Would you like to phone in and talk about a subject? _____

10 Write the numbers of the statements below into the table into one of the two categories.

Most likely to be an opinion	Most likely to be a fact

1 You can actually get very sick from eating fast food.

2 I never have to eat the local muck they call food in some of those places and I can count on quality and never getting sick.

3 I reckon it's still very good value to feed a family on a bucket of chicken with gravy, fries, coleslaw and buns.

4 I've been working since I was 15 and we get pretty low wages, ya know.

5 Did you know we can't join the union, and mostly we get fired as soon as we're 17 and can get adult wages?

6 Well, the fact of the matter is that *E. coli* is a bacteria and it is found in a fair bit of hamburger meat that leaves the big meatpackers.

7 *E. coli* spreads another way and that is from the hands of workers who don't wash them.

8 There are, in fact, cases of real people and they have had settlements from food chains over the deaths of their wee children from eating contaminated meat.

9 I've eaten 'em [hamburgers] all over the world and I've never been sick once.

10 Like I say, I've been eating good ole fast food for ever and I think it's just fine.

11 These days, everywhere ya go, you can get food to go or eat in restaurants run by companies you can trust.

12 It's [the world's] ... changing for the better alright, because, like ya say, we can buy good food no matter what country we're in.

13 Well, you're lucky to have a job, aren't you?

14 He's done the research and it's true as the sun rising.

Task C: Discovering if truth is necessarily fact

Take the same 14 sentences and, using the four categories below, place the letter of the category next to the correct number of each sentence in the table.

A Anecdotal evidence based on experience—sometimes it is an opinion but it can be truth and factual.

B Researched evidence which is truth/fact.

C Truth.

D Opinion stated as truth.

Task D: Factual evidence

Examine the 14 phrases in the context of the listening transcript and decide who you think is the most likely to be providing factual evidence.

- the announcer, Jim
- Barry
- Nerrida
- Luke.

Reading

✓ *Newspaper editorial*
✓ *Purpose or intention of writer: identifying bias, connotations and attempts to influence*

Newspaper editorial

Task A: Defining an issue—global examination of text

Read the newspaper editorial in Task B, on page 126 before you begin to answer these questions:

1 Using your dictionary, define the word 'issue'.

2   What does the bold lettering beneath the name of the paper say and what does it mean?

3   After reading the title, what issue do you believe is going to be discussed in the article?

4   Examine the title and tell your partner what else you think the article is going to discuss.

5   From the title, can you guess which side of the issue the editorial will take?

6   What does the title *Stranded refugees lose again …* imply?

7   Identify the author of the editorial.

8   Examine the name of the newspaper. Are there any clues in the name of the paper that might give you an idea of what the editor may say in this article?

9   Who is the possible audience for this editorial?

Task B: Vocabulary in context 1

Read Editorial 1 on the next page and try to work out the meaning of the vocabulary in the table. If you cannot match the definitions, use your dictionary.

a] stranded (vb)	1 an accusation
b] determination (n)	2 the political party not in power
c] asylum seekers (n)	3 a person who migrates into a country for permanent residence
d] refugee (n)	4 to drive aground on a shore, esp. of the sea, as a ship, a fish, etc.; to bring into a helpless position
e] humanitarian (adj)	5 to follow a course of action
f] indictment (n)	6 people seeking a refuge or a sanctuary—a safe place
g] opposition (n)	7 a going out; a departure or emigration, usu. of a large number of people
h] interned	8 the act of coming to a decision: the fixing or settling of a purpose; the settlement of a dispute by authoritative decision
i] pursue avenues	9 to diminish or destroy the purity of
j] tarnish (vb)	10 one who flees for refuge or safety, esp. to a foreign country, as in time of political upheaval, war, etc
k] immigrant (n)	11 obliged to reside (stay or live) within prescribed limits and not allowed to leave them, as prisoners of war or enemy aliens, or troops who take refuge in a neutral country
l] exodus (n)	12 having regard to the interests of all mankind

The Social Left Herald
News for those who care about the real issues

Stranded refugees lose again ...

1. It is unfortunate, if not downright illegal when a country assumes a position outside international and United Nations determinations. Today, another boatload of desperate people has been towed out of waters near our shores. This country has created a tarnished reputation for itself with regard to the handling and treatment of refugees attempting to enter the country via boats. Asylum seekers are referred to by the current government as 'illegal immigrants' which is ridiculous and incorrect as one cannot be an immigrant when one is a refugee. Additionally, this government most definitely appears to have as an agenda, the elimination of participation in policies which allow new people into the country via any means other than visa application. 5 10

2. The editor of this newspaper recalls the 70s when the Vietnam War necessitated an exodus from some regions of that country via similarly dangerous means as that of the current people fleeing war-torn countries. Leaking boats were rescued by the military (which currently has quite a different agenda) from the seas nearby our shores, humanitarian care was taken with these asylum seekers and processing of their claims for refugee status was carried out efficiently and quickly. 15

3. Not so today. This government has gone so far as to engage the military to 'guard' our shores in a so-called 'border protection policy' and to send ships (even leaking) loaded down with people onwards, rather than allowing them to pursue the avenues that should be open to them. Worse, still, if they do get onshore, the processing times for their claims for refugee status have taken years! The asylum seekers are being interned, they are kept in camps in hostile environments with little or no stimulation. Additionally, children are housed with adults without schooling or entertainment. This is rapidly becoming a human rights issue and is a sad indictment of our government which is heartless at the very least and racist at its worst. 20 25

4. The opposition is not offering solutions through new policies either. Thus, our only power as a people is to question and ultimately, reject both parties and to place support with the *Left Greens Democracy Party* which has made public its humanitarian and legal policies regarding this issue. 30

Task C: Vocabulary in context 2

Read Editorial 2 and try to work out the meaning of the vocabulary in the table. If you cannot match the definitions, use your dictionary.

a] commotion (n)	1 government expenditure which exceeds the money available; also called 'in the red'
b] financial (adj)	2 to deter/discourage through fear or doubt about proceeding

c] budget deficit	3 to set upon with arguments, pleading, entreaties
d] deterrent (n)	4 requests using pleading
e] influx(n)	5 concerning money
f] assailment (n)	6 the arrival of people in great quantity
g] entreaties (n)	7 improve by alteration, substitution, abolition
h] reforms (v.t.)	8 political or social disturbance

The Financial Review

Weekly world financial indicators

1   Despite the current commotion raised by a small minority surrounding the government's policies concerning illegal immigrants, thankfully, there is a wiser, more financial view.

2   The cost burden of processing illegal immigrants has and is becoming an increasing encumbrance upon the taxpayers of this country. The government's   5 sensible border protection policies, although lifting the defence budget considerably and creating a temporary budget deficit, are preferable. Engaging in border protection will prove a deterrent to other illegal immigrants and discourage people smugglers.

3   This country could ill afford an influx of the magnitude that other less prudent   10 policies might give rise to. The continuous assailment upon the government and entreaties from a few bleeding hearts to alter these policies is not viable. Financial markets have responded strongly to the government's stance in a positive way.

4   This editor has observed national division around this issue widen. The press is   15 divided and individuals have strong opinions concerning who has the right to apply to live in their country. The fact is illegal immigrants are queue jumpers. Diplomatic representation in countries of origin, which support the international coalition of nations is the proper procedure to follow. Additionally, many of the claimants are not actually refugees and are merely seeking to short   20 cut an established process.

5   As polling has demonstrated, there is confidence in the wider community and markets will continue to reflect this confidence in the current government and their reforms.

Purpose or intention of writer: identifying bias, connotations and attempts to influence

Bias indicates looking at something in a way that is one-sided or prejudiced in its presentation. Bias is an opinion disguised as fact.

Now that you have read the two opinion pieces which both concern a particular government's policies around refugees entering their country, try to examine the purpose of each writer within each editorial. Begin with *The Social Left Herald, News for those who care about the real issues*.

1 What opinion does the topic sentence in the introductory paragraph express?

2 Write the adjectives and noun groups used to express this opinion.

3 Write the adjective from sentence 2 that describes the editor's opinion of the people seeking refuge.

4 Write the adjective from sentence 3 that describes the editor's opinion of the country's reputation.

5 What does the writer imply and intend you to think about the military in para 2 when he or she writes 'Leaking boats were rescued by the military (which currently has quite a different agenda) from the seas nearby our shores, ...'?

6 When you read 'humanitarian care was taken with these asylum seekers and processing of their claims for refugee status was carried out efficiently and quickly', does the past simple passive 'was taken' and 'was carried out' imply that this is not happening now but it did happen in the past?

7 In para 3, what is the implication of using ' ' (quote marks) around the word *guard*?

8 In para 3, ' ' is used again around '*border protection policy*'. Why?

9 Why does the author choose to write '<u>so-called</u> *border protection policy*' rather than simply *border protection policy?*

10 In para 3, find the exclamation mark and explain what is implied by its use.

11 In para 3, what is the writer's view of the government?

12 In the final paragraph, what <u>statement</u> does the writer make concerning the opposition party?

13 How does the writer attempt to influence the reader?

14 In the last paragraph, the intention of this writer is revealed. Look at the text after the summation or conclusion cue—*Thus*. Write what the author believes is our only option.

15 Based on your reading of the entire editorial comment, what was the author's intention? In other words, why was this article written? You may choose from the following comments:

a] to criticise the current government's policies around refugees

b] to encourage support for the Left Greens Democracy Party

c] to appeal to the public for support for international refugees

d] to question the humanitarian nature of internment

e] all the above.

Read Editorial 2 on page 127 again.

1 What opinion does the topic sentence in the introductory paragraph express?

2 Write the nouns and noun phrases used to express this opinion.

3 What purpose does the word 'Despite' serve as the first word in sentence 1?

4 What purpose does the word 'thankfully' serve in sentence 1?

5 The writer uses an argument beginning in para 2. How does this argument begin?

6 What does 'sensible' refer to?

7 What is the writer's view of the government's border protection policies?

8 What is the financial effect of the government's border protection policies according to the writer?

9 Since the writer says that the policies will lift the defence budget (more money will be spent) and create a budget deficit (the country will be in debt), he or she still argues that they are a good thing. What one key word signals to the reader that this is going to be the argument?

10 Why are the border policies preferable?

11 Is the statement 'This country could ill afford an influx of the magnitude that other less prudent policies might give rise to' a fact or an opinion?

12 Is the above statement in Question 11 worded like a fact? How do you know that it is not necessarily factual?

13 What evidence is there that refugees are actually 'queue jumpers' as the editor states?

14 How does the writer attempt to convince the reader to agree with him/her in the last paragraph?

Critical thinking

Language as power: becoming a critical reader

Task A: Discussion

1 Does your country accept applications from refugees?

2 Does your country accept refugees?

3 If you answered 'yes' to the question above, from which countries do they arrive?

4 What are some of the reasons that people become refugees?

5 Do you believe that any country has a humanitarian responsibility with regard to people from another country who are under threat of death if they remain in their own country?

6 What is your personal opinion about refugees or asylum seekers in the world today?

Read the following text and answer the questions at the end. As in other texts in this book, the paragraphs are numbered.

TITLE: **Becoming a critical reader**

1 Why does language matter? Except for people speaking different languages, don't we all accomplish the same thing with language—communication? No, because some people have power and others do not. Language serves those in power very well and they are often the ones who make the rules as to how language must be used.   5

2 Social conventions about who has power are maintained largely through language. When you examine the feminist movement in the West from the 60s onwards, language had to be changed in order to stop the 'norm' always being male. Textbooks defined scientists, teachers, everyone, really as '... A man who ...' Gender was and (often still is) a determiner in power relations. The naming 10 of things creates our feelings about them and determines how we think about these things. If you refer to a woman as a woman, it is correct and direct. If you refer to a woman as a 'chick' or 'a slut', then the name means something else. 'Chick' often means young or sexy and 'slut' means a woman of loose morals (note that slut is almost never used for a man in English.) These names have power to hurt or offend, yet they all mean woman.   15

3 Whether power is maintained by gender, race, wealth, politics, education or any number of other factors, it is largely maintained by 'dominant meanings' (Janks, 1993) which are often not challenged. When people do challenge the dominant meanings the status quo could be altered.

4 Language rules about who is allowed to speak or write and when, how people 25 are addressed and how long people can be listened to are all governed by social conventions. Language is constructed. It is constructed by making choices from the range we have. It is not natural, nor inherent. It is learned and created and it serves the interests of the users, if they know how to use it.

5 Students of English as well as native speakers, by becoming critical readers, may 30 gain insight into language as power and become more empowered themselves. 'Critical readers resist the power of print and do not believe everything they read' (Janks, 1993: iii).

Reference

Janks (1993) *Language, Identity and Power*. Johannesburg: Hodder & Stoughton

1 What is the main point of the article? Choose from the options below.

a] The main point is that language is constructed.

b] The main point is that readers must not believe all they read.

c] The main point is that people speak different languages.

2 What does the writer want from readers? In other words, what is the writer hoping to teach the readers to do?

_____

_____

3 Who constructs the rules around language and what institutions does language serve?

_____

4 What does social convention have to do with language and its construction?

_____

5 a] Look at para 5. Can you list a few examples of when people are supposed to speak only a certain length of time?

_____

_____

b] Can you list some examples of a situation where someone is not allowed to write or where they might write something, but it would not be read?

_____

_____

6 What is one way that you can become a critical reader?

_____

_____

English for the Internet Age

Refugees: Internet research project

Task A: Finding out about refugees

In the following task, you are to follow the instructions in the table. You need to access the Internet and follow certain links which are provided in order to answer the questions.

Question	Website	Follow these links ...
1 What is a refugee?	www.erc.org.au	■ www.refugeecouncil.org.au ■ enter (over the 'advocacy' button) ■ issues ■ scroll down to 'Justice' ■ Asylum Seekers in Australia

Question	Website	Follow these links ...
	www.refugeecouncil.org.au www.amnesty.org.au	FAQs ■ who are refugees? ■ refugees
2 How many refugees did Australia accept in the 1980s?	www.erc.org.au	■ enter (over the 'advocacy' button) ■ issues ■ scroll down to 'Justice' ■ Asylum Seekers in Australia
3 How many refugees did Australia accept in 2001?	www.erc.org.au	■ enter (over the 'advocacy' button) ■ issues ■ scroll down to 'Justice' ■ Asylum Seekers in Australia
4 What is the ratio of refugees to citizens in the following countries? ■ Australia ■ Pakistan ■ UK ■ USA	www.refugeecouncil.org.au	■ statistics ■ ratio of refugees to host country citizens
5 Why do some asylum seekers come to Australia by boat or air without proper documents?	www.amnesty.org.au	■ refugees ■ questions and doubts ■ asylum seekers are illegal?
6 Are asylum seekers (especially 'boat people' without proper documents) illegal?	www.erc.org.au	■ enter (over the 'advocacy' button) ■ issues ■ scroll down to 'Justice' ■ Debunking the Myths about Asylum Seekers
7 What do the Australian and other governments do with asylum seekers who arrive without proper travel documents?	www.erc.org.au www.dima.gov.au	■ enter (over the 'advocacy' button) ■ issues ■ scroll down to 'Justice' ■ Asylum Seekers in Australia ■ information resources ■ fact sheets ■ pull down menu ■ detention arrangements ■ immigration detention

Question	Website	Follow these links ...
8 What is life like in a detention centre in Australia? There are several different perspectives here. Compare them.	www.dima.gov.au ■ information resources ■ fact sheets	■ pull down menu ■ detention arrangements ■ immigration detention
	Teacher's note: Some of the reports in this site are quite disturbing. Edit first to see if you think they are appropriate. www.chilout.org	■ articles ■ research and reports ■ report of visit in January 2002 (read other reports you can find on this site)
	www.erc.org.au	■ enter (over the 'advocacy' button) ■ issues ■ scroll down to 'Justice' ■ Asylum Seekers in Australia
	http://news.bbc.co.uk/ hi/engllish/world/asia-pacific/newsid 1262000/ 1262393.stm	
9 How many children were in detention centres in 2001?	www.refugeecouncil.org.au	■ statistics ■ number of children and adults
10 How many children were in detention centres with no adult to look after them?	www.refugeecouncil.org.au www.chilout.org	■ statistics ■ number of children and adults ■ articles ■ research and reports ■ asylum seekers in Australia (see box 1 at the very bottom of the site page)
11 What are some options apart from detention centres?	www.erc.org.au	■ enter (over the 'advocacy' button) ■ issues ■ scroll down to 'Justice' ■ debunking the Myths about Asylum Seekers ■ Myth 7
12 Name some refugees found in the Bible.		

(*Source*: Thanks to Liz Nance (original research 2002) from Australian Pacific College.)

Learner independence & study skills

Assignment research skills

> **Task A:** Using an assignment from this course

You might have to prepare a researched oral presentation or essay with references, so go to your library and follow the guide below. Here's some advice.

 LEARNING t i p

> When you are in the library photocopy the cover and the inside page where the date of publication and publishing company appear from every book you refer to as well as the pages you are going to read.

For example, if you used pages 50 through 57 from a chapter in a book edited by Smith, and the writer of the chapter or unit was McPhee, you would photocopy:

- the first page of the chapter;
- all the pages you are going to read (beginning with the last page and working forward to the first page)—this will mean the pages come out in the correct numerical order on the photocopier;
- the cover of the book;
- the inside page where the publisher and publication date appears.

Carry a stapler with you. Staple all these pages together and this will be ONE of your references.

When you begin to complete your bibliography, you can find the information very easily!

Vocabulary for tertiary purposes: university word lists

> **Task A:** University word lists to expand lexis (vocabulary)

At university and in other academic contexts, it will help you to learn the higher lexis (vocabulary) that is commonly used by native English speakers at this level.

1 Visit the following website or simply type in *University Word List*.
http://www.latrobe.edu.au/lasu/eslresour/vocab.html

2 Find the red underlined words Academic Word List and click on them.

3 Examine the headwords of the Academic Word List found at this site.

4 Locate the sublists which are numbered beside each word. Make a list of the family of words beginning with access.

unit 6 a global connection: the environment

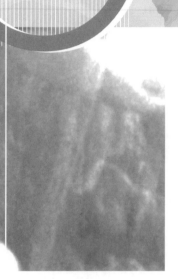

As between the soul and the body there is a bond, so are the body and its environment linked together.

KAHLIL GIBRAN

Skills focus: In this Unit, you will learn and use the following skills:

Speaking 1

What do you know about environmental issues?

Task A: Sharing knowledge about the environment

Copy the table onto a large sheet of paper (one per group). In small groups, share your current knowledge to fill in the table below.

Name of problem	Cause of problem	Possible solutions by government	Possible solutions by individuals	Associated vocabulary
Deforestation				
Greenhouse effect				
Pollution				
Any other problem you like				

Which problem do you think is the most serious? Why?

Compare your table with another group. How similar are they?

Writing

Research reports

Task A: Orientation to research

Answer the following questions.

1 What is research?

2 In what disciplines is it done?

3 Tell your group briefly about as many types of research as you can. Do you think different methods are favoured by different disciplines?

Task B: Stages in a research report

1 Stages in a research report are listed below. They aren't in any order. Put them in the order you would expect to find them in a real report.

- Findings (= what was discovered).
- Background (= background and context of the research, including why it was done).
- Method (= how the research was done).
- Aims (= what the researcher wanted to find out).
- Conclusions (= what the results mean).

2 Check your answers by looking at the headings in the research report written by an undergraduate student for an assignment, on the next page.

3 Sometimes, these stages have different names. Match the words below with the heading with the same meaning in Part 1.

Results   **Introduction**   **Context**   **Procedure**

4 Are reports written in your language divided in the same way?

5 Each stage may have sub-stages. For example, the Findings stage of the report you just looked at has sub-stages *4.1: Findings regarding knowledge*, and *4.2: Findings regarding behaviour*. Look at the following sub-stage headings and decide what stage you would expect to find them in.

Definitions	Research design	Commentary
Discussion	Questionnaire design	Data analysis techniques
Data collection	Analysis	Recommendations
Implications	Literature review	

See Unit 10, page 234.

6 This report (but not all reports) has an abstract. Read the abstract and then the rest of the report and compare the two. What do you think the purpose of the abstract is?

Task C: Identifying language features of reports

1 Read the report starting on the next page again. Which are the most common tenses used in the:

- Background
- Aims
- Method
- Findings
- Conclusions
- Recommendation.

Why are different tenses more common in different stages?

See also
Discourse markers,
Unit 1, page 15;
Unit 2, page 48;
Unit 3, page 66;
Unit 4, page 86.

2 Highlight the discourse markers in a different colour. Do you notice particular types of discourse markers in particular stages?

3 What words are used to mean the people who took part in the survey? What other research-related vocabulary can you find?

TITLE: Knowledgeable but slow to change? An investigation into the relationship between environmental knowledge and behavioural change

Abstract

*Fifty-two respondents were surveyed about their knowledge and the extent of their implementation of the three Rs (Reduce, Reuse, Recycle). Results indicate that environmental advice should be re-directed towards providing practical ideas that can be cheaply and conveniently **implemented** by the public. Further, if efforts are made to reduce the cost and increase the convenience of environmentally sustainable behaviour, this will lead to greater adoption of such behaviour by the public.*

5

1. Background

Environmental **awareness** has been increasing over the last few decades, due to campaigns by environmental **NGOs** and governments as well as education to encourage people to modify their behaviour along more sustainable lines. At the same time, some (but by no means all) businesses have supported this trend by developing and promoting 'green' or 'environmentally friendly' products. However, the trend towards increasing **consumption** has continued, resulting in increased use of packaging and energy. For example, large cars, especially four-wheel drives, with significantly increased fuel consumption, are becoming more popular. It is useful then to know how effective the educational campaigns have been, not only in increasing the public's knowledge but also in **modifying** their behaviour towards greater sustainability, and also to find out how campaigns can increase their effectiveness further.

10

15

20

2. Aims

The purpose of this research was first to investigate how much knowledge a representative sample of people actually have about environmentally sustainable behaviour and secondly, to find out the extent to which this knowledge has led to a positive change in behaviour. A final aim was to look at the factors that are most effective at encouraging people to make their behaviour more sustainable, so that future campaigns can be targeted effectively.

25

3. Method

3.1 The sample

30

The sample size was 52. These respondents were selected from a variety of age, gender and socio-economic backgrounds. They were all residents of urban areas.

3.2 Data collection

This was carried out through the use of a questionnaire. Initially, the questions were trialled with a sample of 10 people. A new improved questionnaire was then **devised**. This comprised 10 questions and focused on some of the most common behaviours. It attempted to **elicit** frequencies of particular behaviours such as re-using items even when buying new ones was more convenient, and choosing to buy goods with less packaging than their competitors.

35

---

implemented
done, put into action

awareness
knowing about something

NGOs Non-government organisation: an organisation, not a company, that is separate from government. Usually they exist for charity or campaigning purposes

consumption
buying or using things, especially things that are not really necessary

modifying
a formal word for *changing*

devised
to write/create something new

elicit
get someone to tell you

4. Findings

4.1 Findings regarding knowledge

Knowledge of what the three Rs represent was reassuringly high. Forty-five of the respondents (87%) could say what the three Rs were. However, only a much smaller proportion (23%, or 12 respondents) could say accurately that reduction of waste and consumption was the most important of the three. As for more practical knowledge, all participants knew how to recycle, but only two-thirds of the respondents (35 respondents) were able to give, without prompting, ways in which they could reduce their consumption. The weakest area of knowledge was in techniques for reusing, with only 16 respondents (31%) able to come up with unprompted ideas. However, when given suggestions such as taking used supermarket bags to the supermarket instead of being given more new ones, or buying reusable instead of **disposable** products, a high 90% said the idea was familiar.

disposable
something that can be thrown away after a single use

4.2 Findings regarding behaviours

Turning to what people actually do rather than just know about, recycling was the largest category, with 79% saying they do this as much as possible and 88% of respondents claiming to do it from time to time. Reducing waste and consumption, however, was a very different matter, with only 69% doing anything in this regard. For example, just over half of all respondents (52%) said they had in the past bought an alternative product because it had less packaging, and 32 (58%) claimed that the energy consumption of products was a major factor in their purchasing decisions.

Re-using again was the least common behaviour, with only 62% able to cite examples of having done this. Just over one-third (18 respondents, or 35%) had reused supermarket bags, despite the high level of awareness of the importance of this, and only 38% of respondents said they never bought disposable products when reusable ones were available.

Despite having knowledge, almost everyone was aware of ideas for following the three Rs that they didn't actually do. Reasons given were as follows:

Inconvenient: 56%

Too expensive: 52%

'Uncool' or 'no one else does it': 18%

(**Note:** These figures add up to more than 100% because respondents were able to specify more than one reason.)

5. Conclusions

5.1 Commentary

discrepancy
an unexpected or illogical difference

It is clear that there is a **discrepancy** between knowledge of the three Rs, knowledge of how to follow them, and the extent to which people actually do follow them in their actions. It is interesting that many respondents who

couldn't suggest a way to follow the three Rs were not only able to do this after 80
prompting, but realised they actually did do it themselves. This suggests that a
lot of knowledge is subconscious. However, it is disappointing that many
people, despite knowing how to recycle, reduce and reuse, don't actually do it.
Expense and lack of convenience are the biggest obstacles to environmentally
sound behaviour. 85

5.2 Recommendations

Because such a large proportion couldn't name ways to reduce or reuse, the
most important of the three Rs, it is recommended that campaigns shift their
focus from recycling and highlighting the three Rs to actually providing
concrete practical suggestions for how to implement them. These suggestions 90
should be as convenient and cheap as possible for the public, in order to reduce
the obstacles to their implementation.

Writing and Speaking

Mini-research project

In this section, you will conduct and write up a small research project.

Many university courses include group assignments, in which the mark for
each member of the group depends on how well the whole group works as a
team. This section gives you experience at doing this.

Because you are working in a group, you will have to negotiate in almost every step of
this project. Everything you learned in previous units about discussion and tutorial
participation skills will help.

See also
Unit 3, page 71;
Unit 4, page 100.

> **Task A: Research questions and hypotheses**

A research project often tries to either:

- answer particular questions (called research questions), or

- presents a statement (called a *hypothesis*) and tries to find out whether it's true
  or false.

1 What are the research questions for the research in the previous section?

2 In groups, choose a topic for your research. Your teacher will give you a general
field. Then, together, decide on a research question or hypothesis.

Task B: Devise the questionnaire

Write a questionnaire with between five and eight questions to investigate your research questions or test your hypothesis. For example, for the research presented on environmentally sustainable behaviour, starting on page 138, one of the questions on the questionnaire may have been 'How often do you recycle?'

Task C: Pilot survey

Trial your questionnaire (conduct a pilot survey) in your class. This is to identify any problems there may be with the questionnaire. For example, there might be more than one way of understanding the question, or you might find it's impossible to draw conclusions from the answers to some of the questions.

After looking at the results of the pilot survey, negotiate together about how to adjust the questionnaire.

Task D: Main survey

Carry out the survey!

When finished, form groups and help each other to collate answers and draw conclusions. A group secretary should record the conclusions.

Task E: Write a report

Write a report to present your conclusions, following the stages you learned at the beginning of this Unit.

Learner independence & study skills

Reading outside class

Task A: Focusing your reading outside class

1 List as many reasons as you can why practising reading outside class is important.

2 Think of useful aims for your reading practice.

3 Put ways that you already read outside class in the top of the following table. Then, compare your table with others in your group and discuss the marks you gave. Choose the ideas you like best and that fit your aims and write them in the bottom part of your table (leaving space for more).

4 Now swap tables with another group. Discuss them as before. When you get your book back, add new ideas to your table.

5 Decide which ideas are best for you and try them out. Next week, you will tell your group which ideas you tried out.

Way of reading	Mark out of 5 for		
	enjoyment	ease of use	usefulness
Your ideas			
Other good ideas			

6 After you have tried out these ideas, you may reject some, change others or try new ones.

Listening and Speaking

✓ *Listening for main purpose: tutorial questions about business and the environment.*

✓ *Tutorial participation skills 2: asking questions in tutorials.*

Listening for main purpose: tutorial questions about business and the environment

> ### Task A: Orientation to topic—alternative energy sources

You are going to listen (Recording number 9) to part of a first year undergraduate tutorial about environmental issues affecting business. All students attended a recent lecture given by the same tutor.

1 Listen to the first segment and write down the topic. Details aren't necessary, and don't expect at this stage to understand everything.

2 Brainstorm in small groups what you know about this topic.

3 Listen to the whole tutorial recording and answer the following questions:

- How many students speak?
- Do you think they are good students? Why?

Task B: Listening for purpose—why are questions asked in tutorials?

▮ Read the listed purposes of tutorial questions and comments in the table below.

 While listening again, tick the appropriate box below each speaker to show the function of each question—**purpose 1 to 3 only!** (4 is used later).

F = female,
M = male

Main purpose	Speaking order						
	1st	**2nd**	**3rd**	**4th**	**5th**	**6th**	**7th**
	Stu 1 F	Stu 2 M	Stu 3 M Daniel	Stu 1 F	Stu 4 F Japanese	Stu 2 M	Stu 3 M Daniel
1 Contradicting the tutor's idea (tutor's reply will help clarify understanding)							
2 Giving an example supporting a previously mentioned idea							
3 Asking for further explanation or information							
4 Checking understanding							

Tutorial participation skills 2: asking questions in tutorials

Task A: Expressions for tutorial questions

9 **1** Listen again and fill in the gaps to complete the expressions the students used.

- I'm not _____ what you _____ when you said that oil companies could gain advantages from _____ in other energy sources. _____ other energy sources are their competitors!

- I _____ what you say about it being _____ for fossil fuel companies to look at alternative energy sources, _____ it seems that there isn't much of this happening! ... What did you mean by this?

- But isn't it the _____ that alternative energy _____ isn't economically viable, ...

- _____ you tell me where I _____ find out more about the predictions that the ...+[reason].

2 Look at the expressions below and indicate their purpose by writing a number from the table on page 143 next to them.
  - When you said that ..., did you mean that ...
  - You mentioned before that ... but what about ...
  - Do you mean that ...
  - So you mean ...
  - If it's the case that ..., why can't ...
  - Could you give me an example?

Task B: Speaking—asking tutorial questions

Choose one of the topics below and explain it to your group. The others must ask the questions from Task A.

- A festival or ceremony in your country—what happens and what is its significance?

- How to prepare some food from your country.

- How to play a sport that's popular in your country.

- How people apply to university in your country, including the exam system.

English for the Internet Age

Using university library catalogues on the net

Task A: Searching library catalogues

1 In the tutorial discussion you heard in the listening section starting on page 142, a book called *The Coming Oil Crisis* by Colin Campbell was mentioned. How would you check whether this is available in your university library?

2 Go to a university web page (eg www.uts.edu.au for University of Technology, Sydney), and find the link for the library and then the catalogue (at some universities, this is labelled OPAC = On-line Public Access Catalogue). Search for this book.

  a] How would you find it on the shelf?

  b] Does the site tell you whether it's available for borrowing?

  c] How can you find out about more books on the same subject?

  d] How can you find out if it's the latest edition?

3 Search for some resources (including journals) on the topic of your oral presentation. To help you find them in the library, fill in the following table.

Author (family name first)	Title	Edition number	CALL number	For loan? Date due back?	Other (eg reserve collection)

4 What further information is required to write references?

Speaking 2

Using visual aids in presentations

Now that preparation for your oral presentation is well under way, it is a good time to focus on something that will help to make your presentation clear—visual aids.

Task A: Sharing knowledge about visual aids

Discuss the following questions.

1 What visual aids can you think of, in addition to overhead transparencies (OHTs) and computer presentations?

2 Why are visual aids useful?

3 Tell your group any useful advice you already know about using visual aids.

Task B: Useful techniques for using OHTs and computer presentations

Building on your answers to Question 3 above, match the comments below with the advice in Tables 1 and 2 on the next page.

Comments

- It's very embarrassing to interrupt your talk to look for the right OHT!

- This is common graphic designers' advice for good layout.

- This helps the audience to focus on the point you're making, and creates a sense of anticipation about what's coming next.

- It's very difficult for an audience to read and listen at the same time, so too much writing on the OHT will take attention away from what you're saying. Therefore it's important for the OHT to be concise, clear and focused. It's not necessary to write in complete sentences.

- 'A picture is worth a thousand words', as long as it's clear and well captioned!

- Making sure that your audience can see comfortably is important.
- A simple trick that will make things much easier when setting up for the presentation!

Table 1: **Making your slides**

Advice	Comments
1 Design your slide with plenty of 'white space'—that is, don't fill it completely with text.	
2 If possible, use pictures, flowcharts, organisation charts, tree diagrams, tables or other visual representations, depending on the topic.	
3 Write only important ideas. Note form, with bullet points, is fine. Indenting is a useful way to show which ideas are the main ideas.	
4 When you have finished making your OHTs, number them in sequence in a corner of the transparency.	

Table 2: **Setting up and giving your presentation**

Advice	Comments
5 Make sure your OHTs are in a pile, in order, next to the OHP, before you start your presentation.	
6 Before you start make sure your projector is positioned so that everyone in the audience can see the screen, and that it's focused.	
7 At the beginning of your talk, cover up everything except the title. During the talk, uncover one point, speak about it, then uncover the next point, explain that, and so on.	

Other oral presentation advice

- Don't give out detailed handouts at the beginning of a presentation.
- Most people speak too fast during their first presentation. Speak just a little slower than feels natural, but not too slow, of course!
- Rehearse to check the timing of your presentation in plenty of time to make changes.
- The best way to overcome nervousness is to make sure you are very well prepared.

3

1 Below is a slide from the talk on families in Unit 2. Read it, and listen again to the talk (and/or read the recording script for Recording number 3), comparing them.

2 Prepare another slide for the next section of the talk.

3 Compare your slide with those from other groups. How can you improve your slide?

4 Can you think of any more advantages to using visual aids now?

1

Family

- Contradictory issues

- All societies

- **Definition**
  - related
  - living together
  - communicating
  - common culture

- **Questions**
  - What is a normal family?
  - Does it exist?

- **Research**
  - Garfinkel (1967)
  - Henry (1989)

Task D: Using visual aids in a mini-presentation and review of oral presentation stages

1 Prepare a short presentation of around five minutes about a familiar topic. Some suggestions for topics are:

- your country
- your home town or city
- places for tourists to visit in your country
- the best ways to travel around your country
- natural attractions or national parks in your country
- your opinion about particular environmental problems

2 Prepare your presentation, remembering the advice, stages and oral discourse markers you learned in Unit 5.

3 Prepare an OHT to accompany your presentation.

See Unit 5, page 108.

4 Give your presentation to a small group of students.

5 Comment on each other's presentations.

Critical thinking

Distinguishing between fact and opinion

> **Task A: Orientation discussion**

Discuss in pairs the following questions:

1 List ten words you associate with the word 'nuclear'. Explain to your partner any words that you know but your partner doesn't.

2 Is nuclear power used in your country? If so, what for?

3 What are the advantages of nuclear power?

4 What do you know about the dangers of nuclear radiation?

5 Have you heard of any nuclear accidents? What do you know about their consequences?

> **Task B: Distinguishing between fact and opinion**

Read the essay below before looking at the questions that follow it.

TITLE: Our world is one place

One country's activities exert influence on others and transgressions against nature affect us all. One country's practices not only influence itself but also impact upon every other country.

One example comes from the highly dangerous and unclean energy source, nuclear power. The risk factor in this industry, although minimised by its   5
proponents, is beyond belief. For example, regarding the 1986 disaster when the Russian Chernobyl nuclear plant experienced a fire which began with an explosion, Gordon and Suzuki (1990:57) report that radioisotopes were 'detected over Sweden within minutes and over Canada's Arctic in hours'. Radioactive contaminated dust poisoned the city and surrounding rural areas   10
and caused miscarriages in pregnant women, and cancer to other unborn as well as living children and adults.

For a huge radius wheat was contaminated, bringing financial ruin to farmers and food shortages for the Russian people. Children who were poisoned and who now have cancers as a direct result are called *the children of Chernobyl* (you can   15
visit their website at www.cofcsd.org) and since this accident occurred in 1986, more than one generation is affected. Some of the children of Chernobyl visit the US and Australia each year under sponsorship programs so they can enjoy sunshine and holidays before they die of the cancers transmitted from the Chernobyl nuclear power accident. Estimates concerning how long the soil will   20
remain contaminated range from 100 years to 250 000 years.

4   Another example of one country's activities seriously impacting upon another's is the notorious Ok Tedi mine, a uranium mine in Papua New Guinea belonging to BHP Billiton of Australia. Careless management of waste (called tailings) resulted in the destruction of an entire river and subsequently all the communities that relied upon that river for fishing. Almost every plant, fish and living organism died as a result of the tailings leaking out of ponds. Soil could no longer grow anything, people could no longer eat any of the fish and soon there was no fish to eat. The ponds (which leaked in heavy rain and ruined the water and plant life) were simply dug out of the earth with no linings on the walls and this was the management system of highly radioactive and poisonous waste by a multi-billion dollar company. The company was forced, by courts of law, to compensate and relocate villagers whose way of life was completely destroyed.

5   Within new theories of physics, a question has been posed and researched—*Does a butterfly flapping its wings affect the weather in another part of the world?* One scientist answers a definite 'yes' to this research question. This is an example of how some scientists believe that all parts of the globe are linked together.

6   The earth is a sphere; we inhabit it together. Regardless of culture, class, race or religion, humankind remains a biological organism co-existing with and dependent upon nature in order to survive. Air and water are as essential to humans as they are to fish, dogs and cats.

Our interdependence as a species with other living organisms is unquestionable, yet both elected and non-elected governments around the world continue to allow and indeed pursue courses of action which are ruining the balance between us and the earth. This balance is a matter of survival for the human race.

8   In conclusion, in the past 200 years a new scientific age has begun, led by Western consumerist, capitalist countries and followed by all developing nations. This model sets out to enslave nature—not work with nature in harmony but to control nature. It is this writer's opinion that nature will not be controlled, nature refuses to be the slave of humankind and will retaliate by simply eliminating the species from the planet.

9   A major nuclear accident or war would cause a nuclear winter from which no person would survive. Continued irresponsible mining of uranium and no facilities for safe waste disposal will contaminate the earth to the extent that all water is poisonous and land unproductive and unfit for food production. Arid wastelands and more desertification will occur as a result of global warming along with rising sea levels which will take whole countries out.

10 People need to unite and fight for their planet. Governments that continue to pollute the earth with no regard to the future should be thrown out of office. Scientists need to gain the respect of decision makers and be listened to, so that the planet and its peoples have a chance for a future where we are not wearing gas masks to breathe nor protective suits to shield us from the polluted air and rain. Will we end up underground or in domed cities like stories of science fiction? Is this what you want?

Questions

1 As a first impression, does the essay express facts or opinions or both?

_____

2 Facts can be things which are commonly known or understood and are accepted as fact, eg humans need air to breathe. Find a sentence which you believe is factual. Why do you think it is fact?

_____

_____

_____

3 Find a sentence that may not be fact. Why might it not be fact?

_____

_____

_____

4 How many references were included in the text? Do you think this is sufficient for factual writing?

_____

5 What language tells you that the author is passionate about the subject? Is this OK?

_____

_____

6 Can factual writing be shocking or surprising?

_____

7 Who is the author? When you read texts that claim to give facts, is it important to know who the author is? Who is the author working for? Is this information also important?

_____

_____

_____

8 Is the writing academic? If so, what makes it so? If not, why not?

_____

_____

_____

9 Has your impression of the essay changed since answering Question 1?

_____

_____

10 What aspects of the essay would you change to make sure it was factual and that the readers knew it was factual?

_____

_____

_____

11 What is your opinion concerning the matters in this essay?

_____

_____

_____

12 Where would you begin your research to write an essay like this?

_____

_____

_____

Grammar 1

Reporting verbs in citation and paraphrasing

> **Task A: Meaning and use of reporting verbs**

See Unit 5,
page 111,
Bibliographies.

1 Look at the referenced idea in the previous essay. Can the idea be written any other way?

2 The following verbs can be used to report ideas. Add to the list by looking at articles in academic journals and noting the verbs that are used.

ask	assert	claim	deny
maintain	report	suggest	

3 For these reporting verbs, find out (using a learner's dictionary if necessary) what the difference in meaning is, if any.

4 Re-write the following as referenced ideas and remember to paraphrase.

a] The end of civilisations in the past has often been caused not by political or economic change as previously supposed, but by climatic change. Harvey Weiss and Raymond Bradley, 2001.

b] The question we should examine is whether logging in the north-west of Govindia should be allowed to continue. J Chakraverty, 2000.

c] Due to climate change, many plants in the UK are flowering many weeks earlier every year than they did 40 years ago. A & R Fitter, 2002.

d] I would like to propose the concept of shifting taxation from positive transactions (such as the receiving of income) towards transactions with more negative impacts such as the purchase of products which are bad for the environment. Özlem Aksu, 2002.

e] Recycling is not the best way to solve environmental problems because it uses plenty of energy in itself—reducing consumption would be much more effective. Hwa Jin Lee, 1998.

Reading

Skimming and scanning

The text in this section is an extract from *Global Environment Outlook 2000: UNEP's Millennium Report on the Environment* (pages 92–3) in which various predictions are given for the future of the environment in South-east Asia. It is taken from the end of a chapter on Asia and the Pacific.

Task A: Skimming race

See Unit 1, page 20.

Read the ideas below. Race to be the first to write down the paragraph numbers in which you might find each idea. Read topic sentences—not every word of the text!

1 How countries are improving waste disposal in cities.

2 Amount of waste generated in a particular country.

3 Population growth in a particular country.

4 Predictions for growth in waste from cities.

5 Effects of dangerous untreated chemicals.

Task B: Scanning

See Unit 2, page 37.

Scan the text to answer the following questions.

1 How many contaminated sites are there in New Zealand?

2 What problems are affecting the South Pacific?

3 Which Chinese cities are 'Environmental Star Cities'?

4 What percentage of Asia's solid waste is expected to be produced in East Asia in 2010?

5 What's the expected total population of Chinese cities in 2025?

6 What's the average proportion of GDP spent on water and sanitation in Asia?

TITLE: **Waste disposal in Asia**

The total waste generated in the region amounts to 2 600 million tonnes a year, of which solid waste accounts for 700 million tonnes and industrial activities generate 1 900 million tonnes (UNESCAP/ADB: 1995). The East Asian sub-region generated 46 per cent (327 million tonnes) of the region's total municipal solid waste in 1992–93; this proportion is projected to increase to 60 per cent by 2010   5 (UNESCAP/ADB: 1995). The Republic of Korea produced a 50 per cent increase in industrial waste in the period 1991–95 alone (Government of Republic of Korea:

contaminated
made dirty or poisonous

hazardous
dangerous

discharged
allowed to flow into the outside world, used for gases or liquids

sewage
waste from human bodies carried away from houses through pipes

1998). In New Zealand, many of the country's estimated 7800 **contaminated** sites are in urban industrial areas (New Zealand Ministry for the Environment: 1997).

A large percentage of industrial wastes in South-east Asia, including **hazardous** chemicals, are **discharged** without treatment. These wastes affect not only the health of workers who handle them but also residents living near factories. However, many countries now have effective legislation for the safe handling, treatment and disposal of these substances (ASEAN: 1997).

Many urban waste disposal systems are inadequate. Disposal of untreated waste water is spreading water-borne diseases and damaging marine and aquatic life. In response, investment in domestic waste water treatment systems has been accelerated in many South-east Asian countries, including Malaysia. High rates of urbanisation in the island states of the South Pacific has also resulted in serious waste management and pollution problems, particularly with respect to their impacts on groundwater resources. Environmentally safe disposal of solid waste and **sewage** is a major concern for the island states of the region where land and therefore available disposal sites are limited and sewage systems are lacking.

In most countries, the urban population is likely to grow threefold in the next 40 years (UNESCAP/ADB: 1995). China alone is expected to have 832 million urban residents by 2025.

As urban areas, especially megacities, expand further, increases in traffic congestion, water and air pollution, and slums and squatters settlements can be expected. Most large Asian cities already face an acute shortage of safe drinking water and a fivefold increase in demand is anticipated within the next 40 years (UNESCAP/ADB: 1995). Public expenditure on water and sanitation is around one per cent of GDP for most countries of the region, and is likely to rise.

In East Asia, many governments are attempting to reduce the growth of their primary cities by curbing rural-urban migration. A new trend for Chinese cities is represented by Dalian, Zhuhai and Xiamen, Zhangjiagang, Shenzhen and Weihai, the Environmental Star Cities, where great efforts are being made to emphasise urban environmental planning and pollution prevention amid economic development (SEPA: 1998).

Urbanisation is one of the most significant issues facing Asia and the Pacific. How to deal with increasing amounts of urban and industrial waste is a major concern for most of the region. While the proportion of people living in urban centres is still lower than that in developed countries, it is rising rapidly, and is focused on a few urban centres.

References

ASEAN (1997) *First ASEAN State of the Environment Report.* ASEAN Secretariat, Jakarta, Indonesia.

Government of Republic of Korea (1998) *Environmental Protection in Korea.* Ministry of Environment, Kwacheon, Republic of Korea.

New Zealand Ministry for the Environment (1997) *The State of New Zealand's Environment 1997*. GP Publications, Wellington, New Zealand.

SEPA (1998) *Report on the State of the Environment in China 1997*. State Environmental Protection Administration of China, China State Environmental Science Press, Beijing, China.

UNESCAP/ADB (1995) *State of the Environment in Asia and the Pacific 1995*. United Nations Economic and Social Commission for Asia and the Pacific, and Asian Development Bank, United Nations, New York, USA.

Grammar 2

Future predictions

Task A: Tenses for future predictions

1   In the text above, (circle) all the verb groups. In the table below, write the number of times each of these tenses is used.

Tense	Number of times used
'will'	
present simple active	
present simple passive	
present continuous	
'be' verb + (adverb)+ infinitive	

2   Do you find anything surprising?

3   Make a list of the verbs used in the text to express future predictions. How many more, with similar meaning, can you add to your list?

4   What is the difference between: 'is predicted not to ...' and 'isn't predicted to ...'.?

Task B: Reading to identify predictions

1   Find a newspaper article or web page that looks at future trends. Use your knowledge of tenses and verb choice to locate the phrases of prediction.

2   Tell other students the predictions you found and discuss them. Also share your list of language to express predictions.

3   You can use these expressions in your own writing in the future.

Task C: Writing

Write a short report to summarise what you found in Task B. Pay particular attention to verb and tense choice.

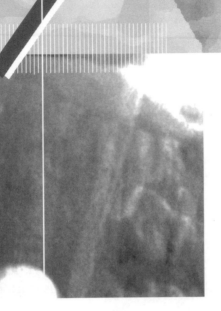

unit 7 on campus

The difficulty we
meet with in reaching
our goal is the
shortest path to it.

KAHLIL GIBRAN

Skills focus: In this Unit, you will learn and use the following skills:

Speaking 1

Campus vocabulary

Task A: Extending campus vocabulary

1 In pairs, look at each set of words below and try to decide whether they are the same or different. If different, what is the difference? If necessary, use a learner's dictionary or ask your teacher.

   a] department/faculty/school of ...

   b] arts/humanities/science/social science

   c] applied science/pure science

   d] apply for a subject exemption/recognition of prior learning

   e] prerequisite/core subject/compulsory/elective (**AuE**), option (**BrE**)

   f] Bachelor/Honours/Master's/Doctorate/PhD

   g] semester/term

   h] pass/credit/distinction/high distinction, third, lower second, higher second, first class honours degree.

2 Next, tell each other about your country's education system. Identify what is the same and what is different. While speaking, try to use as much of the new vocabulary as you can.

AuE Australian English
BrE British English
AmE North American English

Listening and Speaking 1

Academic requests and replies 2

Task A: Listening for purpose

In Unit 1, you looked at some requests that you might have to make in tertiary education.

In groups, list as many purposes for academic requests that you can think of.

Here are some more academic requests. Asking for:

   a] Special time off from your course (leave of absence).

   b] Help with the English in your assignment.

   c] Special treatment in an exam due to injury or disability (special dispensation).

   d] Help with understanding an assignment.

   e] A particular form.

   f] An exam/assignment to be marked again.

See *Academic requests 1*, Unit 1, page 2.

g] Explanation of marking system.

h] Information about using the institution's counselling service.

i] Information about which subjects need to be taken to finish a course.

j] Information about special resources available for your subject in the library.

 Listen to the five requests (Recording number 10) and mark the conversation number (one to five) next to the appropriate purpose listed a] to j] above. You only need to write numbers next to five of the purposes: the other five purposes are not used.

Task B: Understanding replies

Write notes to answer the following questions.

1 *Conversation 1* (student and lecturer)

What are the three steps the student must follow?

a] _____

b] _____

c] _____

2 *Conversation 2* (student and lecturer)

a] What kind of help will the student get? _____

b] Where will it happen? _____

c] Who will the lecturer contact? _____

3 *Conversation 3* (student and lecturer)

a] Where should the student go? _____

b] What should she pick up? _____

c] How many lecturers will look at it again? _____

d] In what circumstances will the mark not change? _____

4 *Conversation 4* (student and receptionist)

a] Which office should she go to? _____

b] Which office is she at? _____

c] Which way should she turn when she finds the pub? _____

d] Write two features of the building with the correct office. _____

5 *Conversation 5* (student and lecturer)

a] How many compulsory subjects has she done already? _____

b] How many more compulsory subjects does she still have to do? _____

Many requests follow the pattern

orientation → problem → question

where **orientation** explains the background to the listener, **problem** is a statement giving the problem, and **question** could ask for permission, information, advice, an explanation or something else.

But sometimes, stages are missed out. Did you notice that sometimes no **question** was necessary?

1 Listen again. Write the number of the conversation next to its pattern below. One pattern has no examples, and another has two examples.

orientation + problem + question	
orientation + problem	
problem + question	
problem	
question	

2 After listening, discuss these questions in pairs.

a] In the conversations with a **problem** but no **orientation**, why was no **orientation** necessary? _____

_____

b] In the conversation with only a **question**, why were two stages missed out?

_____

c] Why is the **question** stage sometimes not necessary? _____

_____

3 Listen again. What expressions are used to introduce:

a] the **orientation**? _____

_____

_____

b] the **problem**? _____

_____

c] the **question**? _____

_____

_____

_____

_____

Can you add other expressions to these?

4 In all these conversations, the student is polite. How does the student make the request polite (other than through choice of expressions)?

Task D: Role play—making academic requests

1 Divide into two groups: 'lecturers' and 'students'.

2 **Students:** Use the information in item 7.1 on page 251 (Appendix B) to make a request to a 'lecturer'. Follow the request stages from Task C above. Listen to the reply and ask further questions as necessary. You may have to use some imagination! After finishing, move to a different lecturer and use item 7.2 on the same page.

Lecturers: Listen to the 'student'. Use the information in item 7.1 on page 249 (Appendix B) to reply, but don't give all the information at once —wait for further questions! When you've finished, another 'student' will ask you about situation 7.2.

3 When finished, 'students' become 'lecturers' and vice versa. Repeat, using items 7.3 and 7.4 on the same page that you used at step 2. Don't change page.

Speaking 2

Further oral presentation skills

Task A: Further features of presentations

See also
Unit 5, page 108;
Unit 6, page 145.

From each pair of instructions below, choose the best advice.

1 a] Hold your notes in front of your face so that you don't miss anything written on them.

 b] Hold your notes in one hand, to leave one hand free for gestures.

2 a] Use small notes, the size of your palm. On these, write only main points and any details that are difficult to remember, such as statistics and references. These are called palm cards.

 b] Write everything you're going to say on your notes so that you don't forget anything.

3 a] Speak as quickly as you can to fit as much as possible into your presentation.

 b] Speak a little slower than your normal speed, but not too slowly.

4 a] Use gestures and move around.

 b] Stand in the same place so that everyone focuses on you, and wave your hands as much as possible to make it look exciting.

5 a] Ask questions during your talk to involve the audience, and respond to their answers.

 b] Use plenty of questions but don't wait for answers.

6 a] Make eye contact with everyone in the room, without lingering for too long on each person.

b] Look just below the level of people's eyes to show respect.

7 a] Make a special effort to make eye contact with people on the edge of the room as well as those in the middle, because people on the edge can easily get missed out.

b] Look especially at people in the audience who appear to be the most interested.

Task B: Dealing with questions

Questions after a talk are an important part of the presentation—tutors often give marks for asking as well as answering questions.

1 If you asked a question, and the presenter didn't know the answer, which of the following would you prefer the presenter to do?

a] guess the answer;

b] admit honestly to not knowing, or not being sure about, the answer;

c] explain why he or she doesn't know, eg no one knows;

d] suggest where to look for the answer;

e] explain that the talk doesn't address the issue.

2 Match the expressions below with the functions in Question 1.

i] I'm afraid that's beyond the scope of this presentation.

ii] That's a very interesting question—but I'm afraid I don't know, though I think the answer might be in Richards and Rogers.

iii] That would be an interesting research topic! I'm not sure anyone has done that yet.

iv] I'm not sure, but I'll try to find out for you.

v] I think it might be around 80, but I'm not sure. I'll check for you.

 LEARNING t i p

The best way to deal with difficult questions is to be well prepared!

3 For homework, predict at least three questions that you might be asked at the end of your presentation. Make sure you can answer them!

Task C: Speaking—differences and similarities between presentations here and in your culture

You have covered many aspects of oral presentations so far. To review, tell your group what is the same and what is different about presentations in your country.

Task D: Practice!

Give a short talk (two or three minutes) on one of the topics below.

■ Differences between English lessons in your own country and here.

- Your expectations about education in this country before you came here, and any differences you've found since arriving here.

- Educational experiences in your own country that help you to learn about your traditional culture, eg school trips, dance classes.

- How do you apply to university in your country?

1 During each talk, the audience should mark the features in Task A that the speaker includes.

2 At the end of each talk the audience ask questions.

3 Then, the audience should tell each speaker which features from Task A they used. Does the speaker agree?

See Unit 6, page 143, *Asking questions in tutorials.*

If you missed doing anything during your talk, try to remember to include it in your main presentation!

English for the Internet Age

Referencing from Internet sources

Task A: Referencing from Internet sources

See Unit 5, page 114.

1 Look at this typical reference to an Internet site.

Columbia University Press (2002) Basic CGOS Style. *The Columbia guide to online style.* http://www.columbia.edu/cu/cup/cgos/idx_basic.html (8 Dec 2002).

Complete the first line of the following table with the details from the reference.

Author	Year of writing/ last update	Title of web page/ document	Title of website/ complete work	Web address	Date of access
Columbia University Press				www.columbia.edu... etc.	

2 Go to the following websites and fill in the next two lines of the table for these pages.

www.dfes.gov.uk/highereducation/
www.studyinaustralia.gov.au/Sia/en/StudyCosts/Scholarships.htm

3 Write a bibliography using this information.

4 Look up some references related to your oral presentation, ensuring you have a record of all the bibliographic details.

> Oral presentations should include a list of references, just as an essay does.

Reading

✓ *Examining texts from different points of view*
✓ *Using texts to assist in making and supporting judgments*

Examining texts from different points of view

In this section, you will read an adapted version of a document published by UTS (University of Technology, Sydney, Australia), giving its anti-discrimination and anti-harassment policy.

Task A: Orientation discussion—what is discrimination and harassment?

Discuss the following questions:

1 List as many kinds of discrimination as you can.

2 For each, give an example (eg sexism: a company may be reluctant to promote women with children because it thinks they will have too much focus on their family to work hard).

3 What does 'harassment' mean? Use a dictionary if necessary and give examples.

4 Which of the following situations do you think are examples of discrimination, harassment or neither?

  a] A well-qualified and experienced woman is trying to get a job but, again and again, instead of her, a man is chosen. She is in her late twenties and recently married.

  b] A man with a scruffy hairstyle and rough manner but good qualifications and experience is finding it difficult to get a job.

  c] A male student often touches female students—this is considered 'normal' in his culture. The male student doesn't realise that one particular female hates this, because in her culture, people smile in all situations and, in public, hide any negative feelings they have. However, she would prefer the male student to keep his hands to himself.

  d] Someone who has a different political opinion from her boss is repeatedly passed over for promotion.

  e] A male in an office makes sexual jokes in front of female colleagues, and forwards emails containing sexual jokes to many colleagues, both male and female.

  f] A student who has to use a wheelchair is told that he can't do a particular course because lectures take place in an old building with no wheelchair access.

  g] A student and a lecturer fall in love with each other. They continue a relationship even though one of them is the other's teacher. At the end of the course, several students apply for a scholarship to a higher level course, including the student who's involved with the lecturer. One important factor in getting the scholarship is a reference from the same lecturer, and only one scholarship is available.

h] Charging a high fee for a course, which only the rich can afford.

See also
Unit 1, page 20;
Unit 2, page 37,
*Skimming and
scanning.*

Task B: Reading—skills practice

1 Read only the headings in the following text, to familiarise yourself with the structure of the text (30 seconds). It is from a university's student handbook.

2 Find and in pencil definitions of discrimination, direct discrimination, indirect discrimination and harassment (2 minutes).

3 What punishments are given for harassment?

4 What does the text say you should do if you're a student at this university and you feel you're being harassed?

5 For each of Questions 1 to 4, did you skim, scan or read in detail?

LEARNING tip

Every time you look at a new text, quickly reading the headings, introduction and the conclusion first can give you an overview of the text which will help you find information more quickly later.

TITLE: Preventing discrimination and harassment

1 What is discrimination?

1.1 Direct and indirect discrimination
Both direct and indirect discrimination are unlawful in all aspects of employment and education at this institution. Discrimination means treating someone unfairly because they happen to belong to a particular group of people.   5

1.2 Direct discrimination is the result of beliefs and stereotypical attitudes some people may have about the characteristics and behaviour of members of a group. It occurs when a person or group is harassed or excluded because of a personal characteristic such as gender or ethnic origin. For example:
- a selection committee refusing to consider applicants with family   10
  responsibilities
- refusing to employ or enrol Aboriginal people or people whose first
  language is not English
- assuming that a person with a disability would not be capable of
  undertaking a course of study because of their disability.   15

1.3 Indirect discrimination occurs where a rule, work practice or decision is made which applies to all persons equally and appears to be non-discriminatory, but which in practice significantly reduces the chances of a particular person or group of persons from complying with it. For example:
- recruitment or promotion based on seniority or length of service may   20
  indirectly discriminate against women applicants, because women are more
  likely to have taken career breaks to accommodate family responsibilities

- selection criteria requiring a specific number of years of previous experience may also constitute indirect age discrimination.

Indirect discrimination provisions recognise the structural inequalities some groups encounter in employment, and require the university to examine all its policies and practices, to ensure that not only the **intention** but also the **impact** of the rule or practice is non-discriminatory. However, indirect discrimination is not illegal if the condition, requirement or practice which indirectly discriminates is seen to be reasonable in the circumstances.

1.4 Areas of discrimination
UTS is committed to ensuring the elimination of any discrimination or harassment in employment, education and service delivery on the grounds of:
- sex
- race, colour, descent, national or ethnic origin, ethno-religious background
- marital status
- pregnancy or potential pregnancy
- family responsibilities
- disability (includes physical, intellectual, psychiatric, sensory, neurological or learning disabilities and illness such as HIV/AIDS)
- homosexuality
- transgender status
- age
- political conviction
- religious belief.

The Equity and Diversity Unit provides confidential, equity-related grievance advice to both students and staff who feel they may have been discriminated against or harassed on any of the grounds listed above.

2 What is not unlawful discrimination?
- **Administrative action.** Managers and university staff frequently have to make difficult decisions, for example, course changes. These decisions may not please everybody but they do not normally constitute discrimination.
- **Student assessment.** Academic staff have a responsibility to students to assess their work fairly, objectively and consistently across the candidature for their particular subject/course. A poor assessment is not discriminatory, provided the criticism is reasonable and constructive. Giving appropriate criticism and taking appropriate corrective action when an individual's assessment is unsatisfactory is a standard part of academic life.
- **Consensual relationships.** A relationship of a sexual nature based on mutual attraction, friendship and respect does not constitute discrimination, **providing the interaction is consensual, welcome and reciprocated.** However, consensual relationships may lead to conflict of interest (see later).

3 UTS Policy on the prevention of harassment
UTS is committed to ensuring that all students and staff are treated fairly and equitably, and can work and study in an environment free of harassment. Discrimination, harassment and victimisation are unlawful, undermine

professional relationships, diminish the experience of university life, and will not be tolerated at UTS.

All students and staff have a responsibility to contribute to the achievement of a productive, safe and equitable study and work environment by avoiding practices which lead to, support or condone harassment.

3.1 Legislation

Provisions relating to unlawful harassment are outlined in both federal and state anti-discrimination laws. These laws prohibit discrimination and harassment in employment, education and service delivery on the grounds previously listed. The legislation also prohibits racial, homosexual, transgender and HIV/AIDS vilification, dismissal because of family responsibilities, and victimisation resulting from a complaint.

3.2 What is unlawful harassment?

Unlawful harassment is any unwelcome conduct, verbal or physical, which has the intent or effect of creating an intimidating, hostile or offensive educational, work or living environment, and which happens because of a person's sex, pregnancy, race or ethno-religious background, marital status, age, sexual preference, transgender status or disability.

Unlawful harassment can include:
- verbal abuse or comments that put down or stereotype people
- derogatory or demeaning jokes intended to offend on the basis of stereotyped characteristics
- offensive communications (such as posters, letters, emails, faxes, screen savers, websites)
- offensive telephone or electronic mail or other computer system communications
- insults, taunting, name calling, innuendo or bullying
- persistent or intrusive questions or comments about an individual's personal life
- unwelcome invitations especially after prior refusal
- orientation activities that involve unwelcome sexual, sexist, racist or other discriminatory behaviour
- non verbal behaviour such as whistling, staring and leering
- uninvited sexual or physical contact such as embracing, kissing or touching
- intrusive questions about sexual activity
- demeaning jokes of a sexual nature
- promises, propositions or threats in return for sexual favours
- engaging in behaviour which is embarrassing, humiliating or intimidating
- derogatory comments about race, religion and customs
- teasing or offensive language and racist behaviours
- mocking customs or cultures.

The offensive behaviour does not have to take place a number of times: a single incident can constitute harassment.

What is important is how the behaviour affects the person it is directed against. Unlawful harassment can occur even if the behaviour is not intended to offend. Students and staff should be aware that differing social and cultural standards may mean that behaviour that is acceptable to some may be perceived as offensive by others.

4 Procedural guidelines

The University's procedures for handling complaints are based on confidentiality, impartiality, procedural fairness, protection from victimisation and prompt resolution. Any complaints of harassment or discrimination will be dealt with promptly, seriously, and without victimisation of those involved. Processes for handling complaints are outlined in the Policy on Handling 120 Student Complaints (for complaints made by students).

Disciplinary action may be taken against students or staff who are found to have harassed other students or staff. Breaches of the policy will be considered to be 'misconduct' or 'serious misconduct' in the case of employees, and 'non-academic misconduct' in the case of students, and may result in the most 125 serious cases in permanent expulsion (for students) or dismissal (for staff). Formal warnings about inappropriate behaviour are a common outcome for first offences, unless the behaviour is of a very serious nature.

4.1 What to do about harassment?

Students should seek advice from the Equity and Diversity Unit (if the complaint 130 relates to unlawful harassment) or the Student Services Unit (for counselling and support). The Students Association also provides advice and advocacy for students.

Source: Adapted from: UTS Equity and Diversity Unit (no date given) 'Preventing discrimination and harassment', Sydney: UTS Equity and Diversity Unit. Internet site available at: http://www.uts.edu.au/div/eounit/unit/discrim.html, accessed 25/08/02. A variation is also published in Lambert, T & Barreto, L (2001) *UTS Students' Association Postgraduate Handbook 2001,* Sydney: UTS Students' Association, pages 36–39.

Using texts to assist in making and supporting judgments

Task A: Using the text when making and supporting judgments

Complete the table below, with evidence from the text.

	Mark if yes			Support for your answer	
Situation (in Task A, question 4, on page 162–163)	Discrimination?	Harassment?	Neither?	Section no.	First and last words of section of text supporting your answer
a]					
b]					
c]					
d]					

| Situation (in Task A, on page 162–163) | Mark if yes | | | Support for your answer | |
	Discrimination? Harassment? Neither?			Section no.	First and last words of section of text supporting your answer
e]					
f]					
g]					
h]					

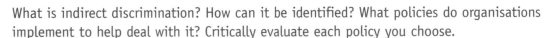

Task B: Critical thinking—analysing the cultural content of a text

▊ In small groups of mixed nationality (if possible), discuss the following questions.

1 Read the lists of discriminatory and harassing behaviour in the text again and explain any that would sound unusual in your culture. Also, explain any points that would be considered discriminatory in your country but which aren't listed here.

2 Do you think that ideas of what constitutes discrimination should vary from culture to culture, or are they universal, that is, do they apply to all humans? Why?

3 What advice would you give a university student who's used to ideas like those in the text, before he or she goes to study in your country?

Task C: Reading to research an assignment—note taking practice

1 Imagine that the text above is one of several that you are reading for an assignment which asks:

What is indirect discrimination? How can it be identified? What policies do organisations implement to help deal with it? Critically evaluate each policy you choose.

Read the text again and make notes that will help you with this assignment.

See *Note taking* Unit 2, page 50.

2 Reading a text often causes new questions to come into mind. What questions are raised by this text? For example, section 1.2 states 'indirect discrimination is not illegal if ... [it] ... is seen to be reasonable in the circumstances', but what is regarded as 'reasonable'? Add these questions to your notes.

3 If you were researching the assignment and wanted to answer the new questions, what could you do?

4 Compare your notes with another student. Together, either:

■ prepare a new set of notes that combines the most important ideas from both of your notes, or

■ highlight the ideas from both your and your partner's notes which are especially relevant.

1   Take notes again in relation to the following question.

Compare and contrast policies affecting the employment of women in a multinational organisation, a medium-sized business, an academic institution, and a branch of government. Look also at the implementation of these policies. Which would you expect to be most effective at recruiting and retaining women?

2   You have now read the same text for different purposes. In the different tasks, did you read different amounts of the text? Did a part of the text have a different meaning to you in the different tasks?

 LEARNING t i p

> When reading a text, write main points, your opinions and reactions **in pencil** in the margin. Later you may need to read the text again for a different subject or assignment, in which case you will probably be looking at the text from a different point of view. Therefore, your notes will be different. The advantage of using pencil is that you can erase old notes and make new notes.

Speaking and Listening

✓ *Giving constructive criticism*
✓ *Critical listening and peer marking of presentations*

Giving constructive criticism

Task A: Constructive criticism

1   Imagine someone is talking about an oral presentation you've just given. Which of the expressions below would you prefer to hear?
   ■ You should have made clearer OHTs.
   ■ Your talk was generally very good, especially the way it was structured, but making the OHTs clearer would help.
   ■ I didn't understand your OHTs.
   ■ Your OHTs weren't so clear.
   ■ It might be useful next time to make the OHTs clearer.

2   Read the expressions below. Add the more positive comments from above under the most appropriate heading below.

Positive feedback
   ■ I liked the way you (explained the ...)
   ■ It was great how you (made it clear with your OHTs)
   ■ (Your OHTs) really helped me to understand your presentation because ...

- It was an interesting presentation because ...
- ... I'll do the same in my presentation

Suggesting alternatives

- (I think) it might help to ...
- One thing you could do is work on ...
- How about ...?
- What do you think about ...?
- It might be useful to ...
- I would suggest ...
- It'd be better to ...

Replacing negative words with positives

- It was difficult to understand that section → It wasn't so easy to understand ...
- There were very few references → There weren't so many references.

Mitigating the not so good by also mentioning the better

- Your first point was easy to follow because you used plenty of discourse markers, but the next section, I think, needed a few more of them.

De-personalising

- Your OHTs could have been better ... → The OHTs could have been better ...

3 Underline syllables that might carry sentence stress.

4 Practise saying these with pleasant, polite intonation. Your partner will tell you whether you sound polite!

Critical listening and peer marking of presentations

Task A: Observing oral presentations

Now is the time to give the presentation you've been preparing for the last few weeks!

The audience should observe in pairs.

1 During the presentation, one member of each pair should fill in the *Oral Presentation Observation Sheet: Content* from Appendix C. The other member should use the *Oral Presentation Observation Sheet: Technique,* also in Appendix C.

 LEARNING tip

> One of the best ways to learn to do something well is to watch other people doing it, and notice their good points. Then you can use these good points yourself!

2 After the presentation, explain to your partner what you've written. At the same time, the person who gave the talk should also fill in both Oral Presentation Observation Sheets.

LEARNING tip

> Reflecting on your performance is an excellent way to improve!

3 Then, using techniques from the previous section (*Giving constructive criticism*) and the sheets from the previous task, give feedback to the presenter.

Task B: Reflection on oral presentations

- What three (or more) things did you do best in your presentation?
- What three (or more) things will you do differently next time?
- Are there any things that the class, in general, needs to improve on?

Critical thinking

What is the purpose of education?

In traditionally English-speaking countries the following are often said to be benefits of tertiary education.

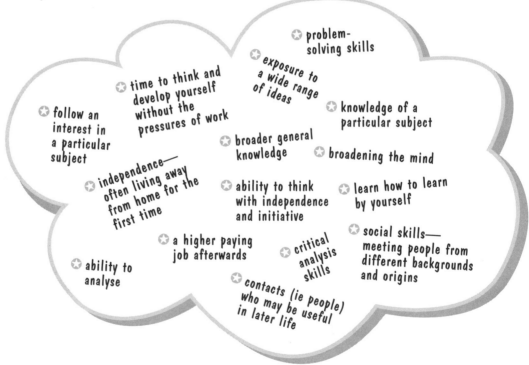

Task A: Evaluating purposes

1 Can you add more ideas to these?

2 In your culture, which ones are most important? Of medium importance? Of little or no importance? Why?

3 Is your personal opinion different from number 2?

4 Do these benefits help the whole of society, or just the individuals who go to university? Give reasons.

5 What for you is the most important benefit of education? Give as many reasons as you can.

6 Do you think that some subjects teach this benefit better than others?

Listening and Speaking 2

Tutorial participation skills 3: various discussion techniques

Task A: Orientation discussion and predicting

You are going to listen to an undergraduate tutorial in which two students, Eleanor and Hamid, discuss who should pay for education, and whether all subjects should be funded the same way. They are studying Arts Management, a subject offered to students in the School of Management as well as the Arts Faculty. But first, discuss:

1 Should education be available to all students with sufficient academic ability, irrespective of who they are or how much money they can spend? Why?

2 With other student(s), discuss whether you believe government funding for tertiary education (or government scholarships) should be provided for:

a] only students studying subjects that are directly relevant to jobs with higher salaries, such as accounting or business administration;

b] students studying any subject;

c] no students at all—only students whose families can afford to pay, or are rich enough to afford it themselves, should be able to study.

3 Look again at the description of the tutorial at the beginning of this task and predict arguments on each side of the discussion you're going to hear.

Task B: Listening for main ideas

  Listen to Recording number 11 and answer the **gist** questions below.

1 Briefly describe Eleanor's opinion. What side or view does Hamid take?

2 Which arguments are given in favour of Eleanor's opinion?

gist general meaning

3 Which arguments are given against?

Task C: Listening to identify tutorial discussion techniques

1 Read the list of functions below.

- [ ] asking a question that expects agreement in reply;
- [ ] indicating understanding, but not agreement;
- [ ] steps in a logical argument;
- [ ] illustrating using a **hypothetical** situation;
- [ ] making a new point;

hypothetical
a possible consequence of an action, which isn't happening yet

☐ supporting a point with examples;

☐ showing understanding by restating the other person's point in own words;

☐ referring back to a previous argument.

 2 Listen again, and tick the functions you hear on the list above.

3 In pairs, try to write down expressions which can be used for each of these functions. Use words you remember from the recording, expressions you already know, and ones that you create from your own knowledge of English.

4 Listen again. Tick the expressions from your list that you hear, and adjust any that are a little different from the recording. You can also add new expressions from the recording.

5 Add any other expressions with the same function that you can think of.

6 Why do you think the tutor doesn't speak much?

Task D: Speaking and critical thinking

Predict ideas the two speakers might use to continue their discussion.

Task E: Tutorial discussion practice

See also
Unit 4, page 100;
Unit 6, page 143.

1 Together, prepare a conversation, like a tutorial discussion, that you can present to the class. Choose from the list of discussion topics at the end of the Unit, or your own topic. Try to include as many of the functions covered above (and in other Units) as you can.

2 Present your conversation to other groups. Your audience will use the list in Task C as a checklist and tick off the functions that they hear you use.

3 Which group used the greatest number of functions? Which group had the strongest arguments? Why were these the strongest?

Task F: Further discussion practice

Choose another topic (your own choice or from the list at the end of this Unit), to carry out further discussions. Ensure that you (and each other!) use a variety of functions from earlier in this section. Feel free to suggest expressions to each other!

Grammar

✓ *Hypothesising and speculating*
✓ *Conditionals*

Hypothesising and speculating

Task A: Verb forms for hypothesising and speculating

Look at the following examples from the written and spoken texts in this Unit.

a] 'A relationship of a sexual nature based on mutual attraction, friendship and respect does not constitute discrimination, providing the interaction is consensual, welcome and reciprocated.'

b] 'But what about the arts and pure sciences? Where would our society be without them? We'd be in a cultural black hole! There'd be nothing in the way of art except for the mass-market stuff like Hollywood movies that simply follow the same old boring formula.'

Questions

1 From your experience of English, which example above—(a) or (b)—feels the most hypothetical?

2 Which describes a 'timeless' situation (that is, something that applies to any time, past, present or future)? Which refers to the future?

3 Which verb forms (or tenses) express the realness or otherwise, and time reference, of these examples? Complete Table A below.

Table A

	real/likely	hypothetical/speculative
past time reference	various past tenses	would have + past participle
'timeless' time reference		would + bare infinitive
present or future time reference	various future tenses	

In the right-hand column of the table, 'would' can be replaced by could, may, might, should etc.

4 How are the weak forms of the hypothetical/speculative verb groups pronounced?

 LEARNING t i p

> **SPEAKING:** A useful conversation pattern is as follows: The full form of 'would' is used to introduce the concept of unreality, but after that, it is contracted to "d' (as shown above in the second example (b)).

Conditionals

Task A: Verb forms in conditionals

▌ The examples from the previous task can be rewritten using 'if':

a] A relationship of a sexual nature based on mutual attraction, friendship and respect does not constitute discrimination **if** the interaction is consensual, welcome and reciprocated.

b] **If** we didn't have arts and social sciences, where would our society be? We'd be in a cultural black hole ...

Notice that the 'if' clauses use different tenses from the main clauses. Again, fill in Table B (the 'main clause' columns are the same as in Table A above).

Table B

	real/likely		hypothetical/speculative	
	'if' clause	main clause	'if' clause	main clause
past time reference	N/A	various past tenses	past perfect	would have + past participle
'timeless' time reference			past simple	would + bare infinitive
present or future time reference	present simple	various future tenses		

'Will' and 'would' in Table B can be replaced by other modal verbs, and other tenses are possible, eg *If it's raining later, I might not go out*. Note also that, traditionally, 'was' isn't used with conditionals. Instead, 'were' is used for all subjects.

Task B: Practice

1   Choose the correct verb form for the gaps in the conversation below (between two students from the same country, studying in the UK). Main verbs are given in brackets, if necessary, and some have been done for you as examples.

   A: Imagine if by some chance our language (be) *were* more popular in the world than English, and if people from many countries (come) _____ to our country to study our language. That (be) _____ interesting, *wouldn't* it!

   B: Yeah! It (be) _____ great! We (come) *wouldn't have come* here, _____ we! I guess we _____ already (be) _____ at university, without spending all that time it takes to learn English.

   A: But the great thing is that it (be) _____ easy to travel for fun if everyone in tourist resorts (speak) _____ our language ... no problems! Or, for a career, we *could teach* our language to international students coming to our country to study ... so we _____ still (can, meet) _____ people from other countries!

   B: Good idea! That (be) _____ an interesting job ... though we (need) _____ to study another course!

2   Discuss how your lives would be different if:

   a] tertiary education were free for everyone of sufficient ability;

   b] we could live to 120 years old;

   c] you were rich enough that you didn't have to think about money;

   d] you could choose to live in any country in the world.

3 Choose three issues of interest to you. Discuss them by speculating about what would happen if each side of the issue was true. For example,

Issue: English should be studied from early in primary school in your country.
Discussion: What would be/is the effect of this policy happening? What would be/is the effect of English not being studied until much later (or not at all) in your country? (Choose the tense according to the situation in your country.)

Learner independence & study skills

Speaking outside class

Task A: Sharing and evaluating ideas

1 In small groups, list as many ideas as you can for speaking practice outside class, such as speaking with other overseas students in English, or working with native English speakers.

2 Do you find these easy to do? Why (or why not)? Which situations are easier than others? Tell your group.

3 Do some situations help your English more than others? For example, when you tell other students what you did over the weekend, you don't need to use complex language, and you've probably described similar things many times before. However, if you explain to a friend how to cook some food from your country, you have to express yourself more accurately because your friend has to understand you very clearly.

 LEARNING t i p

> It will help your speaking practice outside class if you choose situations in which:
> ■ you express complex ideas or abstract ideas
> ■ someone else has to follow your instructions or explanations.

4 Mark your ideas from Question 1 according to how complex the language is likely to be, and whether someone has to follow what you say.

Writing

Extended essay assignment

Task A: Starting the assignment

You will now begin an extended essay assignment. Your teacher will give you information to complete the form below—this is information you should know before you start **any** assignment (at university the question you're given will tell you which genre. You'll look at how to do this in the next Unit.)

Look at the Essay Assignment Cover Sheet in Appendix C (page 257). This shows which aspects of the essay you will get marks for, so make sure you address all these points!

 LEARNING t i p

> In your tertiary course, it's important to find out as much as you can about how an assignment will be assessed before you start writing it!

Your essay will be read by your classmates before submission (Unit 10, page 234).

Writing and Speaking

Issues in education

The following are questions for writing and speaking practice.

- Should all tertiary level students be required to take part in sport?

- Increasingly, university departments and research projects are being sponsored by business. Could this become a source of bias?

- Extra money from business sponsorship will enable universities to provide a greater range of subjects and increase the breadth of their research. To what extent do you agree with this point of view?

- Should entry requirements to university be lowered for students who can pay higher fees?

- The university experience includes benefits beyond academic study; for example, involvement in clubs, political activities or meeting new people. To what extent do you agree with this point of view?

8

a global connection: economics

Representative
governments were,
in the past, the fruits
of revolutions; today
they are economic
consequences.

KAHLIL GIBRAN

Skills focus: In this Unit, you will learn and use the following skills:

Reading and Writing

✓ *Compare and contrast essays*
✓ *Cause and effect*

Compare and contrast essays

When a writer has two or more ideas about a topic, the writer must be able to contrast their ideas in such a way that readers can understand what is being compared and why. The reader must also be made to understand where and how the contrast begins and ends.

Should those ideas express different points of view, all viewpoints must be examined. A writer could begin by comparing a sunny day to a rainy day.

With a partner:

1 Describe a sunny day (mention temperature, light, the sky).

2 Describe a rainy day (mention temperature, light, the sky).

3 Now, compare the two descriptions.

Questions:

■ How does your comparison differ from the plain description you wrote in 1 and 2?

■ What did you have to do to create a comparison or a contrast?

Task A: Converting description into comparison

1 Describe the characteristics of a rich country (in terms of economic wealth).

2 Describe the characteristics of a poor country.

3 Turn your description into a comparison. (Use comparison and contrast connectives such as: but, whereas, although, on the other hand, similarly, likewise, correspondingly, in the same way, on the contrary, conversely, in comparison, while, instead.)

Task B: Orientation discussion and reading around world economics and global trade

Discuss with your group what you know about world economics in terms of global debt. In the course of your discussion, define the IMF and the World Bank. Do you know if or how your own country is affected by these organisations? Next, read the essay below titled *Economics and inequality* and complete the tasks that follow.

Vocabulary notes: Your teacher has cards with definitions for the following terms. Find the person who has the card that matches your word. It should fit into the sentence on the card which is below the definition.

1 squander

2 disposable income

3 inequality

4 debt servicing

5 economic analysts

6 national autonomy

7 deforestation

1 Why do you think it is that a small, privileged group of people who live in developed countries squander food, drive enormous cars that consume huge quantities of petrol (gasoline), take 45-minute hot showers and buy consumer goods daily, while the majority of people in the world go to bed hungry, don't own a car, have little or no access to hot water and no disposable income? Why, 5 too, do the people of many countries walk miles to collect drinking water that other countries would not even consider fit to wash their dogs in? Why in many countries do children as young as five or six years old have to work like adults do instead of going to school and playing games in their spare time?

2 If one acknowledges the inequality that exists in the world, the next logical 10 step is to question the reasons behind it. There needs to be an exploration of cause and effect and a questioning of the powers that control the circumstances of people in all countries. Usually, governments are expected to find solutions to economic problems which may give rise to poverty, child labour, poor working conditions and low pay. Governments are meant to consider and address 15 problems concerning environment and progress.

3 But do governments actually control their countries? Do governments have real power on the global stage? What forces lie behind governments? According to some historians, researchers and economic theorists, it is not individual governments that hold power, it is actually the world banks and/or international 20 monetary funds. Debt servicing in terms of interest payments on money lent to entire countries is the largest single controlling factor on the planet.

4 According to some economic analysts, servicing debt to the so-called First World countries has meant the demise of those countries in the form of eroding social, economic and environmental conditions. These claims are supported by the 25 following argument: the banks charge interest rates which cannot ever be paid. Some countries have been paying back loans for 30 years and have paid the initial debt back many times over. It is the interest that can never be met. Further, many countries are actually re-borrowing money from the same banks in order to pay that bank their interest payments. In other words, the World 30 Bank and the IMF lend money to pay their own selves back. In these instances, so the arguments go, the lenders make decisions which affect the government policies of the countries in debt. Thus, it may be argued that national autonomy is seriously affected by debt servicing.

A few examples follow: 35

5 Tanzania, 1983: Farmers required imported sprays for their oxen against deadly ticks and tsetse flies and pumps to administer the sprays. 'To conserve funds needed to pay its foreign debt, the government has had to impose restrictions on these and other desperately needed imports' (George, 1990:101).

6 Brazil, 1984/2002: 'The country has been shedding jobs by the hundreds of 40 thousands' (due to the government having to pay back debt). A parallel

economy of crime is the result and it may oblige shops and business premises to maintain armed guards ... (Ibid:128).

7 Indonesia, Zaire, Peru and Colombia: Deforestation is increasing due to loans from the World Bank and other sources. 'Environmental issues become totally marginal' when governments face huge debts (Christine Bagdanowicz-Bindert, an economist who used to work with the IMF, Ibid:167). 45

8 In Bolivia in the 1980s 'the government froze salaries for school teachers under pressure from the IMF' (statement from a Bolivian teacher to Susan George, Ibid:151). 50

9 On the other hand, there are those who argue that the IMF and World Bank lending policies have brought enormous benefits to countries that were barely developed. Their economies were lagging far behind the First World nations and their populations had little opportunity for any sort of industrial development. Without the aid, assistance and funds from these lenders, many countries could never have enjoyed the economic profitability that industrialisation and investment can bring. 55

10 There is evidence to support both positions. Solutions for difficult conundrums like those described are neither simple nor easy to discover. However, programs that concentrate on a shift to self-reliance, community action and production of local goods, less debt to governments by allowing longer times to pay back or by cancelling interest payments altogether could be, and presently are, a starting point. 60

Task C: Global examination of texts for six main purposes

Analyse the **first paragraph** of the text in the following ways;

1 What is the theme in the first sentence?
2 Where might it be written?
3 Who might have written it?
4 Who is it written for?
5 What is the author's bias or opinion?
6 What is the effect of a question to the reader in the form of 'Why' at the beginning of each sentence?

Task D: Contrast and comparison words—juxtaposition of ideas

juxtaposition
placement of (things) side by side

1 Find all the question and contrast words in the first paragraph and list or highlight them.

2 Write the things being done by people which are contrasted in each example from paragraph 1.

People in rich countries   *People in poor countries*

a] _____/_____

b] _____ / _____

c] _____ / _____

d] _____ / _____

e] _____ / _____

f] _____ / _____

Cause and effect

See also
Unit 3, page 66;
Unit 4, page 86.

Task A: Cause and effect; result and reason

To support the claim in the essay '... that national autonomy is seriously affected by debt servicing ...', the following examples showed cause and effect. The contrast is with what *should* be happening as opposed to what *is* happening. Examine Example 1 and then complete the exercise using the other Examples:

1 Tanzania, 1983: Farmers required imported sprays for their oxen against deadly ticks and tsetse flies and pumps to administer the sprays. 'To conserve funds needed to pay its foreign debt, the government has had to impose restrictions on these and other desperately needed imports' (George, 1990:101).

Effect—*(result) is that the farmers could not obtain the sprays they needed.*

Cause—*(reason) is that the government had to impose restrictions on imports.*

2 Brazil, 1984/2002: 'The country has been shedding jobs by the hundreds of thousands.' (due to the government having to pay back debt). A parallel economy of crime is the result ... (Ibid:128).

Effect—(result) _____

Cause—(reason) _____

3 Indonesia, Zaire, Peru and Colombia: Deforestation is increasing due to loans from the World Bank and other sources. 'Environmental issues become totally marginal' when governments face huge debts (Christine Bagdanowicz-Bindert, an economist who used to work with the IMF, Ibid:167).

Effect—(result) _____

Cause—(reason) _____

4 In Bolivia in the 1980s 'the government froze salaries for school teachers under pressure from the IMF' (statement from a Bolivian teacher to Susan George:151).

Effect—(result) _____

Cause—(reason) _____

Write each discourse cue which serves to establish cause and effect and which illustrates reason or result.

1 In Sentence 1, there are no cues. The cause and effect is gained from the content or ideas of the sentences. 'In order to' is implied where "To" is stated.

2 **Effect**—(result) _____

   Cause—(reason) _____

3 **Effect**—(result) _____

   Cause—(reason) _____

4 **Effect**—(result) _____

   Cause—(reason) _____

Task C: Metaphor and simile

Another way to compare or contrast is through **metaphor** and **simile**:

- a metaphor calls one thing, another thing;
- a simile compares two things using *like* or *as*.

Examine the following phrases, note whether they are a metaphor or a simile and then make up some of your own!

1 That woman is an angel (<u>metaphor</u>).

2 Mark my words, that man's a dog! _____

3 His eyes were like diamonds _____

4 A butterfly is like a small, lightweight bird _____

5 Her head felt as heavy as lead _____

6 His speech was as rapid as a machine gun _____

7 The moon was a pale pumpkin glowing over the celebrations _____

8 You are a flower seen today _____

9 You are a sparkling rose in the bud _____

10 My soul is a patient onlooker _____

11 The queen was a she-wolf of France _____

12 Thy bright mane for ever shall shine like the gold ... _____

13 *The moon, like a flower* _____

   In heaven's high bower,

   With silent delight

   Sits and smiles on the night

   (extract from William Blake 1757–1827, *Night*)

14 *From thy bright eyes <u>love</u> took his fires, _____*

Which round about in sport he hurl'd;

But 'twas from mine he took desires

Enough t' undo the amorous world.

(extract from Aphra Behn, 1640–1689, *Song*)

Task D: Writing contrasting texts

Write a paragraph using your own knowledge (or speculate) to contrast a typical morning of a young adult from a country with an 'approved' emerging or established economy (perhaps your own country) with that of a poorer neighbour or foreign country. An observation might be that while one adult walks from their bed to their bathroom and shower, another walks a half an hour to the nearest water source which may be a pump or faucet. Continue to the morning meal, the day's possible schooling and so on. Use contrasting sentences and connectives. Think of at least five differences.

Writing

Exposition schema: discussion and argument

schema
stages and
language features

When undertaking tertiary study in an English medium, you will be expected to compose essays using researched information which argues a case for something. When you argue, you must persuade. This happens in both speaking and writing. You must persuade your listener or reader that your point of view is correct. You must have a point of view and you must convince the listener or the reader of it. In argument, people are said to 'take sides'.

Task A: Identifying an issue

With a partner:

1 Think of something that you believe in very strongly. It could be about food, religion, family, politics.

2 State that belief to each other.

3 Write the belief _____

4 Is there a different belief about the same thing? In other words, is there any other possible position/belief that could be held?   Yes ☐   No ☐

5 If you answered 'Yes' to Question 4, then you have identified an 'issue'.

Task B: Defining an issue

1 From the definitions below, choose what you think is an 'issue'.

a] A point in question or dispute—it has to have two or more viewpoints.

b] A personal belief that is challenged.

c] A factual report that has been researched.

d] A solution to opposing viewpoints.

2 Make a list of three things that you believe are *current issues* both in your own country and in your host country, if you know any here. Remember that an issue needs to be a belief or a point that is arguable. In other words, different people hold different opinions about an issue.

a] _____

b] _____

c] _____

Now that you have considered the idea of an issue, read on in order to discover how to write or speak your argument to express your belief, your claim, your contention, your side or your own case! You will use exposition.

Task C: Exposition: an argument that will express your belief, claim, contention, side or case!

Exposition is one of the most common essay forms that you will be required to produce. An exposition is a factual text which carries forward an argument or puts forward a point of view. You will write essays and give oral presentations based upon reading and the research of others.

An essay must be logical and the staging within its structure follows the pattern:

Notice that exposition includes arguments and discussions (see Unit 2, page 43 and Unit 3, page 61).

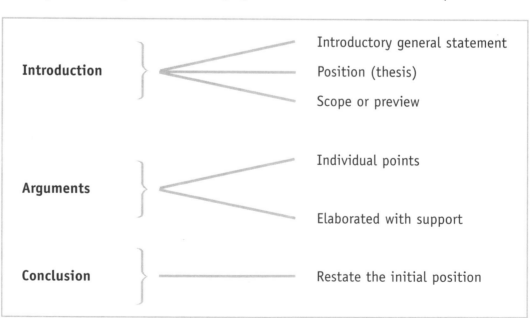

Notice that this includes argument and discussion:

■ Expositions often use simple present tense and logical sequencers rather than temporal (time).

- A model/an example of an exposition about the reasons for a successful international business follows Task D.

Task D: Staging in exposition and predicting text content from a title

1 Read the model below and match the stages of the writing to the exposition schema provided above.

2 Before you begin reading, paraphrase the title in order to predict what the writing will be about

Causes of Aqua Blue Surfgear International's success in 2003

1 Whenever a business is enormously successful, other companies and the general public want to know why. Aqua Blue Surfgear is an international success story for the first decade of the 21st century. For a business to be successful, it is necessary to have strong consumer sales, leading to big profits which in turn inspires investor confidence. Many success stories are also based around   5 international expansion. These elements of strong sales and profits, plus investor confidence are really key components. A business example of these principles in action is Aqua Blue Surfgear International (ABSI).

2 Initially, ABSI was a Spanish company driven by local sales. They expanded offshore, and it was this expansion that really launched the group. Companies   10 require continuing investor confidence and with ABSI, this confidence had waned. Now there is certainly renewed confidence in Aqua Blue Surfgear International's earnings. The causes for this confidence are strong sales, and a possible profit upgrade. Reports of strong sales in the company's major offshore markets of the US, Australia and Europe bolstered faith in market forecasts that   15 the surfwear apparel company will earn $110 million in the year to 30 June 2003.

3 If this figure is reached, or is even close to it, it will be a large profit upgrade for ABSI due to the fact that investors believed in a target of only $85 million. Floating on the stock exchange is a sure-fire way to be successful in business. But, naturally, it takes a certain amount of success to float in the first place.   20 Aqua Blue joined the stock market only two years after forming. The measure of success once on the stock market is the rising value of the shares. Investors are thrilled because Aqua Blue company shares have risen this quarter more than 9% to $8.90 surging clear of long-term lows. When Aqua initially floated, there was interest, and then it died down.   25

4 So, what caused renewed interest in their product lines? One reason Paul Minnow, company director, believes is that presently there is a resurgence of interest in his company because surfing movies have hit the US again, and young people are buying up big in a wave of enthusiasm and rekindled interest in the surf scene. Consumers have to enjoy the brand and repeat buy for a company to be successful   30 and with ABSI, their consumers are girls, and girlswear is the primary driver in their remarkable recovery. The rally is predicted to continue for two to three years.

5 The company offices will expand to Los Angeles in July of this year providing evidence that success in retail business, and ABSI in particular is primarily based around consumer and investor confidence plus international expansion.   35

Grammar

Nominalisation: moving towards more academic writing

In English, there is a specialised grammar of writing. This is 'a grammar that has evolved over hundreds of years, with science at its cutting edge, to construct the world in different ways than talking does' (Martin, 1991:55).

Task A: Nominalising verbs—changing verb forms to nouns

Change the following verb forms to nouns. The first one is done for you.

1 To educate becomes: _education_

2 To inform becomes: _____

3 To distribute: _____

4 To cite: _____

5 To solve: _____

6 To predict: _____

7 To communicate: _____

8 To introduce: _____

9 To transport: _____

10 To produce: _____

11 To pollute: _____

12 To conserve: _____

13 To govern: _____

14 To develop: _____

15 To detain: _____

Task B: Removing personals from writing—creating a more academic text

1 Look now at how to remove personal pronouns from your writing to make it more academic. Do you use the word 'people' often in your writing? Do you use, 'I', 'we', 'us', 'them', they' in your writing? Read the text below and circle all the personals you find.

In my country, there are very rich people and very poor people. People in the government are corrupt because they take bribes. We cannot live a good life and feel free all the time. I love my country because it is mine and many people feel the same way. We just wish our government would make more jobs and people could be more equal in their lives.

2 Now, begin to rewrite without the words you circled, ie remove every: *my, people, they, we, I, mine, their, etc.*

For example: *In <u>my country</u>* becomes: *In (<u>the name of the country</u>), there are the very rich and the very poor.*

_____

_____

_____

_____

_____

Do you see what happens when you remove the personals? Often the end of a sentence must become the beginning! Also, you must use higher lexis (vocabulary) to make the writing more academic. In academic writing, there are more nouns and noun groups than there are verbs and verb groups.

3 With the next exercise, you will learn how to move from spoken language to the passive and then to nominalisation.

Read the following table and complete the empty boxes.

Spoken language	>	How we make paper
Passive form	>	How paper is made
Nominalisation	>	The process of paper making

Active	Passive	Nominalisation
How people make paper	How paper is made	Paper making
First, people fell trees	First, trees are felled	Felling trees is the first step
Then they remove the branches and leaves	Then the branches and leaves are removed	The second step is the removal of branches and leaves
After that, they transport the logs to the sawmill	The logs are transported to the sawmill	The next step is the transportation of the logs to the sawmill
Next people strip the bark from the trunks		
Saw the trunks into logs		
Convey the logs to the paper mill		
Cut into small strips		
Mix the strips with water and acid		
Clean wood pulp		
Bleach the pulp with chemicals to whiten and flatten with rollers		

Active	Passive	Nominalisation
Produce sheets of wet paper		
Press and dry sheets		

4 Now write the paper making process as a text in your notebook.

Task C: Using multiple drafts—unpacking the meaning of noun groups and nominalisations

The next text is a paragraph from the essay titled: *Economics and governments: who calls the shots?* from page 179, but it is the first draft before nominal groups and nominalisation were introduced.

Examine the table and continue to 'unpack' the meaning in the nominalised sentences. You are working from the academic back to the non-academic to discover the writer's original thinking. This is the opposite of moving from the active to the passive to the nominalised forms as you did in the paper making exercise.

- Here you will put the personals back into the text, eg, *people*.

- You will change nouns back to their verb forms, eg. *solution = to solve*.

- You will change the higher language back down to lower language, more spoken, eg, *acknowledges = admits to knowing*.

Academic and nominalised	Non-academic with personals
If one acknowledges the inequality that exists in the world	If a person admits to knowing that in the world, people are not equal
the next logical step is to question the reasons behind it.	people need to ask why other people are not equal. What are the reasons?
There needs to be an exploration	People need to explore
of cause and effect	what causes things to happen
and a questioning of the powers	and people need to question the powers (powers are people who make decisions and who have power)
that control the circumstances of people in all countries.	people have circumstances, circumstances are their living conditions, their employment etc. These circumstances are controlled by someone in every country
Usually, governments are expected to find solutions	
to economic problems which	
may give rise to poverty, child labour, poor working conditions and low pay.	
Governments are meant to consider and address problems	
concerning environment and progress.	

Here is the academic text:

If one acknowledges the inequality that exists in the world, the next logical step is to question the reasons behind it. There needs to be an exploration of cause and effect and a questioning of the powers that control the circumstances of people in all countries. Usually, governments are expected to find solutions to economic problems which may give rise to poverty, child labour, poor working conditions and low pay. Governments are meant to consider and address problems concerning environment and progress.

Task D: 'Unpacking' meaning

Unpack the meaning of the following nominalisations. You must use complete sentences. The first one is done for you.

1 Debt servicing—this means that someone or some country borrows money and is obligated to pay it back. To service a debt means that you must do whatever it takes to 'make the debt good'. In other words, whoever borrowed money must pay the money back.

2 National autonomy— _____

_____

3 A country's self-determination— _____

_____

4 Economic sanctions— _____

_____

5 Dissuasive taxes— _____

_____

Speaking and Listening

✓ *Orientation discussion about global trade*
✓ *Listening to predict main focus, understand key points and take notes*

Orientation discussion about global trade

Task A: Discussion

Based upon your reading in this Unit and your own knowledge or research, what does your group think about global economics? You could bring into your discussion:

■ The public protests throughout the world that have taken place since 1998 concerning the European Union and the World Trade Organisation.

■ What you can purchase in your own country.

■ What you can purchase in the country where you are now.

- Whether it is possible to produce and buy goods made in your own country only or whether we all need imports.
- If you try a web search for 'global economics', use information from that search to add to your discussion.

Listening to predict main focus, understand key points and take notes

Task A: Note taking

See also
Unit 2, page 52;
Unit 4, page 98.

Refer back to Unit 2 and Unit 4, where some abbreviations for note taking were given.

Here is a suggestion for note taking that may use numbering and lettering underneath each heading, but which is a clearer method.

Organise your paper with the following headings, like this:

Main ideas	Supporting ideas and definitions	Authors or researchers mentioned by the lecturer
1	1. A	
	B	
	C	
2	1. A	2
	B	
	C	

Before you listen to the lecture and take notes, consider PREDICTION!

What is prediction? It means that you should try to anticipate or guess what the lecture will be about before you listen to it.

1   Read the title—*Effects of global economics: trade and more trade, what's all the fuss about?* and make a list of three things you know (due to the title and common sense) that must be covered in this lecture.

   a] _____

   b] _____

   c] _____

Did you think of the definitions that the lecturer ought to include? Surely they will explain the meaning of 'global economics' near the beginning of the talk. The talk will have to 'scope' or narrow down the topic, because even if your lecture was five hours long, everything to do with global economics could not be discussed. Therefore, the lecturer will tell you that he or she will focus on two or three major points around the topic of global economics.

2   Think of anything you can that you might know about the subject. Make a quick list of points.

   ■ _____

   ■ _____

   ■ _____

Task C: Listening for discourse markers to understand key points and main ideas in a lecture

Look back at previous lessons and note the discourse markers you have learned. Listen hard for them in this lecture!

See also
Unit 1, page 15;
Unit 2, page 48;
Unit 3, page 66;
Unit 4, page 86.

Listen, also for markers you can expect to hear from the lecturer's mouth and try to listen, then write what is said, using your paraphrasing skills and abbreviations:

■ Today, I am going to discuss _____

■ There are three main _____

■ Let me explain _____

■ Let me repeat that _____

■ So _____

■ It is important to note that _____

■ I'd like to emphasise _____

■ Although it seems that _____ actually _____

■ Crucial to this argument is that _____

- Let me say in passing, though _____ (this will be a digression and you do not necessarily need to write here—just listen and rest your hand for a moment)

- Now _____

LEARNING t i p

> Take a hand-held recorder to every lecture and listen to it again. You can take notes from the recording as well as when listening for the first time. With today's technology, this is a very effective tool to help you.

Task D: Note taking from a lecture

 Now listen to the lecture (Recording number 12) and take notes.

Reading and Critical thinking

✓ *Vocabulary and scanning*
✓ *Issues around globalisation*
✓ *Skimming for main ideas*

Vocabulary and scanning

Task A: Three-part task

1 There are three parts to this task. First, you are to scan the written version of the recording for the following nouns, noun phrases/groups and nominalisations contained in the text. They are underlined. Once you locate the words, write the number of the paragraph where you located the words next to the word in the list below.

2 With a partner, match the underlined word groups to their definitions on page 198.

Words and word groups list

1 _____ degradation of developing countries' environments

2 _____ a commodity

3 _____ globalisation

4 _____ consumerism

5 _____ global economic integration

6 _____ very good track record

7 _____ conspicuous consumption practices

8 _____ a cursory glance

9 _____ the maxim

10	_____	excessive higher dependence on foreign capital inflows
11	_____	the trade deficit
12	_____	liberalised trade
13	_____	advocates
14	_____	integration of the international economy
15	_____	the continuing advocacy
16	_____	the assumption
17	_____	prudent master
18	_____	emerging nations' economies
19	_____	dergulated global trade
20	_____	consumption poverty

Recording script

  RECORDING NUMBER 12 (17 MINUTES, 5 SECONDS)

TITLE: Trade and more trade, what's all the fuss about?

Lecturer:

Good Afternoon to students, visitors and guests...

In my talk today, I hope to clarify some of the issues that surround the topic of <u>globalisation</u>. A great deal of the world's focus over the past decades, has been concerned with developed and <u>emerging nations' economies</u> and the links between *them* and the more developed, *established* economies or countries 5 which are capable of huge <u>consumerism</u>. So, what's meant by 'economy' and what do we mean when we mention 'globalisation'?

Well, let's start—according to the *Macquarie Dictionary*, a discussion of economics will be a discussion, and I quote, 'pertaining to the production, distribution and use of income and wealth'. Globalisation has not made its way into the dictionary 10 as yet as it appears to be a term (a nominal or noun term—a nominalisation) based upon the noun, 'global' which pertains to the whole world. Now, according to an article at the Center for Trade Policy Study's website entitled, 'The Benefits of Globalisation', 'Globalisation describes the ongoing global trend toward the freer flow of trade and investment across borders and the resulting <u>integration of the</u> 15 <u>international economy</u>'. So, let me repeat that definition for you....'Globalisation describes the ongoing global trend toward the freer flow of trade and investment across borders and the resulting integration of the international economy'.

Now, <u>global economic integration</u> is a goal of the policy makers who advocate liberalised or free trade around the world. Another common term for free trade 20 or <u>liberalised trade</u> is <u>deregulated global trade.</u>

4 Advocates of free trade try to explain that the reason globalisation is so good for countries is that it expands their economic freedom and spurs competition thereby raising both the productivity and the living standards of the people in countries who participate. 25

5 Hmmm, and that's where the debate really begins. Because, if that's true, then the countries involved in globalisation over the past 10 or 20 years will surely be able to demonstrate those promises—that is that their productivity and living standards are raised or improved. And that there are fewer poor people and those who are poor have a better standard of life. Now, before we examine 30 that aspect of the claims for a particular economic policy, I'd like to outline briefly what I intend to cover in the talk.

6 Now, there are three main points—

1 First, I'd like to offer a brief overview of some positions concerning free trade.

2 Secondly, I'd like to point out some examples of countries who are seen to 35 benefit by advocates of globalisation policies.

3 And, thirdly, I would like to point out some of the examples of countries who are seen not to benefit by reformers and critics of globalisation policies

4 And then to wrap up, I would like to test the truthfulness or otherwise of the statement that globalisation raises both productivity and the living 40 standards of the people in the countries who participate.

7 Now it's beyond the scope of this lecture to discuss in depth some of the economic policies which comprise globalisation, well, for example, open or closed capital accounts, capital controls, inflation targeting, reserves and supplementary reserves and so forth. So, I'll limit my talk to issues around trade and whether or 45 not this most important aspect of globalisation is, in fact, delivering its promise.

8 Now, by whatever term you call free trade and the push to increase it, it either has a very good track record or a very poor track record, and that depends entirely upon which side of the fence you sit upon, be that politically, financially or academically. 50

9 So, let me explain this a bit further. The main drivers for free trade are the richer, industrialised countries led by the IMF, you know, the International Monetary Fund and the World Bank. Now these advisors meet at the World Economic Forum where changes have recently taken place. Interestingly, all of these organisations state that they are committed to reducing world poverty 55 and to increasing the wealth and well being of the poorer, less industrialised or, let's call them, developing nations (as countries without the conspicuous consumption practices of the other nations are referred to).

10 Now, even a cursory glance at the World Bank's home page on the World Wide Web reveals that its position statement or motto, if you like, is 'Our dream is a 60 world free of poverty'. Well, regardless of the side if I may call it that, that you are on, this is the stated aim of both the opposing sides. Now, the method for the achievement of that aim is the thing that seems to be in dispute.

11 Now, deregulated, liberalised free trade in order to integrate economies is the goal of both the World Bank and the IMF. For example, the World Bank in September 2001, argued that, and again, I quote 'globalisation reduces poverty because integrated economies tend to grow faster and this growth is usually widely diffused'. (World Bank: 2001a,1) 65

12 Now, the IMF's First Deputy Managing Director, Mr. Stanley Fischer, states that he believes that 'Asia needs the Fund if it is to continue to benefit as it has so spectacularly over the years from its integration into the global economy'. Well, his position is clear enough. The IMF has benefited Asia in a spectacular way. Korea, for example was one country that may have agreed, but only for a short while. They appeared to be benefiting until the Asian crisis in the late 1990's. 70

13 Another point of view, James Glassman, a columnist for the Washington Post and a fellow at the, what is it, the ... American Enterprise Institute in Washington stated that free trade creates wealth, which he says ... get this ... is 'more important than jobs'. So, here he is entering a debate with fellow Americans in the United States who oppose free trade because many of their own industries and there are many (such as textiles)—are being destroyed. Now, in this theory, imports are why people trade and they are in fact the important factor. He uses Adam Smith's argument of 200 years ago that, and I quote Smith, 'It is the <u>maxim</u> of every <u>prudent master</u> of a family never to make at home what it will cost him more to make than to buy ... If a foreign country can supply us with a <u>commodity</u> cheaper than we ourselves can make it, better buy it off them.' So, in his view, exports are only traded in order to gain the benefit of imports. 75 80 85

14 So, just returning for a minute to claims that global economic integration has great potential to combat poverty and economic inequality ... and as I stated earlier in this lecture if this claim were true, then that could be demonstrated. But, it isn't. Listen a moment to these statistics which are provided in a research paper by Weller, Scott and Hersh in 2002. It goes like this ...' In 1980 median income in the richest 10% of countries was 77 times greater, 77 times greater, than in the poorest 10%; and by 1999, that gap had grown to 122 times. The number of poor people actually rose from 1987 to 1999. The world's poorest 10%, and that's 400 million people, lived on 72 cents a day or less. In 1998, that figure had increased ... to 79 cents and in 1999 had dropped again to 78 cents'. This represents no improvement for a decade of trade. 90 95

15 Now, while many other 'social, political and economic factors contribute to poverty, the evidence shows that unregulated capital and trade flows actually contribute to rising inequality and in fact impede progress in reducing poverty.' How? I hear you asking. Well, it goes like this ... when trade is liberalised there is more import competition—which in turn leads to lower wages for locals. Deregulated international capital flows can lead to rising short-term capital inflows certainly and increased financial speculation. But this causes instability which causes more frequent economic crises. We only have to think of the so- 100 105 called Asian crisis back in the late 90's. Governments cannot cope with crises as they do not have the reserves. Now, as we all should know, any economic problems within any country harm the poor to a greater extent than others. Poor people are not being helped by free trade, even though that could be the desire and is, indeed, the stated claim of the IMF and the World Bank. 110

16 Hang on a minute, I hear you say .... What about somewhere like India and the IT industry there? Surely, this unrestricted globalisation there has proved to be a boon in India. Many business opportunities for India would be the result. And they now have lots of technology. Yes, but firstly, it does not belong to them and secondly, there is no infrastructure to provide it to people outside of a very 115 small area of the country, and thirdly, only a very few workers benefit from it and even they work for far lower wages than they should.

17 In a detailed analysis of the IT revolution and the opening up of India to globalisation in South Asian Voice, it appears that FDI (that's Foreign Direct Investment) benefits the multinationals far in excess of the benefits to India and its 120 own people. For example, the MNCs receive huge tax breaks that are not available to competing local companies. So not happy with tax breaks, the MNCs also evade tax. The Minister of State for Finance in India named a number of very large and very well known companies as having been charged for serious income tax violations so, obviously, this means that the government has lost money to these huge companies. 125

18 And, privitisation has meant that in areas such as power supply—companies like Enron charge double to the State Electricity Board than a local supplier. And also, Enron uses imported fuels, making India even more dependent on the international market. Now, it also means again that the Indian government has lost capital. This results in a lack of funding to important infrastructures within 130 the country, the obvious ones like education and healthcare. So once again, the poor get poorer and the rich get even richer.

19 Now, in the same article from the South Asian Voice, we have Dr. DM Nanjundappa in the Deccan Herald in 1998, now he's a noted economist and also happens to be the Deputy Chairman of the State Planning Board in India, and he stated the 135 following, and I quote from Dr Nanjundappa: '_Excessive higher dependence on foreign capital inflows_ and a rise in exports is likely to be dangerous. Unless there is a sustained growth in exports arising from improvement in the competitive strength of the Indian industry, our hope to recover will be the will o' the wisp'.

20 And to support that, the trade deficit in India widened to a record four billion 140 dollars in the last quarter of 2002. It grew by a staggering 27% and this was in spite of an increase in exports. And at the same time the rupee shrank in value as well. Africa has many similar tales to tell to the Asian situation.

21 Now, the point of all of these criticisms is that economists themselves are actually questioning the value to their countries of unrestricted and deregulated 145 trade. Certain geographical areas may benefit and certain individuals will most certainly benefit from those policies. But in terms of the overall nations who are supposed to be assisted by having markets for trading—that is a place for

their exports and the development of technology within their own countries, there's not really much concrete evidence to support that that is in fact happening. So, the benefits go to the rich countries and it is on the rich country's terms that the whole concept of globalisation is constructed. 150

22 Now, to the second point, as for combatting poverty, the World Bank has this to say in its own report published in 2001. And this is straight from the report, 'In the aggregate, and for some large regions, all...measures suggest that the 1990's 155 did not see much progress against <u>consumption poverty</u> in the developing world' (Chen and Ravallion, 2001:18) and also the IMF, in its 2000 report, ... Part IV reports that progress in raising real incomes and alleviating poverty has been so disappointingly slow in many developing countries." It also states that "the relative gap between the richest and the poorest countries has continued to 160 widen" (IMF 2000, Part IV, p.1). What is not mentioned in all of that is that not only has poverty increased, but the <u>degradation of developing countries'</u> <u>environments</u> has also increased dramatically. To put that another way, there is greater poverty of lifestyle conditions as well. Note the air, water and land pollution as a result of demand for exports produced cheaply and with great cost 165 to the local environment.

23 So, and I'll close here, despite the <u>continuing advocacy</u> of rich nations that poor countries must trade and trade on the terms of the more powerful nations and that in turn this trade will and must lead to greater wealth, prosperity and more equality, it appears that the number of poor people has actually risen. So, the 170 promises of poverty reduction and more equal income distribution have actually failed to occur. Now I'd like you to consider whether or not the economic policies need to be a little newer than 200 years old and could, in fact incorporate the economies they deal with, rather than making <u>the assumption</u> that there is but one way to create wealth and reduce poverty. It is not working. The evidence is 175 there. Now, the theory may work, but the practice doesn't. It seems that the ideas for globalisation must take into account the infrastructures which currently exist in developing countries and work respectfully with them to create meaningful solutions to and for the ever increasing poor around the globe rather than exploiting them in an opportunistic way to create ever more poor. Thank you. 180

Task A: Question 3

3 Last, place the underlined word groups into the correct sentences which contain blanks.

So, in conclusion, despite _____ of rich nations that poor countries must trade and trade on the terms of the more powerful nations and that this trade will and must lead to greater wealth, prosperity and more equality, it appears that the number of poor people has actually risen.

_____ on _____ and rise in exports is likely to be dangerous. Unless there is a sustained growth in exports arising from improvement in the competitive strength of the Indian industry, our hope to recover will be the will the wisp'.

_____ in India widened to a record of $4 billion dollars in the last quarter of 2002.

Interestingly, all these organisations state that they are committed to reducing world poverty and to increasing the wealth and well being of the poorer, less industrialised or developing nations (as countries without the _____ of the other nations are referred to).

What is not mentioned is that not only has poverty increased, but the _____ of _____ has also increased dramatically.

A _____ at the World Bank's home page on the World Wide Web reveals that its position statement or motto, if you like, is 'Our Dream is a World Free of Poverty'.

According to an article at the Center for Trade Policy Study's website titled 'The Benefits of Globalisation', 'Globalisation describes the ongoing global trend toward the freer flow of trade and investment across borders and the resulting _____

In my talk today, I hope to clarify some of the issues that surround the topic of

_____

A great deal of the world's focus over the past decades and coming decade, is aimed at and concerned with developed and _____ and the links between them and the more developed, established economies or countries which are capable of huge _____

_____ is a goal of the policy makers who advocate liberalised or free trade around the world. Another common term for free trade or _____ is _____ .

_____ of free trade explain that the reason globalisation is so good for countries is that it expands economic freedom and promotes competition thereby raising both productivity and living standards of the people in countries who participate.

'In the aggregate, and for some large regions, all ... measures suggest that the 1990s did not see much progress against _____ in the developing world' (Chen and Ravallion, 2001: 18).

Now, by whatever term you call free trade and the push to increase it, it either has a _____ or a very poor track record, depending upon which side of the fence you sit upon politically, financially and academically.

He uses Adam Smith's argument of 200 years ago that 'It is _____ of every _____ of a family never to make at home what it will cost him more to make than to buy ... If a foreign country can supply us with a_v cheaper than we ourselves can make it, better buy it off them.' In his view, exports are only traded in order to gain the benefits of imports.

_____ on _____ and rise in exports is likely to be dangerous.

Definitions for words and word groups list (Task A, page 192)

1 To degrade or lower the environment of a country which is emerging.

2 Anything of value which may be bought or sold.

3 Describes the ongoing global trend toward the freer flow of trade and investment across borders and the resulting integration of the international economy.

4 To buy—the power to obtain goods and to do so.

5 Where economies join or become integrated into the world's economic policies.

6 A positive result of actions.

7 To consume a great deal, to purchase new things constantly and to have the buying power to do so.

8 A quick look at something.

9 The saying or belief.

10 For a country to rely too heavily on other countries in terms of cash/money coming into the country.

11 Money owed to other countries as a result of trade.

12 Free trade or trade which is unrestricted, trade without controls.

13 People who believe in something and ask that it be accepted—to put up an argument in favour of something.

14 For economies around the world to become integrated, to work together.

15 For people to continue to advise and argue a case.

16 A belief.

17 Wise person.

18 The economy or money base of nations which are developing along an industrial line.

19 Trade around the world which is not regulated by governments.

20 When people do not have buying power and are poorer than others who consume a lot.

Skimming for main ideas

See also
Unit 1, page 20;
Unit 2, page 37.

In Unit 4 (pages 96–98), under note-taking skills, you learned how to examine a book or text, including the index, bibliography, table of contents and chapter headings. When quickly looking over these areas, you were skimming the book for a general idea of what it might provide for you.

■ In skimming, you are floating over the surface as a rock skipping over water when thrown.

■ In scanning, you may scan for *specific information* and the following exercise is to assist you and train your eye and brain to be able to do that more quickly. After you scan and locate the information, you then skim the paragraph where you found it and then stop and read slowly.

Task A: Skimming and scanning for key language signals

Take no more than 10 minutes for this exercise. Look for keywords such as:

1 Issues.

2 Sequencing words such as *first, second*.

3 Arguments and their counter-arguments—cued by words such as *however, but, now, let me explain*.

4 Conclusions and recommendations.

Write what you located in Task A next to each of the four main headings found in that task. In other words, match your scanning and skimming by *noting down* the issues; the concepts that follow *first, second*; arguments found that were cued by words such as *however, but, now, let me explain*; and the conclusions and recommendations.

English for the Internet Age

Internet research project

Task A: Issues and views, Earth Summit 2002

Conduct an Internet research project based upon the *Earth Summit* held in Johannesburg in 2002. You can use the techniques from English for the Internet Age sections in Unit 1 (page 28), Unit 2 (page 42), Unit 3 (page 69) and Unit 4 (page 104).

1   What were the key issues set down for the summit by UN Secretary-General Kofi Annan?

2   Which two countries did not sign the protocol for the EU's (European Union's) renewable energy target?

3   What was the reaction and action of Greenpeace activists to the *Earth Summit*?

From your research, what are your conclusions around the summit?

- Was it successful?
- Who benefited the most?
- Was trade an important issue?
- Was the environment an important issue?
- What is your opinion concerning the Earth Summit?

Learner independence & study skills

Faculty requirements within different disciplines

Task A: Using a university/faculty handbook

1   If you have chosen your university or further study institution, then contact them and obtain a handbook for your own faculty or chosen area of study.

2   From this handbook, locate and note down the following:

- assessments in terms of assignments;
- course materials;
- examinations and their dates for the current session;
- essay writing requirements;
- tutorial presentation;
- referencing style;
- bibliography requirements.

unit 9 language

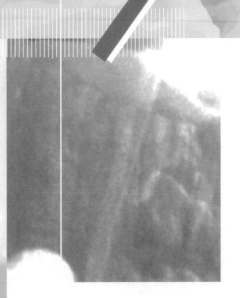

Every language is a temple, in which the soul of those who speak it is enshrined.

OLIVER WENDELL HOLMES

Skills focus: In this Unit, you will learn and use the following skills:

Speaking 1

Languages quiz and introductory discussion

Task A: Languages quiz

Together, discuss and choose the answers to the following questions that you find the most realistic or likely.

1   How many languages are there in the world?

   a] around 23 000

   b] around 16 000

   c] around 6 000

   d] around 2 000

2   Which country has the greatest number of native languages?

   a] India

   b] Indonesia

   c] Papua New Guinea

   d] Kenya

3   How many countries have, between them, half the world's languages?

   a] 95

   b] 50

   c] 20

   d] 8

4   Which languages have the greatest number of native speakers?

   a] Mandarin Chinese (Pǔtōnghùa), Spanish, Portuguese

   b] Spanish, English, Hindi

   c] Mandarin Chinese (Pǔtōnghùa), Arabic, English

   d] Mandarin Chinese (Pǔtōnghùa), Spanish, English

5   Vanuatu, in the South Pacific, has a population of only around 180 000—the size of a large town in most countries. About how many native languages do you think exist there?

   a] 100

   b] 50

   c] 20

   d] 8

6 The island of Guinea, which comprises most of Papua New Guinea and also the province of Irian Jaya in Indonesia, has 0.1% of the world's population, but about how many languages?

a] 3000

b] 1100

c] 550

d] 200

7 Approximately how often does a language 'die' (that is, have no native speakers left)?

a] once every six months

b] once every month

c] once every two weeks

d] once a week

8 Which of the following languages have been, or are being, 'raised from the dead', that is, have increasing numbers of speakers when once they were expected to die? (You may give more than one answer for this question.)

a] Hebrew (the language of Israel and the traditional language of Jewish people)

b] Welsh (the native language of Wales, part of Britain)

c] Hawaiian

d] Irish Gaelic

9 What proportion of the world's population is raised bilingually or multilingually, that is, they learn more than one language in early childhood from their family and the people around them, not through formal education?

a] 3%

b] 20%

c] 45%

d] 66%

10 Approximately how many languages have been recorded as influencing the vocabulary of English?

a] 350

b] 100

c] 35

d] 10

Listening, Speaking and Critical thinking

✓ *Language of persuasion*
✓ *Critical thinking: reflecting on cultural aspects of persuasion*

Language of persuasion

You are going to hear a conversation between two students. At the beginning, one (Roger) doesn't see any benefit in preserving minority languages, but his friend, Kate, has a different opinion.

Task A: Discussion—orientation to the topic

In pairs, briefly discuss the following points:

1 What's your first language? Is it the main language of your country? What do you think will be the status of the language in a few decades? Will English be more popular?

2 In your country, do some people speak minority languages? Do you have any idea how many people speak them? Do you think these languages will die? Does the government of your country give these languages support? If so, why? If not, why not?

3 Think of as many reasons as you can why:

   a] some people might think minority languages should be supported and preserved, and why;

   b] some people might think it's better to support more major languages, such as the language of the country, and give no support to minority languages, or even try to suppress them.

Task B: Listening for main ideas

Read the list of reasons to preserve dying languages, below.

a] Because a person's language provides a sense of identity and a connection with previous generations.

b] Because knowledge of languages can help the study of other subjects, such as anthropology and history.

c] We might still learn things, for example, medical uses of some plants, if we study the knowledge that is held by native speakers of these languages.

d] Because the more languages there are, the more culturally rich humanity is.

e] Living languages are better than languages that appear only in books.

f] Preserving unique cultures and preventing them from becoming influenced by other cultures is good for tourism.

g] Different languages involve different ways of thinking, and this diversity is good for humanity.

  Listen to the discussion and mark the four main points from the list a] to g] above that Kate uses in her argument.

Task C: Identifying techniques for persuasion

Look at persuasion techniques (a) to (g) below. Match them with extracts from the recording script labelled (i) to (x). Two techniques have more than one example, and another has no clear example listed.

Persuasion techniques

a] Acknowledge another's point of view, but then refute it.

b] Ask questions which expect a positive answer.

c] Use dramatic language, to give the argument more force.

d] Make strong statements of opinion.

e] Add emphasis, for example, by repeating words or using a signposting expression.

f] Relate the argument to the other person's experience, or to a similar idea that's more familiar to them.

g] Appeal to the listener to imagine a situation.

Extracts from recording script

i] ... I know it sounds _____ er ... , but ...

ii] ... it's a bit like losing the Mona Lisa, or a Van Gogh painting ...

iii] ... but don't you think there's something missing if it's just ... a story in a book?

iv] ... it's just like looking at a dead animal in a museum ...

v] ... the most interesting thing ... is how people express ideas

vi] Have you ever studied another language? ➔ *answer* ➔ *development of argument*

vii] ... But there's an even more important reason than that.

viii] ... just imagine how you'd feel if ...

ix] ... just look in most countries at ... who ...

x] ... not really fitting in—not fitting in to the dominant culture.

 LEARNING t i p

It's important to recognise when these techniques are being used in an attempt to persuade you. However, you don't have to use them all yourself!

(13)

Task D: Listening for intonation in persuasion

Listen to the conversation again, and focus especially on the persuasion techniques. Notice the intonation patterns used.

Critical thinking: reflecting on cultural aspects of persuasion

Task A: Critical thinking—reflecting on persuasion; cross-cultural comparison; identifying attempts to persuade

1 **a]** Together, list some situations in which people might attempt to persuade.

   b] Do you think it's acceptable to try to persuade in these situations?

2 In which academic situations do you think the persuasion techniques in Task C of the previous section above might be used?

3 **a]** Do you use many of these techniques in your own language?

   b] Are there some that you wouldn't feel comfortable using in your own culture?

   c] Do your answers depend on the situation, eg who's speaking?

   d] Can you add other techniques that are used in your language (it may be useful to write your own conversation, in your own language, with someone else from your own culture).

4 **Homework:** Listen to the television or radio, or read some advertisements or political leaflets, and see how many of these techniques you read or hear.

Speaking: persuasion

Task A: Practice in persuasion

Take it in turns to persuade your partner of the following points. When it's your turn to listen, identify the technique that your partner uses, and tell your partner when he or she finishes. You can vary these, or choose your own points.

1 Food from your country is the best food in the world.

2 Every time someone in the class speaks their own language, they have to pay money into a chocolate fund.

3 The class should organise a social activity after class next week.

4 Cats are better than dogs.

5 Everyone should learn a language other than English.

6 Cars should be taxed much more heavily than they are now to reduce their use and therefore the problems they create.

7 Media such as newspapers and televisions shouldn't have any financial connection with politicians.

Grammar

Articles 2

> ### Task A: When are 'a' and 'an' used?

▮ Look at the following example with some noun groups bolded.

When **a language** dies, it's clearly **an unfortunate event**, but it may at first glance be difficult to understand why some people consider it so catastrophic. However, when we examine carefully what has been lost with **the passing of the language**, **a different picture** emerges ...

With 'a language', you probably already understand that 'a' was chosen because this particular language is introduced here for the first time. The audience doesn't know which language at this point. However, when the same language is mentioned again ('the passing of **the language**'), the writer shows the audience that he or she means the same language by using 'the'.

However, why was 'an' chosen in 'an unfortunate event'? It appears that we know which unfortunate event because the writer just said which one—'a language dies', so 'the' seems the clear choice. However, 'an unfortunate event' is a wider category than 'when a language dies', that is, it's less specific. That's why 'a' is chosen. If the author had chosen 'the unfortunate event', it would appear to be an event mentioned in a previous sentence, but there is no previous sentence!

A common pattern is that 'a' or 'an' follow it/this... + 'be' verb

Another way of looking at it is that:

> 'a/an ...**X**...' means 'one ...**X**...', but the focus isn't on which ...**X**....

> ### Task B: Practice

▮ Now, apply the hypothesis at the end of the previous task to help you fill the following gaps in a description of an English course, adapted from part of an assignment written during a postgraduate course for English teachers. Choose the most likely article for each gap but also think about how the meaning would change with a different article.

The English for Business course is aimed primarily at students intending to enter business courses running at the college, though (1) _____ course is also open to those intending to work in business or corporate jobs. It is basically (2) _____ ten-week course, with one topic-based unit of work lasting one week. It fulfils (3) _____ standard accreditation requirements for (4) _____ full time course, consisting of 20 hours classroom study and 5 hours self access study per week, making (5) _____ 250 hour course.

Students either enter (6) _____ course from Pre-Intermediate General English classes at (7) _____ college, or students new to

(8) _____ college, if demonstrating an intermediate level of English in the college placement test, may start in this class if they express (9) _____ preference for Business English as opposed to General English. Enrolment, as determined by college policy, is continuous: students can begin any Monday. After completing this course and passing a proficiency test within (10) _____ college, students can progress to the Upper Intermediate English for Business class.

Task C: Speaking practice with articles

1 Choose a topic for discussion, for example, the questions at the end of this Unit.

2 In pairs, record a short conversation on this topic.

3 Listen to the recording, focusing on noun groups containing articles.

4 Decide where articles were and weren't used appropriately. Ask your teacher if necessary.

English for the Internet Age

Internet directories

When searching the Internet, the first things people often think of using are search engines. However, most of the sites found by search engines are inappropriate for academic work. A more efficient way of finding academic information is to use academic directories or virtual libraries. All sites listed on these have been reviewed and found to be of an appropriate academic standard. Also, they are organised in a systematic way, making it easy to find particular sites.

Task A: Demonstration of an Internet directory

Imagine you want information about Chinese culture.

1 Go to http://bubl.ac.uk/link/, the index page of BUBL Information Service.

2 Click on the main heading Language, Literature and Culture.

3 You will see many links in alphabetical order. Choose the one for Chinese culture.

4 The page you come to will give you summaries of various sites about Chinese culture. These summaries will help you to choose useful links.

Task B: Evaluating and selecting directories for your field

See Unit 4, page 104, *Evaluating credibility of internet sites.*

1 Look at the right hand column of the table below. Do you think that knowing these kinds of information about websites will help you to choose which ones to visit? Is there anything you would add or change?

2 Look for pages related to **the subject of your future studies** in the directories mentioned in this table, and fill in the table below with 'Yes' or 'No'.

	BUBL	Infomine	Librarians' Index to the Internet	Virtual Library	Internet public library
	bubl.ac.uk/link	infomine.ucr.edu	www.lii.org	www.vlib.org	www.ipl.org
Does it give summary information of each site listed?					
If there is summary information, is it helpful?					
Does it give the author of each site?					
Does it give the date each site was last checked?					
Does it give resource type for each site (eg journal article, list of links)?					
Is other useful information given for each site?					
Does the directory have the field you want?					

3 Which is/are the best directory(ies) for information in your field?

Writing 1

✓ *Dissecting essay questions for meaning*
✓ *Expositions revisited and expanded*

Dissecting essay questions for meaning

Task A: Model of a multi-part essay question

1 Look at the following essay question:

> Evaluate the usefulness to business of having employees with ability in a variety of languages. Is language training in the nation's education system adequate to cope with the need for businesses to have speakers of other languages? If necessary, suggest methods of improvement.

'Evaluate', 'Is ...' and 'suggest' are key question words. What do you think they tell you to do in your answer?

2 Look on page 210 (bottom) to check your answer.

In the *Key question words* box below are common words used in essay questions. Write them in the *Key question words and genre* table (below) next to their common meanings. Using a learner's dictionary may help.

Key question words

account for	(critically) analyse	assess	comment on
compare	contrast	criticise	critique
describe	discuss	evaluate	explain
justify	yes/no question	to what extent do you	

The genres in the table below were introduced in the following units: Explanation—Unit 1, page 14; Argument—Unit 2, page 43; Discussion—Unit 3, page 61; Compare and contrast—Unit 8, page 178; and Exposition—Unit 8, page 184.

Key question words and genre table

Key question words	Meaning	Genre
describe	give information without analysis or judgment (answers most 'what' questions)	information report
_____	give factual information about how something works, how something is done, or why something happens (answers most 'how' or 'why' questions)	explanation
account for	give reasons for something	explanation
_____ _____	show similarities (and sometimes differences) show differences	compare and contrast
justify assess _____ _____ _____	make an overall judgment (perhaps by looking at strengths and weaknesses and deciding which are stronger)	argument or discussion (exposition)
_____ criticise _____ _____ _____	find strengths and weaknesses, advantages and disadvantages, etc	discussion

Answer to Task A

1 You would discuss or argue this point, ie you would give reasons for and/or against language ability being useful to business.

Evaluate the usefulness to business of having employees with ability in a variety of languages. Is language training in the nation's education system adequate to cope with the need for businesses to have speakers of other languages? If necessary, suggest methods of improvement.

2 This is a yes/no question, so you would choose to agree or disagree with this, with reasons, ie **argument.**

3 You would **give ideas**, **explain** them if necessary and then **argue** for them, ie say why you think they would work

LEARNING tip

> Note that while these are standard conventions, not every lecturer follows them. If you're not sure about the meaning of an essay question, check with your lecturer as early as possible.

Task C: Analysing essay questions

1 Look at the following questions and analyse them in the same way as Task A. Write your comments against the arrows coming from the questions. You don't need to know the models and theories mentioned!

a] **Critique** Porter's Five Forces Model of competitive advantage. **To what extent** can it still be applied in today's rapidly changing business environment of globalisation, deregulation and increasing use of technology?

b] **Briefly explain** the Teaching-Learning Cycle. **Compare and contrast** this with Task-Based Learning. **Evaluate** the strengths and weaknesses of each. **How** would you adapt them to your own teaching situation? It may be useful to choose (and describe) a group of learners you have recently taught.

c] For a listed company of your choice, use recent annual financial reports to **compare** its performance over two financial years. **Evaluate** this against its business plan. **Critically analyse** the performance of the company in terms of consistency of value to shareholders.

LEARNING tip

> The golden rule is if you give an opinion, always support it, even if the question doesn't directly ask you to!

LEARNING tip

- If the question says 'describe and analyse', more of the marks will be for the higher level skill (analysis) than the description, so you should spend more time on that.
- Ensure you answer all parts of the question!
- Ensure every paragraph connects to the question!

Expositions revisited and expanded

Task A: Orientation discussion

Together, discuss the following questions.

1 When did you begin to learn English, or another foreign language? Did you wish you had started earlier?

2 What do you think is the best age to begin to learn another language? Why?

3 On a different topic, if you worked for an organisation in your country, in which language would you expect negotiations with organisations from other countries to be carried out? If you had two potential suppliers, one of whom was happy to negotiate in your language, while the other insisted on using English, which would you prefer to deal with (all other things being equal)?

4 What other benefits can employees with high level language skills bring to organisations?

Task B: Review of essay structure

1 Read the essay question below and the introduction to the answer (opposite, para 1). The question is the same as the one in Task A of the previous section. Assume that the answer was written in an English-speaking country for a university lecturer. Identify the stages in the introduction and draw boxes around them (see Unit 2, page 43).

Essay question

Evaluate the usefulness to business of having employees with ability in a variety of languages. Is language training in the nation's education system adequate to cope with the need for businesses to have speakers of other languages? If necessary, suggest methods of improvement.

2 Are each of the three parts of the question addressed in the Introduction? What is the relationship between the question and the preview/scope?

3 Predict the ideas that will be given in the body: write a list.

4 If you were about to read the essay and wanted to find a suggestion for a long-term improvement to language education, where in the body would you start to look? What reading technique would you use?

5 Now, read the body of the essay on the next page (paras 2–7). How well does the body fit your predictions?

6 Draw boxes around the topic sentences of the body paragraphs.

7 What are, usually, the two stages of the conclusion?

8 Write your own conclusion for this essay.

9 Compare your conclusion with the one given in Appendix B, page 250.

TITLE **The road to diversity: The economic benefits of universal second language education from primary school**

1　Due to the increasingly globalised business environment, companies are more than ever before finding it necessary to communicate with people and organisations from other countries. Traditionally, people in English-speaking countries have relied on English as a language of communication, but the advantages of knowing other languages are rapidly becoming better known. It 　　5 is now extremely important that companies employ people with high level language skills, and that improvements are made in the education system of the country to supply people with the right skills for this. This essay will elaborate some ways in which language ability is directly and indirectly useful to business, and then put forward a long-term and a short-term suggestion for how 　　10 the education system can be improved in order to provide the skills needed.

2　International trade depends on an ability to negotiate deals, and clearly this is much easier if a company's negotiators speak the language of the people they are doing business with—after all, this motivation is one of the reasons for the enormous size of the English language teaching industry around the world. It is 　　15 true that English is a very common international language, but a company can gain an advantage over its competitors by speaking its customers' own languages. This would not only impress the customers and provide an extra tool for developing rapport, but would also enable companies to take opportunities that would otherwise be closed to them, for example dealing with organisations 　　20 which have little or no English language skill. However, this is something that seems to have passed businesses in English-speaking countries by, to their disadvantage. Research by the Centre for Information on Language Teaching found that 'a third of British exporters miss opportunities because of poor language skills' (Crystal, 1997). Even in English-speaking countries, therefore, 　　25 there would be considerable benefit from greater knowledge of other languages.

3　Language learning also leads to greater understanding of other cultures, that is, the cultures of a company's suppliers and customers, thus providing further competitive advantage. 'Language is part of culture' (Kramsch, 1998: 3), and therefore learning a language automatically means increased cultural knowledge, 　　30 understanding and insight. This is clearly a valid educational objective in itself, but is also of great importance to business. A deeper understanding of motivations and thinking in customers' and suppliers' own countries will clearly give an advantage over other companies not only in trade negotiations, but also in dealing with all levels of government to do things such as getting permission 　　35 to build new factories, and also in the public relations sphere, which can be important for allowing acceptance of the company in a foreign country.

4 Linked to the argument above is the idea of flexibility of thinking and being open to ideas which are different from your own or from the people and culture around you. In many cultures, flexibility and originality of thought have long been considered an asset in business, and the ability to think in different languages strongly helps this. To take an ideal example, bilingual children have, given the right circumstances, been shown to have greater abilities in flexible and creative thinking than monolingual children (Saunders, 1988: 19). Therefore, bilingualism, or at least the learning of a second language during the early years of a child's life, should be encouraged systematically across the country, and an efficient way to do this would be through the public education system.

5 Now that it has been shown how important language ability is to business, ways in which the language ability of the nation can be improved will be suggested. Native speakers of English traditionally complain that they are not good at learning languages. But perhaps the reason for this is that languages are often not taught seriously until very late, that is, after finishing primary school. It is common knowledge that language learning is most effectively done from a much earlier age—young children, if given sufficient need to learn a language, pick it up much more easily than adults. Therefore, it is imperative that language learning not only begins in primary school but also becomes an important part of the primary school curriculum.

6 However, for this to be successful, primary schools need to be sufficiently resourced. This includes the training of teachers. Presently, most primary school teachers are generalists, trained to teach a wide variety of subjects. But language education requires teachers who are fluent in the language, and the best way to provide this is to train primary school language specialists who have lived in the country where the language is spoken. While this would entail considerable investment, it is essential in order to successfully achieve a higher level of linguistic competence across the nation.

7 This is, however, a long-term solution. What is needed in the short-term is an increase in the prestige and perceived benefits of learning languages. This would increase the number and quality of students in language courses. One way forward with this is through large-scale in-school promotion campaigns which pick up on the current fashion of being interested in business and emphasise the relevance of languages to business success. Another is to emphasise the cultural and communicative aspects of language learning and to get away from the image of learning language as memorising vocabulary lists and tricky grammar rules full of annoying exceptions.

(This essay's conclusion is in Appendix B, page 250: see question 9 above.)

Task C: Essay and paragraph development—further features

1 Look again at the topic sentences. Does each paragraph answer a part of the question? (In the fourth paragraph, look also at the second sentence.)

LEARNING t i p

Every paragraph **must** answer some part of the question. Check this before submitting every assignment—it's easy to get carried away!

To help you with this:

 LEARNING t i p

Put your essay question or thesis statement on the wall in front of where you write. Look at it frequently!

2 **a]** Which body paragraphs answer the first part of the question?

b] Which answer the second and third parts of the question?

3 **a]** In Task B, we noted that there are two parts to this essay, each of which answers a different part of the question. Which sentence shows the transition between these parts?

b] Would the essay be as easy to read if this sentence was missed out? Why, or why not?

c] How important is this sentence?

 **LEARNING** t i p

If your essay changes direction, tell your reader this with a special sentence (called a transition sentence)—it will make your essay easier to follow.

The first part of the essay (paragraphs two to four) is like a standard argument essay. However, the second part is more complex. The next two questions look at this.

4 Look at the sixth paragraph of the essay. This is like a mini-essay. Write the sentences which provide the following functions in this paragraph:

Stage/purpose	Wording
Link to previous paragraph	However,
Opinion	for this to be successful, primary schools need to be sufficiently resourced
Preview/scope	
Problem (2nd part of question)	
Solution (3rd part of question)	
Acknowledgment that problems exist	
Conclusion	

5 Look at the seventh paragraph. This is developed in yet another way. Fill in the table below, noticing how it mixes argument and explanation.

Stage/purpose	Wording
Link to previous paragraph	
Opinion (suggestion: 3rd part of question)	
Support (argument)	
Explanation I: how?	
Explanation II: how?	

LEARNING t i p

> **WRITING:** The genres given in this book provide building blocks to be combined and adapted as necessary. Use them flexibly and intelligently!

Task D: Answering a multi-stage question

See also page 209, *Dissecting essay questions for meaning.*

1 Choose from one of the essay questions below.

2 Analyse the question: will you have to describe, explain, argue, discuss, or do a combination of these?

3 Write the answer!

Questions

a] Suggest and evaluate two ways in which English can be taught from early in primary school in your country. Which one would be most feasible and effective? Justify your choice.

b] Compare and contrast three grammatical features of your first language and English. Using these as evidence, state whether you agree with the opinion that speakers of different language think in different ways. Justify your opinion.

Reading

Finding implied meaning

Task A: Finding implied meaning

Look at the preview/scope of the essay in the previous section again. Does it answer the second part of the question:

'... Is language training in the nation's education system adequate to cope with the need for businesses to have speakers of other languages?'

This is an example of *implied meaning* (sometimes called *implicit meaning*), that is, a meaning contained in the writing, but which isn't stated directly.

A further example: 'He's not very British—he's a good cook' implies that British people generally aren't good cooks, even though this isn't stated directly.

Using the essay in the previous section, answer the following questions, giving evidence.

1 Does the author believe that skills developed in childhood continue into adulthood?

_____

_____

_____

2 Does the author believe that native speakers of English have low ability to learn other languages?

_____

_____

_____

3 Currently are languages taught at primary schools at all?

_____

4 If languages are taught, is it done to a high standard?

_____

_____

5 Does the author believe that individual students studying languages at university should pay for their own education?

_____

_____

_____

6 In the author's opinion, do languages currently have high status as subjects among school children?

_____

_____

_____

Listening

Listening skills: interview with a student

Task A: Orientation discussion—listening

You are going to listen to a Japanese student being interviewed about listening in English. The questions she answers are printed on the next page. Before you listen, answer them for yourselves in groups.

1 What do you think about pauses in speech when you are listening? Things like 'umm', or speakers backtracking and repeating what they've just said? Is it a sign of bad communication or do you think it's just a natural feature of speech?

2 When listening, do you think you hear the whole words or do you listen for the sounds of each word, like the syllables?

3 How important do you think it is to get used to the rhythm and the intonation of a language?

4 In what situations is listening in English easiest for you? I mean, in what places, and with what kind of people?

5 Is listening easier for you when you have some background knowledge of the subject you are listening to?

6 Is there any other advice about listening you would give to someone learning English?

Task B: Listening for main ideas

Listen to the interview (Recording number 14) and answer the following questions. Numbers correspond to the interviewer's questions above and are followed by the main points of the questions.

1 **Pauses in speaking**

   a] Does Keiko believe that pauses in speech are normal? _____

   b] What are pauses in speaking used for? _____

2 **Hear syllables or whole words?**

   a] Does she notice individual syllables, all the words or just key words when listening? _____

   b] What else does she feel is important? _____

3 **Rhythm and intonation**

   a] How do rhythm and intonation help her to understand? _____

4 **In what situations is listening easier?**

   a] What isn't important? _____

   b] What situations are easiest for Keiko? _____

   c] How many people are in her preferred listening situation? _____

   d] What's the problem with more than this number? _____

   e] What's more important than background noise level? _____

5 **Background knowledge**

   a] Does having background knowledge make it easier for Keiko? _____

   b] Why is it difficult for her when she doesn't know the terminology used? _____

6 Further advice

What advice does she give about:

a] how to listen _____

b] a technique _____

c] who to practise with _____

d] what else to do _____

e] what kind of situation is best _____

⑭ (**Task C:** Listening and note taking)

Listen to the last part again. Make notes in the box below about how to follow the technique Keiko mentioned.

┌───┐
│   │
│   │
│   │
│   │
│   │
│   │
└───┘

⑭ (**Task D:** Finishing long answers)

Listen to Keiko's answers to Questions 2, 3 and 5 again. What does she do at the end of each answer to ensure that her points are clear?

Learner independence & study skills

✓ *Listening outside class*
✓ *Poster session about language learning experiences*

Listening outside class

(**Task A:** Ideas for listening outside class)

1 What did you learn from Keiko's answers?

2 Compare the answers you heard on the recording (Task B of the previous section) with your own answers to the same questions (Task A in the previous section). Discuss the differences and similarities.

3 In your experience of learning English, what are the most useful (and least useful) things you've done to help with listening? Why were they so useful (or not useful)?

4 Refer to Unit 7, *Learner independence and study skills* at page 175. That stated that good speaking practice came from situations in which complex or abstract language is used, or in which instructions have to be followed. Do you think this applies to listening too?

5 Can you think of other ways to practise listening that no one in your group has mentioned yet? How would these methods help you?

6 Make a list of things you will do to practise listening outside class. Compare with other students in your group. Set a date on which you will check your lists to see how many of these things you have done.

 LEARNING t i p

> University lecturers and staff have a wide variety of accents—often they are native English speakers with strong regional accents, or non-native speakers of English. Therefore, it is important to practise listening to a wide variety of accents and varieties of English.

Poster session about language learning experiences

Task A: Poster session about language learning experiences

> In your tertiary course, you may be involved in producing a poster session. This involves making a poster about a topic you've researched, and then displaying it with others in a room where people walk around, reading the posters and asking questions.

See also
Unit 2, page 56;
Unit 6, page 141;
Unit 7, page 175.

A good way to learn something is to find out how people who have already learnt it achieved their success. You have achieved success in English—or you wouldn't be using this book! Therefore, you can help other students in your college by sharing how you did this.

1 Make a poster to show the most useful things you've done to improve your English out of class. Work in groups, using ideas from the *Learner independence and study skills* sections of earlier Units, especially about reading, speaking, writing and listening outside class.

2 Hold a poster session with the other groups in your class, and invite other students from your college. Answer questions they ask about your poster.

Speaking 2

Explaining grammar features of languages other than English

As well as giving speaking and listening practice (explanations), this section may also help you to understand more clearly some of the grammatical features of English.

 LEARNING t i p

> One of the best ways to be sure you understand something is to explain it to someone else!

Task A: Discussion—orientation to the field

In groups of mixed nationality, if possible, briefly answer and discuss the following questions.

1 Tell your group about a feature of English that you found difficult to learn. This could be an aspect of grammar, pronunciation or anything else. Why do you think you found it so difficult? Is there an equivalent of the feature in your own language?

2 Which features of English did you find the easiest to learn? Is this because they are similar to your own language? Or is there another reason?

3 Of the languages represented in your group, which sounds the most similar to English? The most different?

Task B: Preparing a short presentation

Choose a feature of your language, perhaps one that you talked about in Task A. Prepare a short talk to your group in which you give a basic explanation of it. Remember to:

- include short example expressions or sentences to illustrate your point, including translations in English;

- give the meaning of basic vocabulary that is necessary for your example sentences;

- use the oral presentation skills from Units 5, 6 and 7;

- think from the point of view of the listeners—are you giving enough information for them to understand what you are saying, and are you staging the ideas in a way that helps the listener?

- predict what questions the audience may ask, and to try to answer them in your talk.

See also
Unit 5, page 108;
Unit 6, page 145;
Unit 7, page 159.

Task C: Giving and listening to explanations

Take it in turns to give your presentations. While listening to other presentations, you should:

- take notes about what you hear (see Unit 2, page 50);

- prepare questions to ask the presenter (see Unit 6, page 143).

After each presentation, you should:

- ask your questions;
- compare your notes with other students, in pairs. How consistent are your notes with those of the other students?
- tell the presenter the best two or three features of their talk.

> **Task D: Critical thinking—should English be simplified?**

Discuss these questions in mixed-culture groups, if possible.

1 If you could change the English language to make it easier to learn or use, what alterations would you make? For example, would you make all verbs regular? Remove third person?

2 Do you think there should be a simplified form of English to be used for international communication? What would be the advantages of this? How about disadvantages?

Writing 2

Short answer questions

> **Task A: Applying guidelines for short answer questions**

Some tertiary level assignments require answers of a page, a paragraph or shorter. You must answer as concisely and accurately as you can, and make sure you answer fully. As with other academic writing:

- Be concise and accurate, but answer all parts of the question.
- Use full sentences and paragraphs (unless your instructions allow bullet points or notes). See Unit 1, page 18 (Task B).
- Avoid personal pronouns such as 'I' and 'you' (unless specifically asked to write about personal experiences). See Unit 8, page 186 (Task B).
- Higher lexis helps to create an appropriate, academic style. See Unit 1, page 9.
- Write in your own words—don't plagiarise, and try to avoid accidents with this! See Unit 5, page 111.
- Nominalisation is useful to make your answers concise as well as sound more academic. See Unit 8, page 186 again.

Practise by answering the following short answer questions on a separate piece of paper.

1 Give three grammar rules that are different in your first language and English.

2 Give a definition of an explanation essay.

3 List the factors in your decision to study in another country.

4 What differences exist between argument and explanation essays?

5 Give a brief reasons why this country is a good one in which to study.

6 Give three examples of thesis statements that could appear in argument essays.

Writing and Speaking

Discussion and essay questions

Here are some extra issues for you to talk and write about.

- Many minority languages are under threat of extinction. Should effort and expense be put into supporting them? Does the preservation of these languages provide any benefit to humanity?

- Everyone should have the right to learn and speak the language of their own culture.

- Everyone should have the right to receive education in their first language.

- Governments should provide legal and financial support to minority languages.

- A second language should be part of the primary school curriculum from the earliest possible age.

- Everyone should learn at least two languages.

- There should be a simplified and standardised form of English, devoid of idioms, grammatical irregularities and difficult phonological features, in order to facilitate international communication. Discuss.

- It has been said that an invented language such as Esperanto is a better choice for a world language than English. What are the advantages and disadvantages of using an invented language in this way? Which language (including 'natural' ones) do you think would be a better choice for a world language? Justify your choice.

unit 10

a global connection: cross-cultural communication

THE ARTS OF THE NATIONS

The art of the Egyptians is in the occult.
The art of the Chaldeans is in calculation.
The art of the Greeks is in proportion.
The art of the Romans is in echo.
The art of the Chinese is in etiquette.
The art of the Hindus is in the weighing of good and evil.
The art of the Jews is in the sense of doom.
The art of the Arabs is in reminiscence and exaggeration.
The art of the Persians is in fastidiousness.
The art of the French is in finesse.
The art of the English is in analysis and self-righteousness.
The art of the Spaniards is in fanaticism.
The art of the Italians is in beauty.
The art of the Germans is in ambition.
The art of the Russians is in sadness.   **KAHLIL GIBRAN**

Skills focus: In this Unit, you will learn and use the following skills:

Writing

Genre overview

> **Task A:** Essay analysis—explanations, arguments and discussions

- Select a text that appeals to you from any Unit in this course book.

- Analyse the selected text by using the form entitled 'Essay genre overview', which follows.

Essay genre overview

Question Topic Aspect Limitation	Explanation	Argument (Exposition)	Discussion
Introduction	Introductory statement	General statement	General statement
	Purpose: rewording of essay topic		
	Definition (optional)	Definition (optional)	Definition (optional)
		Position (thesis)	Issue Statement/ position
	Preview: points that will be in the body paragraphs	Preview reasons or arguments that will be in the body paragraphs	Preview: points for both sides that will be in the body paragraphs
Body	Topic sentence (from points in preview)	Topic sentence (from reasons or arguments in preview)	Point 1—topic sentence—side 1 side 2 Point 2—topic sentence—side 1 side 2
	Elaboration (supporting sentences with:- facts and examples optional concluding sentence (summary of paragraph)	Elaboration	Point 3—topic sentence—side 1 side 2 OR Side 1—Point 1 Point 2 Point 3 Side 2—Point 1 Point 2 Point 3 (points from preview)

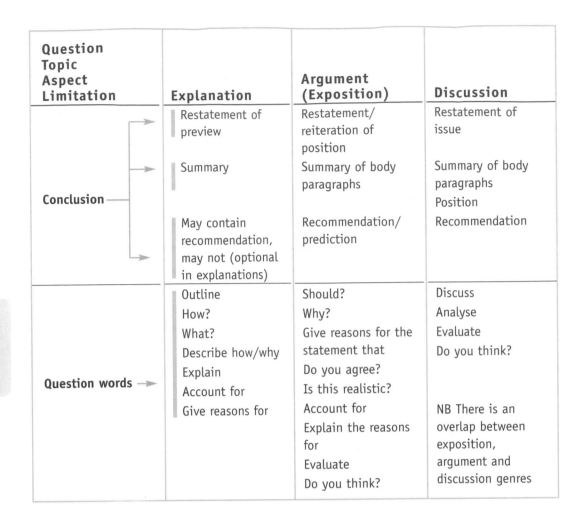

Question Topic Aspect Limitation	Explanation	Argument (Exposition)	Discussion
Conclusion	Restatement of preview	Restatement/ reiteration of position	Restatement of issue
	Summary	Summary of body paragraphs	Summary of body paragraphs Position
	May contain recommendation, may not (optional in explanations)	Recommendation/ prediction	Recommendation
Question words →	Outline How? What? Describe how/why Explain Account for Give reasons for	Should? Why? Give reasons for the statement that Do you agree? Is this realistic? Account for Explain the reasons for Evaluate Do you think?	Discuss Analyse Evaluate Do you think? NB There is an overlap between exposition, argument and discussion genres

See Unit 9, page 209.

Grammar

Reviewing academic writing

✓ *Register*
✓ *Nominalisation*
✓ *Referencing*
✓ *Modality*

Register

> **Task A: What makes a text academic?**

Examine Texts 1 and 2 on page 228 and answer the questions below.

1 What is the theme or main topic or topics of the text?
2 Are there any quotes?
3 Are sources within it reliable?
4 Does it contain more nominalised forms or more verb forms?
5 Does it contain referencing?
6 Does it read like an academic text? Why or why not?

Text 1

Releasing butterflies at weddings and christenings has created a wonderful business for Jody Kissle and her partner Mark. As local lepidopterists, they decided to use their knowledge of butterflies and are now quite happy about their success. 'We make around $400 each wedding and we are beginning to do some christenings as well!', said Jody. Mark added that the idea occurred to them when they were watching people throw rice and confetti over a bride and groom. He said they thought '... it was wasteful and not good for the environment'.

Text 2

The cecropia moth, like most moth species, is a destructive pest in terms of crops. Very few butterfly species, however, attack what is referred to in this study as 'important' plants. The consideration of these plants has been aided by a group of amateurs to whom I am indebted. 'Amateur lepidopterists have produced a large body of biological and distributional information for a century or more and this has contributed to ecological and evolutionary research' (Bertomi, 2003: 265).

With your teacher, examine the two short texts and make comparisons using the following grid. List all the sentences and words which apply in the columns provided. The theme is done for you.

	Text 1	Text 2
Theme/topic/s	*Using butterflies in a business*	*A study about butterflies and plants*
Nominalisations/noun groups		
Verbs/verb groups		

	Text 1	Text 2
Theme/topic/s	*Using butterflies in a business*	*A study about butterflies and plants*
Quotes Who is being quoted?		
References		

Task B: Differences between academic and non-academic texts

What conclusions can you draw concerning the differences between Text 1 and Text 2?

1 _____

2 _____

Nominalisation

See Unit 8,
page 186.

You have studied nominalisation previously and since then you have been attempting to recognise and to use it as a feature in academic writing. Below is a review around constructing and deconstructing nominalisations and noun groups.

Task A: Constructing nominalisations

Construct nominalisations for the following concepts and statements following the two examples.

For instance, 'a student understands something and is familiar with it'. So the nominalisation would be **student familiarity**.

'A group of people who have come to and settled in another country from different parts of the world are called migrants. They have formed a group and become associated legally.' The nominalisation would be a **migrant association**.

1 In a forest all the trees have been cut down. This is a process that people made happen over time and where that *forest* was, now there is nothing. The nominalisation would be: _____

2 A government wishes to make changes in the *tax* system of a country. They consider these changes a type *of reform*. The nominalisation would be: _____

3 Women in many countries, but particularly in the West, believed they should have completely equal rights with men. They were labelled 'feminist' as opposed to 'masculist'. Their activities became known as a *movement*. The nominalisation would be: _____

4 This refers to the custom of respecting your elders, in particular, your parents. A person should not place their own values over those of their parents. They should be obedient and act piously. *Filial* refers to the children who must act in a *pious* and obedient manner. The nominalisation would be: _____

Task B: Deconstructing nominalisations

Examine the following paragraph and locate all nominalisations and noun groups which need 'deconstruction' or 'unpacking' to make their meaning clear.

Text 1

Lack of familiarity with a country's customs, especially those around showing respect, may lead to cultural misunderstanding. For example, in the case of Chinese students, 'Teachers need to remember that learners are likely to use relative age and status as a primary determinant of the level of politeness to be used and this may result in socially inappropriate speech' (Brick, 1999).

Write all the nominalisations and noun groups and explain them:

1 _____

_____

2 _____

_____

_____

3 _____

_____

4 _____

_____

5 _____

_____

Referencing

Task A: Listing references

See Unit 5, page 111.

Review the texts you have read thus far in this unit. List all the references.

1 _____

2 _____

Modality

Read the following statements from A to H.

A. Most angels have wings.

B. That angel could have wings.

C. That angel may have wings

D. That angel might have wings.

E. An angel has wings.

F. Angels have wings.

G. It's possible that angels have wings

H. Perhaps angels have wings.

Write the probability (degree of certainty) on the line below of A to H as definite to not so definite. F is first—it is a definite 'yes' statement. The writer is certain that all angels have wings!

F
_____

Definite   Unsure

Task B: Using modality in your writing

Opinion: *should, must, may*

Recommendation: *should, must*

Argument: possibly, *perhaps, most, might, would, could, some, most, many, usually, often, slightly, almost all*

Using the guide words above and your own knowledge, re-write the following essay by adding modal words. A discussion must allow the reader a space to argue or discuss what is written. This essay expresses too much certainty, even though it is a good discussion. There is not enough modality. Words that are too certain are underlined. You must remove underlined words and replace them with others. Add changes where the ^ symbol appears. You may have to change the word order in places.

ESSAY QUESTION: **Although each religion is different, religions around the world share many commonalties. Discuss.**

There are thousands of belief systems around the world. They ^ are animism, shamanism, monotheism and polytheism. They all have totally ^ different images, rituals, festivals and architectural styles in their places of worship. However, when we examine the basic beliefs and moral systems of these religions, they are ^ all the same. The most ^ important feature/s of religions are their moral codes. They are stated directly, such as in the Ten Commandments of Christianity and in Islam.

5

2 ^ Interlinked with the setting of moral codes is the guidance of social relationships. This guidance is stronger in some religions, such as those in the Judeo-Christian-Islamic tradition, and weaker in others such as Shinto in Japan.

3 ^ Religions teach respect for elders. ^ In Confucianism, respect is a part of the 10
basic tenets. Australian Aboriginal cultures also emphasize respect for older people. ^ <u>This</u> promotes social harmony and reduces conflict.

4 In ^ <u>all</u> cases religions include rituals to mark the special events of life. It's very rare to find traditional societies that do not have a religious focus to ceremonies for special events such as the naming of new babies, marriage and funeral ceremonies. 15

5 Thus, religions are ^<u>all the same.</u>

6 It is clear therefore that, although religions appear very different on the surface, they are <u>in fact</u> fairly uniform in that they emphasize positive relations and tolerance between people and that this is facilitated through systems of ethics and rituals and ceremonies. 20

Speaking

Cross-cultural discussion of common beliefs and practices

Students: Since you are learning another language, you are working in a cross-cultural way. You use your own native language and you possess your own cultural knowledge, beliefs and practices. The 'target' language (English, in this case) also contains cultural knowledge and its users have varying beliefs and practices transmitted through their own native language (English).

> ### Task A: Discussion—considering your own culture

In every language and in every culture, there are ways to do the things listed below. With a partner or in your groups, explain how your language would deal with them. Use the bullet points to help you in your discussion.

- How do you do this in English?
- How do you do this in your own language?
- Bring into your explanation the differences you can think of between your own language and carrying out the communications in English:

1 Introduce someone to someone else in a casual social situation.

2 Greet someone you know very well.

3 Greet a relative.

4 Greet someone you have never met and who is superior to you in the situation.

5 Apologise to someone who is 'above' you.

6 Apologise to someone who is 'below' you.

7 Farewell someone who is a loved one.

8 Farewell someone who is a business associate.

9 Enter into a business contract.

10 Write a letter of complaint.

11 Write an essay for an academic situation.

12 Write a letter of friendship talking about your current situation.

Listening

Note taking from a lecture: cross-cultural communication

(**Task A: Note taking**)

Take notes while listening (Recording number 15) to the lecture on cross-cultural communication. This is a shortened version of an actual conference presentation (Cox, 2000).

See Unit 2, page 50, *Listening & note taking.*

(**Task B: Test**)

Take the test your teacher gives you based upon the lecture. Use your notes to assist you in answering the questions.

Critical thinking

Critical cultural consciousness: political protest

(**Task A: Cross-cultural comparison around political protest**)

In this section, you will consider political protest. You need to think about what it is, where it occurs, the sorts of issues that give rise to it, what type of people carry it out and whether or not, in your culture, it is ever an appropriate response to governments and their policies.

Your teacher will lead your discussion and set up the tasks around this important concept.

Reading

Peer review of extended essays

This marks the final stage of the extended essay assignment started in Unit 7, page 175.

As with the oral presentation assignment, finished also in Unit 7, it is useful to evaluate each others' assignments, because you may learn something from the other students, and discussing your work with others will help you reflect on, and improve, your own work.

Throughout this section, it's particularly important to ask your teacher about anything you're not sure about.

Task A: Checking essays against criteria

Swap essays with another person. Check the essay against the assessment criteria on the assignment cover sheet in Appendix C, page 257.

Task B: Discussing extended essays

In small groups, point out the three best features of the essay you are looking at. Also, point out three features which may need extra work. Do the other members of the group agree with you?

See Unit 7,
page 168.

Task C: Giving feedback to the writer

Explain to the essay's author the good points of the essay and points that may need more work. Remember to do this sensitively. A good method is to mention good points first, then things that need more work, then finish with another good point.

Reading and Writing

✓ *Precis, abstracts and introductions: reading to discover the usefulness of texts for assignments*
✓ *Extended introductions*
✓ *Conclusions and summaries*

Precis, abstracts and introductions: reading to discover the usefulness of texts for assignments

Both precis and abstracts are a type of summary. They are used to summarise research and essays. You might write an abstract or a precis of your own work (a long essay, for example) or someone else's work in order to recall what you have read. Both types of summaries are a kind of paraphrasing. This means you must re-write what has been written. You must make it much shorter.

Precis

What must be included in a precis?

- your own wording of the author's writing;
- the main ideas;
- the main arguments;
- the main conclusions.

Abstract

An abstract must include:

- the author's wording—the author's exact words;
- the main ideas—in the author's exact words;
- the main conclusions—in the author's exact words;
- don't forget to reference those exact words.

Further features

Note that you may link the two together by using transitions and connectors/discourse markers.

- A **precis** can summarise an **abstract**. It is a summary of a summary!
- An **abstract** pulls out (extracts) the main concepts using quotes from the original.
- A **precis** has to be written by you, in your own words, incorporating the main concepts.

When researching by using journals that are written by specialists within your own field, you will find a format that will assist you to understand what you are reading. Articles within journals begin with an abstract or an introduction which will outline exactly what the article will be about.

By reading the abstract/introduction alone, you should be able to discover whether or not the research or the theory put forward in that particular article will be useful to you.

> **Task A: Reading to discover usefulness of texts for assignments**

Read the following introductions (Text 1 and 2). Text 1 introduces a test of some kind. Text 2 introduces a paper, either written as in a journal or spoken as presented at a conference. Decide whether they would be useful to you if your assignment was to *Discuss various learning style theories.*

Text 1

When attempting to learn anything new, it is advantageous to maximise your understanding of your own learning. All individuals have learning styles and there are differences. You can discover which learning style you feel most comfortable with (concrete, reflective, abstract or active) and explore different learning opportunities for yourself. The following test was devised to analyse individual abilities.

Answer: _____

Text 2

A great deal of research has been carried out around learning styles of individuals. All individuals have learning styles and there are differences. Four major styles which have been in the literature for a number of years are concrete, reflective, abstract and active. In this paper, in addition to a thorough examination of these categories, the concept of multiple intelligences is explored.

Answer: _____

More review!

In English, texts make themselves known in the introduction. They explain what they will be about in the final stage of the introduction.

Task B: Staging

See also
Unit 1, page 14;
Unit 2, page 43;
Unit 3, page 61.

Using the staging you learned in Units 1, 2 and 3 and for recognising introductions in essays, highlight using different coloured pens, or *circle*, underline and lightly xxx the three stages of the introduction from the two texts you just read (reproduced below).

Text 1 and Text 2

The three stages of an introduction or abstract:
- general statement which orients the reader to the topic;
- definition of terms, explanation or viewpoint of the author;
- preview, scope (what the text will actually be about).

Text 1

When attempting to learn anything new, it is advantageous to maximise your understanding of your own learning. All individuals have learning styles and there are differences. You can discover which learning style you feel most comfortable with (concrete, reflective, abstract or active) and explore different learning opportunities for yourself. The following test was devised to analyse individual abilities.

The final stage informed you of the content of the writing to come, did it not? So in an essay around Learning Style Theories, this test would probably not be useful for your essay.

Text 2

A great deal of research has been carried out around learning styles of individuals. All individuals have learning styles and there are differences. Four major styles which have been in the literature for a number of years are concrete, reflective, abstract and active. In this paper, in addition to a thorough examination of these categories, the concept of multiple intelligences is explored.

Extended introductions

In an extended introduction, each stage is far longer than the introductions covered elsewhere in this book. The principle, however, remains the same, that is, there are three main stages that must be included. You can write more background information and include longer and more thorough definitions. You can include some historical background in the second stage which orients the reader to your point of view.

Task A: Recognising an extended introduction/model

Examine the recording script on cross-cultural communication from this Unit (your teacher will give you a copy) and write the paragraph number where the (extended) introduction ends.

Task B: Writing an extended introduction

Write or revise the introduction for the extended essay you began in Unit 7 page 173.

Conclusions and summaries

When writing essays or reports, stories or letters, novels or articles, you must end them eventually. (All good things must come to an end!) An ending is the conclusion. Within any conclusion, there is a summary of the main points from the body of the text. You signal to your reader that you are about to begin your conclusion with a discourse signal, for example: *in conclusion …*

Task A: Concluding discourse markers

Choose the appropriate discourse signals that might indicate a conclusion from the list below by placing a tick next to them:

1	Next		**5**	Finally
2	After that		**6**	However
3	In conclusion		**7**	Sometimes, it occurs that
4	Thirdly		**8**	In summary

Task B: What makes a conclusion a conclusion?

1 Is the following extract an introduction, a part of the body of an essay, or the conclusion?

2 Why?

It is clear therefore that, although religions appear very different on the surface, they are in fact quite uniform in that they emphasise positive relations and tolerance between people and they facilitate this through their systems of ethics and their rituals and ceremonies.

Task C: Writing conclusions

Using your skills and knowledge of paraphrasing and summary writing, summarise the following information within each text, as briefly as possible in order to write the conclusion stage of the essay. Make a recommendation, if required.

TITLE: **Text 1: Bangkok ferries**

Introduction

1   The problems with the traffic in Bangkok are that the roads are crowded, the river is congested by both private and public transport, there is pollution, not enough public boats and those provided are not regular. So by closing the river between the hours of 7:30am and 5:30pm to private boats and only opening the river for use by ferries and express boats we will hopefully increase the number of people using public transport on the rivers and reduce traffic on the roads.

2   Our overall plan for the river is to extend a small section to increase tourism, and have fast express boats for the early morning and after work commuters into the Central Business District. We hope by doing this we can decrease road traffic problems and pollution.

Display

3   Our display is a model of where the new river has been proposed to be extended and of the bypass walkways which will connect to tourist attractions such as the new Botanical Gardens, the Zoo etc.

4   Our express boats will have a red stripe across them to indicate that they are express. Our tourist ferries will have a yellow stripe and our all-stop boats will be green.

5   The ferries will have such facilities as bathrooms, cafés and newsagents. The 'all stops' and express will also have light snack bars.

6   The tourist fares are cheap—costing $10 for a family of 4 for an all day pass; $5 single; $4 concession; and small fees for one or two stops, or return tickets.

7   The tourist ferries are to seat 100–150 people, the express 50–70 and the all-stops 80–120 people.

8   The timetable for the ferries will be posted clearly at each station. The express will come every 15 minutes, the all-stop every 20 minutes and the tourist every 30 minutes. There will be a total of 15 express boats, eight tourist ferries and 12 all-stops.

Conclusion

9   _____

    _____

_____
_____
_____
_____
_____
_____
_____
_____
_____
_____

TITLE: **Text 2: Capital punishment: right or wrong?**

1 Capital punishment is the execution of a criminal under a death sentence imposed by a qualified public authority. But one question for those of some faiths and those who live in modern, civilised society is, is capital punishment right or wrong?

2 Capital punishment is an ancient practice, and existed in the ancient middle eastern kingdoms. The death penalty was usually for murder, and some religious or sexual offences. In Israel it was declared that 'whoever sheds the blood of a man, by man shall his blood be shed' (Gen. 9.6). It is also said 'If injury ensures, you shall give life for life, eye for eye, tooth for tooth, hand for hand' (Ex. 21.23–24). It was understood that this principle of revenge was to stop offenders by excessive punishments. When the death penalty was given in these ancient times it was by stoning, hanging, beheading, strangling, and burning.

In primitive times death and mutilation were frequent penalties. Capital punishment has a long history, but is it too old fashioned to be used in today's society? Are prison cells overflowing and are there too many crimes being committed? And if they are, is that reason enough to kill people? Is capital punishment the way to fix our modern day problems about murder, crime etc? These are some of the questions at stake.

4 In conclusion, _____
_____
_____
_____
_____
_____

5

10

15

20

25

Writing and Reading

Interpreting and describing information from charts and graphs

> **Task A:** Interpreting numerical information

1 Look at the following numerical information, relating to multicultural aspects of a fictional country, Govindia. Which figure is:

a] a pie chart?

b] a line graph (often just called a graph)?

c] a bar chart?

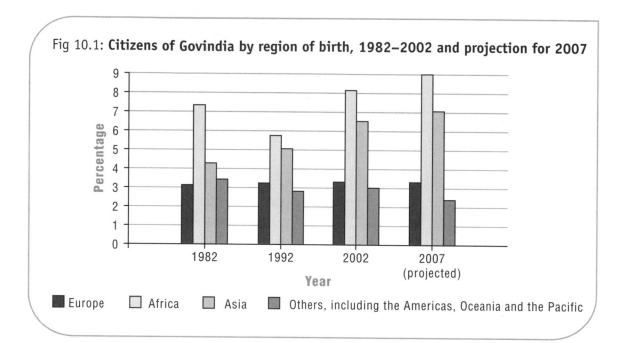

Fig 10.1: **Citizens of Govindia by region of birth, 1982–2002 and projection for 2007**

■ Europe   □ Africa   ■ Asia   ■ Others, including the Americas, Oceania and the Pacific

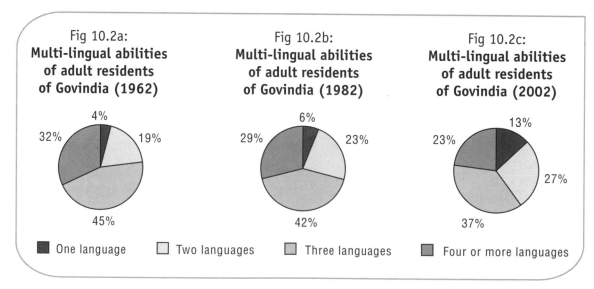

Fig 10.2a:
**Multi-lingual abilities
of adult residents
of Govindia (1962)**

Fig 10.2b:
**Multi-lingual abilities
of adult residents
of Govindia (1982)**

Fig 10.2c:
**Multi-lingual abilities
of adult residents
of Govindia (2002)**

■ One language   □ Two languages   ■ Three languages   ■ Four or more languages

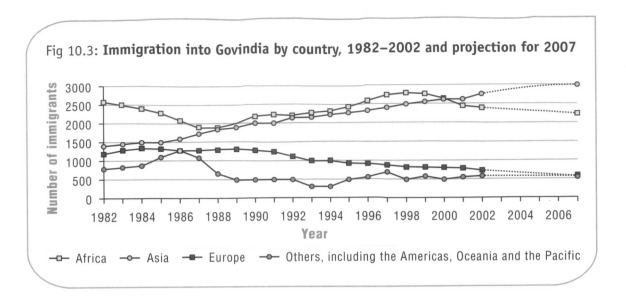

Fig 10.3: **Immigration into Govindia by country, 1982–2002 and projection for 2007**

Number of immigrants

3000
2500
2000
1500
1000
500
0

1982 1984 1986 1988 1990 1992 1994 1996 1998 2000 2002 2004 2006

Year

–□– Africa   –○– Asia   –■– Europe   –●– Others, including the Americas, Oceania and the Pacific

2 Look at the titles of Figures 10.1 to 10.3. What information do they include (eg place, reason, person for whom the research was done, time, or what the figures show)?

_____

_____

3 a] Using your answer to Question 2, write a sentence or two for each graph or chart to explain what it represents. The first has been done for you as an example.

Figure 10.1— *This bar chart shows the percentage of Govindia's citizens who were born in each of four regions of the world, in 1982, 1992, 2002 and forecasts for 2007.*

Figure 10.2—_____

_____

_____

Figure 10.3—_____

_____

_____

b] Compare your writing with a partner. Are the meanings the same? Together, prepare a single answer for Figure 10.2 and another single answer for Figure 10.3 which combine the best features of each individual answer.

> **Task B: Features of written descriptions of numerical information**

1 Read the following description of Figure 10.1, comparing each feature described with Figure 10.1 itself. This is an answer to the question given below. What can you identify that you think might be a feature of description?

Question: Use recent census data and government demographic predictions to show trends in the cultural origins of the citizens of Govindia.

This country is widely known as being multicultural, an opinion borne out by data from the last three 10-yearly national censuses (1982, 1992 and 2002) and also projections for 2007. Figure 10.1 shows the figures broken down into four regions of the world: Africa, Asia, Europe and Others, which includes North and South America as well as Oceania.

5

The most common origin of immigrants during this period was Africa. Despite a significant fall from nearly 7.5% in 1982 to just below 6% ten years later, the trend over the period was towards a general increase, with proportions of over 8% in 2002 and over 9% projected for 2007.

Migration from Asia also showed a strong upward trend. In 1982, only 4.3% of Govindians claimed Asian origin, but this figure rose to 5.1% in 1992 and to 6.6% in 2002. A figure of 7.1% is projected for 2007, which would mean a considerable increase of nearly two-thirds over the 25-year period.

10

Europe and the 'other' regions showed the least noticable changes. Europeans represented 3.2% of the population in 1982, rising minimally to 3.4% in 2002. No further increase or decrease is forecast over the next five years. The contribution of 'other' regions to the country's population was the only fall over the whole period. In 1982, 3.5% of citizens were from the 'other' countries, falling to 2.9% in 1992. The proportion was virtually constant over the next ten years, reaching 3.0% in 2002, but a drop is anticipated to 2.5% by 2007.

15

20

The census data demonstrates that the population of this country is becoming more diverse, at least in terms of origin, and this trend is anticipated to continue for the foreseeable future.

2 Answer the following questions, which focus on identifying common features of written descriptions of numerical information.

a] What main point is represented in each paragraph? The first has been done for you.

Paragraph 2 *Migrants from Africa*

Paragraph 3 _____

Paragraph 4 _____

Paragraph 5 _____

b] How do you think the author chose the order of paragraphs? (Remember the principles of *theme* in English)

c] Which tenses are used in the following situations:

■ to describe the actual chart, not the data on it? (line 3)

_____

_____

- to describe the data in the bars representing 1982, 1992 and 2002?

_____

_____

- to describe the data in the bars representing 2007?

_____

_____

d] Locate words from the text which describe change and no change, then fill in the table.

	Verbs	Nouns
to go up		
to go down	—	
to have no change		—

e] Fill in the boxes in the diagram below using the following words. 'n' means noun, 'adj' means adjective, and some boxes will contain whole expressions. Ask your teacher for help with the difficult ones.

climb	gentle	rapid	sharp
decline	gradual	reach a peak	slight
drop	increase	remain constant	slow
fall	level off	remain stable	steep
fluctuation	peak	rise	

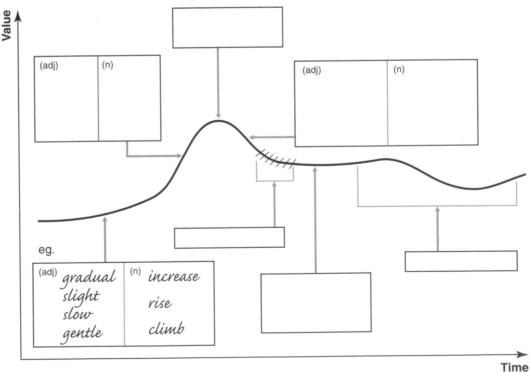

Task C: Common mistakes to avoid

What is wrong with the following statements, related to Figure 10.1 on page 241? They are all gramatically correct; the mistakes are in the meaning. Can you make corrections?

1 The proportion of people from other regions of the world dropped down from 1982 to 1992.

2 There were more citizens from Europe in 2002 than in 1982.

3 Govindians from Africa increased significantly between 1982 and 2002.

Task D: Writing to describe numerical information

1 Write a description of:

a] Figures 10.2a, b and c together.

b] Figure 10.3.

Use the work you did in the rest of this section to help you.

2 Swap your writing with another student. With your partner's essay, check whether the features from Task B have been included. Your partner will do the same with yours.

3 Exchange ideas about how each other's writing can be improved. For example, you could suggest different words to increase the variety of vocabulary.

4 Write a second draft, incorporating ideas from your partner that you like.

Task E: Reading descriptions of numerical data

1 Find an article in a magazine or newspaper which describes the results of a survey.

2 Reconstruct a graph or other graphical method of representing the data.

 LEARNING t i p

Descriptions of numerical information like this are often embedded in longer pieces of writing.

English for the Internet Age

How does and will the Internet affect you, as a student?

Task A: Comparing a student from the past with the present

Read the following explanation from a student as to how they might research, write, prepare, and submit, an assignment for a university in the early 1900s.

1 I parked my bicycle on the green lawns of the campus, straightened my tie, placed my cap carefully over my head, and headed through the giant oak doors to the library. I had an important paper to write for Professor Rodeen and I would begin my research this morning before lectures began.

2 My subject was *Science and the future of transportation* and I had decided to examine not only the history of the shipping lines and their future development (which was familiar to us), but to try to find some information about the recent experiments and minor successes around flying. Some were saying that one day in the future, people might fly in aeroplanes and use them as a method of transportation. I considered this somewhat ridiculous and just a visionary speculation but was fascinated by the idea. 5

10

3 I began my search with the letter 'F' for 'flying' by pulling out one long, narrow box drawer which had from 'fa' to 'fm' displayed on its front. It slid out of the wooden chest which held at least 50 other drawers just like it and I began sorting through the cards using the tips of my fingers. Ah—here was something. *Flight—the Wright Brothers' experiments*. I would begin by reading this. 15

4 The catalogue number was displayed on the card and I began to search the library shelves for the paper that had been written on the subject. Once found, I took my seat and began to read.

5 My ink pen was ready and I had bought a fresh ink bottle and so I began making my notes in black ink on my pale, brown paper. I would have to revise them and write the final paper once all my research was completed and my conclusions were drawn. 20

6 Weeks later, and my paper completed, I tied the bundle together with a small ribbon used for the purpose and submitted it, in person, to my professor. 25

Task B: Write an explanation of you as a modern day student

Using your own knowledge, compose an explanation as to how you, as a student will research, write, prepare, and submit an assignment for a University.

_____

_____

_____

_____

_____

_____

_____

_____

_____

_____

Choose a recent development in your future field of study (or, if you are not sure, choose one of the following fields as a topic for your discussion):

- banking
- marketing
- retail management.

1 Do you think the Internet is useful in your field?

2 What is the Internet used for in your field (or the fields above)?

3 How is the Internet changing the way people do business?

Learner independence & study skills

End of course: friendship, compliments!

Good luck in the future, each and everyone!

Task A: Compliments activity

1 Write your name in the box at the top of the diagram. Write the other students' names in the other boxes.

2 Pass it around the class. Each time you receive another book, write against your name, comments about the book's owner, such as:

- A compliment for that person. This can be anything, for example 'You had a great sense of humour,'; 'I was impressed by your determination.'

- What you learned from that person during the course, for example, 'I learned from you that determination is very important,'; 'You demonstrated that a sense of humour makes academic study more fun and motivating.'

3 When you receive your book back, you can keep the grid and comments as a memento of your classmates—your fellow travellers on the EAP journey you have just completed.

Appendix A—Correction codes

Symbol	Kind of error	Example	Correct sentence
c	capitalisation	*c* I went to england, once.	I went to England, once.
P	punctuation	*P* She said, yes, that's right.	She said, 'yes, that's right'.
//	new paragraph	// (start a new paragraph)	
S	spelling	*S* My freind is here.	My friend is here.
PS	word form (part of speech)	*PS* She was hope.	She was hopeful.
○	plural/singular mistake	I have three sister°	I have three sisters.
#	subject-verb agreement	*#* She like swimming.	She likes swimming.
T	verb tense mistake	*T* Last week I <u>have</u> a great party.	Last week I had a great party.
[ ]	delete (erase)	I'm going [to] shopping tonight	I'm going shopping tonight.
↑	add a word	They are my house. ↑	They are (coming to) (going to visit) my house.
W	wrong word	*W* Turn write at the corner.	Turn right at the corner.
A	wrong or omitted article	*A* We're studying good book.	We're studying a good book.
↶○	reverse word order	That was a movie long.	That was a long movie.
○↷	word order mistake	I <u>you see will</u>.	I will see you.
/	separate these words (new sentence)	They'll eat dinner/ they'll go home.	They'll eat dinner. Then they'll go home.
⌒	should be one word (combine sentences)	There was rubbish every where	There was rubbish everywhere.
∿	rewrite (meaning unclear)	I very often trying new.	I often try new things.

Appendix B—Information gap activities

Unit 3: Graph I—Retention versus time without review

This is how much is remembered as time passes after a lesson if no reviewing is done. To see what happens if reviewing is carried out regularly, see Graph II on page 250.

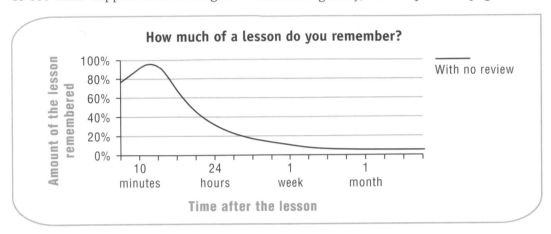

Source: Adapted from Tony Buzan (1995) *Use Your Head*, 4th ed, BBC Books, London, p. 65.

Unit 7: Role play

Student A's parts (Lecturers)

The following are the prompts for the student–lecturer role pay

7.1 (Lecturer role) **How to apply for a further degree?**
→ Must obtain a distinction or high distinction in current studies.
→ Must have reference from your tutor to say your work is of sufficient academic standard—I'll be happy to give you one!
→ Fill in Further Studies Application Form.
→ Submit to department office. Deadline: 23 December.

7.2 (Lecturer role) **Advice—problems at home, worried about assignment deadlines**
→ Fill in 'Genuine Reason for Extension of Deadline' form.
→ Explain problem to counselling service—someone will sign the form for you.
→ Give a copy to each of your lecturers.

7.3 (Student role)
You feel you are falling behind in your studies. Other students have finished their first assignment of the term, but you've hardly started. Ask for advice from your lecturer.

7.4 (Student role)
You need a particular piece of equipment to carry out your research. You have heard that if you get your lecturer's permission, you can buy it and the university will pay. Ask for permission from your lecturer.

Unit 9: Conclusion to essay

In conclusion, it is clear that there would be great economic benefit for English   75
speaking countries if they improved the ability of their population to speak
other languages. It is also clear that this has to be done from the earliest levels
of primary school, and that this requires significant investment. Investment is
also needed in campaigns to promote and increase the prestige and intrinsic
interest of language learning. It would be beneficial therefore if these changes   80
were set into motion as soon as possible.

References

Crystal, D (1997) *English as a Global Language*. Cambridge: Cambridge University Press.

Kramsch, C (1998) *Language and Culture*. Oxford: Oxford University Press.

Saunders, G (1988) *Bilingual Children: Guidance for the Family*. Clevedon: Multilingual
    Matters.

Unit 3: Graph II — Retention versus time when reviewing

This graph shows what happens when review is carried out at regular intervals.

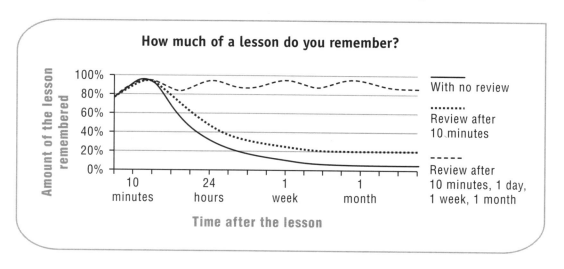

Source: Adapted from Tony Buzan (1995) *Use Your Head*, 4th ed, BBC Books, London, p. 65.

Unit 7: Student B's parts (Students)

The following are prompts for the student–lecturer role play.

7.1 (Student role)
You want to apply for a further degree in the department you're studying in now. Find out from your lecturer how to do this.

7.2 (Student role)
You have urgent family problems in your own country and dealing with them will make your assignments very late. Find out from your lecturer what you can do.

7.3 (Lecturer role) **Advice—study problems**
→ I understand the problem—it affects many first year students.
→ Thank you for letting me know before it's too late.
→ The academic advice service can provide excellent advice and help.
→ It's on the third floor of the Collingwood building, which is on South Road, on the left about ten minutes' walk past the university library.
→ There's also an English language support service available if you want to make use of that.

7.4 (Lecturer role) **Permission for equipment purchase**
→ Yes, that's within the department's budget.
→ I need to give you a letter which explains why it is necessary.
→ I'll prepare that by the end of the week.
→ Take it to the requisitions section—they will order it for you.

Appendix C—Assessment sheets: Oral presentation and essay

Oral presentation observation sheet 1: content

Write notes, not sentences!

Introduction

Background

Definitions

Thesis/discussion point

Main points to be covered (preview/scope)

Body

Main point 1
Support

Main point 2
Support

More supported ideas

Continued ...

<table>
<tr><td colspan="2">Conclusion</td></tr>
<tr><td>Summary</td><td></td></tr>
<tr><td>Recommendation</td><td></td></tr>
</table>

<table>
<tr><td colspan="2">Question time</td></tr>
<tr><td>Question 1</td><td></td></tr>
<tr><td>Answer</td><td></td></tr>
<tr><td>Question 2</td><td></td></tr>
<tr><td>Answer</td><td></td></tr>
<tr><td>More questions</td><td></td></tr>
</table>

After the presentation:

- Were the main ideas in the preview/scope, body and summary the same?

  _____

- Comment on the strength of support for the opinions expressed.

  _____

- Were there sufficient references?

  _____

- Did the talk sound well researched?

  _____

- Were ideas from the literature questioned and analysed (critical analysis)?

  _____

- Write down the most interesting things you leaned about the topic of this presentation.

  _____

Oral presentation observation sheet 2: techniques

Signposting

Stage	Function	Signposting expressions used (X = none used)
Definitions	To define	
Thesis/ discussion point	To give opinion(s)	
Preview/ scope	To introduce preview/scope	
Body	To move on to new main idea	
	To move on to a new supporting idea	
Conclusion	To summarise	
	To recommend	
	To give sources	

Presentation techniques

Start time: _____   Finish time: _____

Technique	Notes
Use of visual aids	What used? Comments
Gestures, eye contact etc	Eye contact with all sections of the audience? Other paralinguistic features used? Comments
Involvement of audience	How? Comments
Voice and clarity of expression	Comments
Timing	Comments

After the presentation:

- What techniques did the presenter use most effectively?

  _____

  _____

- With which techniques is there room for improvement?

  _____

  _____

Oral presentation observation sheet 3: outcomes

Outcome/competency	Achieved? (Yes or No)
Can provide appropriate background and context	
Can define technical terms used	
Can clearly give thesis/discussion point	
Can give preview and scope of talk near beginning	
Can clearly state main points of the talk	
Can provide adequate support	
Can summarise the talk	
Can give recommendations based on ideas mentioned	
Can deal adequately with audience's questions	
Can ensure overall coherence to the talk	
Can argue logically	
Can sustain an argument throughout the talk	
Can critically analyse the issue	
Can research a topic using library resources	
Can provide clear signposting throughout	
Can use a visual aid effectively	
Can use appropriate paralinguistic features, such as gestures and eye contact	
Can involve the audience, eg by asking questions	
Can express ideas clearly and audibly	
Can present within a time limit	

Extended essay assignment cover sheet

Assignment Cover Sheet

Student's name	Family .... Given ....
Assignment title	
Class/course	
Date due..	Date submitted ....

I hereby declare that:

  i] this work is entirely my own.

 ii] all sources used in the preparation of this assignment are fully referenced.

iii] no part of this work has been submitted for assessment in any other course of study.

Date: _____   Signature: _____

ASSESSMENT:

AREA	GRADE
Clear argument	
Strong support	
Appropriate staging throughout	
Key concepts and terms defined	
Evidence of extensive library research	
Critical analysis	
Full and appropriate in-text referencing	
Full reference list	
Vocabulary (use, register and variety)	
Sentence structure (accuracy and variety)	

General comments (continue on other side if necessary):

_____

_____

_____

Final grade	**Teacher's signature:** _____

Appendix D—IELTS Grid: Preparation tasks for IELTS Academic module

Introduction

The following grids will assist and guide you in acquiring skills and knowledge and help with your IELTS test preparation. The exercises are open–ended in some instances and you, your class mates and teachers must take an active role in preparing and practising the work outlined. In the main grid, the location of each task in the body of this book is given and each skill which will be enhanced is explained, then the relevant IELTS test section is pointed out, followed by instructions for using and/or adapting the existing material for IELTS test preparation.

Quick reference table

Starting on the next page, in Unit order, are instructions on how to use activities in the book as preparation for the IELTS test.

Part of IELTS test	Location in the Students' Book
Listening	Unit 7, page 156, Tasks A and B Unit 9, page 204, Task B
Reading	Unit 1, page 28, Task A Unit 3, page 62, Task B Unit 5, page 117 Unit 6, page 152, Tasks A and B
Writing Task 1	Unit 4, page 102, Task A Unit 10, page 240, Tasks A to D
Writing Task 2	Unit 2, page 46, Task E Unit 3, page 75, Tasks A and B
Speaking: all parts	Unit 8, page 178, Tasks A–D
Speaking part 2	Unit 1, page 2, Task A
Speaking part 3	Unit 2, page 36, Task A

Location in course book	Skill	Relevant IELTS test section	Instructions for students
Unit 1, page 2 Speaking Task A: Discussion —Exploration of previous education system	Speaking unsupported for 1 to 2 minutes	IELTS Middle stage of Speaking test	■ After completing Task A: Exploration of previous education system **In pairs:** ■ Ask a partner to time you speaking for two minutes about the following topic: *Talk about the most important thing that you have gained from your education.* Explain: ■ Why it is important ■ When you realised it was important ■ Who made it important for you ■ Is it still the most important thing now? You have one minute to make notes on the topic before you begin speaking. The partner who is timing the task does not speak at all.
Unit 1, page 28 English for the Internet Age: Task A: Identifying stages in an explanation essay and skimming—further practice	Reading Matching headings to paragraphs	IELTS Reading	Follow these instructions under timed, silent conditions. You should spend a maximum of 10 minutes on this activity. ■ The reading passage on pages 29 to 31 has numbered paragraphs. Label them A to I. ■ Create an answer sheet for yourself by writing the numbers 1 to 6 down a page. ■ Read the passage, and choose the most appropriate main idea from the list at part 2 of Task A on page 28 of this book for each of the paragraphs B–I. Write the correct number i to vi next to numbers 1 to 6 on your answer sheet. Question numbers apply to paragraphs as below. 1 Paragraph B 2 Paragraph C 3 Paragraph D & E 4 Paragraph F & G 5 Paragraph H 6 Paragraph I
Unit 2, page 36 Speaking Task A: Orientation discussion	Answering questions and engaging in discussion	IELTS Final stage of Speaking test	■ After the group discussion, work in pairs and ask each other the questions again. This time, try to answer at length and engage in a two-way conversation around the questions. (Spend no more than five minutes discussing.) ■ Speculate on the future of education in your country and compare your education and opportunities to that of your grandparents' day. In other words, how is education different for you than it was for an older generation? ■ Discuss the question: How will technology influence education in the future?

Location in course book	Skill	Relevant IELTS test section	Instructions for students
Unit 2, page 46 Writing and Reading Task E: Writing an argument essay	Essay writing—practise writing 250 words in 40 minutes expressing your point of view and agreeing or disagreeing with a statement	IELTS Academic Writing Task 2	■ Follow the instructions for writing an essay using the statement: *It is to the benefit of society for family units, living together, to include the older generation.' To what extent do you agree or disagree with this statement?* ■ Write 250 words. Time your writing and allow only 40 minutes to complete the task.
Unit 3, page 62 Writing Task B: Reading—example discussion essay Title: *Genetically Modified Foods*	Reading comprehension; ability to select correct words to complete a summary Preparing answers on a different sheet of paper Recognition of different types of questions	IELTS Academic Reading	**In groups:** ■ Create 12 questions using the example essay titled *Genetically modified foods.* The questions must not require answers of over three words. ■ In groups, draw a box and insert the following words: GM, process, consumers, multinational, controversial, scientific, atoms, genes, dangers. Three words aren't used. Complete the summary below by choosing words from the box: The _____ of genetically altering foods means that _____ have been spliced to create _____ food. The method and its ramifications are very _____. One side believes there are _____ involved in the introduction of _____. The other argues there will be benefits to _____. manufactured crops. The other argues there will be benefits to _____. ■ Each group then exchanges their questions. ■ Individually, read the essay again and answer the questions on a separate sheet of paper. Allow only 20 minutes for this task. ■ Write no more than three words for each answer. ■ Be careful not to make mistakes in spelling or grammar.
Unit 3, page 75 Writing 3. Task A and B: Analysing questions —which genre?	Responding to essay questions; recognising genre and instruction cues within questions	IELTS Academic Writing Task 2	Choose an essay question different from the one you have previously chosen from Task A and B. Write 250 words in 40 minutes answering the essay question you chose.

Location in course book	Skill	Relevant IELTS test section	Instructions for students
Unit 4, page 102 Learner Independence and Study Skills: Time management Task A: Examining your use of time	Writing about a table, graph or chart for an educated reader	IELTS Academic Writing Task 1	After completing the weekly timetable from Task A, write 150 words in 20 minutes describing the information in the table. Write for a university lecturer. ■ Compare obvious differences. ■ Mention anything that stands out (for example, if you watch TV 50 hours per week, this should be noted as a large amount of time). If Saturday is very different from Monday, make comparisons and point out what the differences are.
Unit 5, page 117 Grammar: Tense Review: Perfect Tenses Text 1: *Narrative of the most extraordinary and distressing shipwreck of the whaleship Essex,* by Captain Owen Chase, 1821		IELTS Academic Reading section 1	■ Text 1 has seven paragraphs. Label them A–G. ■ Create an answer sheet for yourself by writing the numbers 1–8 down the page. ■ Now answer the question: Which paragraph contains the following information? Write the correct letter from A–G next to 1–8 on your answer sheet. NB You may use any letter more than once. **1** The Captain makes a decision that every man must look after themselves **2** The whale has damaged the ship beyond repair by striking it on the windward side **3** The Captain tries to avoid the ship being hit by the whale **4** The whale hits the ship and swims off **5** The Captain first sees a huge whale **6** A whale strikes the boat after being harpooned **7** The whaleship Essex was captained by a man named Pollard **8** The crew realizes that they are going to be hit by the whale a second time Spend only 10 minutes on Questions 1–8.

Location in course book	Skill	Relevant IELTS test section	Instructions for students
Unit 6, page 152 Reading Title: *Waste disposal in Asia* Use the questions from Tasks A and B	Creating and answering different question types around a reading passage	IELTS Academic Reading	You need to consider the following question types: Type A: Read the statements below. Decide whether each statement agrees with the views of the writer (Yes), disagrees with the views of the writer (No), or represents a view which isn't given in the passage—not given (NG). Type B: Read the statements below. Decide whether each is true or false, from the information in the text. **In groups:** Using your knowledge of the passage from Task A: Skimming race and Task B: Scanning, re-work the questions and answers into the question types above and add some of your own. Create 10 True or False questions. Create 10 Yes, No or Not Given questions. ■ Exchange questions and write your answers on a separate sheet of paper.

Unit 7, page 156
 	
Listening and Speaking 1
Tasks A and B:
Academic requests and replies 2
Recording number 10
	Listening and matching content to ideas
	
	Restricting answers to four words
	
	Understanding gist of information given
		IELTS
		Listening test
		—All sections
			You must listen to the recording once only.
			
			■ Complete Task A: Listening for purpose.
			■ Complete Task B: Understanding replies (five conversations).
			■ Use no more than four words and/or a number for your answers.
			
			After listening, choose the correct letter A, B or C:
			
			1 In a personal emergencies a student may
			  A quit university and re-apply
			  B request leave of absence
			  C request emergency assistance
			
			2 Special dispensation in exams for students is
			  A possible by request **B** not possible without a fee **C** possible for a broken arm
			
			3 Re-marking of an exam is
			  A always possible **B** never possible **C** sometimes possible

Location in course book	Skill	Relevant IELTS test section	Instructions for students
Unit 8, page 178 Reading and Writing Task A–D: Compare and contrast essays Title: *Economics and Governments: who calls the shots?*	Speaking Extending range of discourse markers Pronunciation Improving fluency and ability to paraphrase Expressing opinions	IELTS All stages of Speaking Test	Complete Tasks A to D from Unit 8, pages 178–181, as preparation for the tasks below. **In pairs:** ■ Ask each other the questions which follow the directions below. ■ The student listening to the answers corrects everything they hear which needs correction. When speaking: ■ Is your partner using comparison words? ■ Is their pronunciation clear? ■ Are they speaking fluently without too much hesitation or slowness? ■ Can you hear any grammar errors? Questions: **1** Now that you have read the reading *Economics and Governments: who calls the shots?* compare one government policy in your country to that of any of the countries mentioned. **2** Do you agree with the author that economics controls governments? Why or why not? **3** Paraphrase and further explain the argument around deforestation in Indonesia, Zaire, Peru and Colombia. **4** What is your opinion concerning the world bank and the IMF?
Unit 9, page 204 Listening, Speaking and Critical Thinking Task B: Listening for main ideas	Listening Selecting main ideas	IELTS Stage 2 Listening Test	Listen to Recording number 13 about saving languages. ■ Complete Task B: select four main ideas from the list A to G in the Students' Book.
Unit 10, page 240 Writing and Reading Tasks A–D: Interpreting and describing information from charts and graphs		IELTS Academic Writing Task 1	Complete Tasks A to D from Unit 10, pages 240–244, then: ■ Using the bar chart in Fig 10.1, p 240, write 150 words describing the information found in the chart. Write for a university lecturer. ■ Take no more than 20 minutes to complete the writing.

References

BBC (2001) Secondary Schools, BBC News.
http://news.bbc.co.uk/hi/english/education/uk_systems/newsid_115000/115872.stm
(6 May 2002).

Billington R & Stanford P (1988) *Child Workers Around the World*. London: Fount.

Brown, K (1999) *Developing Critical Literacy*. Sydney: Macquarie University (NCELTR).

Burns, RB (1994) *Introduction to Research Methods*. Melbourne: Longman Cheshire, p 2.

Butt, D, Fahey, R, Feez, S, Spinks S, & Yallop, C (2000) *Using Functional Grammar: An Explorer's Guide* (2nd ed). Sydney: Macquarie University (NCELTR).

Buzan, T (1995) *Use your head* (4th Ed). London: BBC Books.

Campbell, C (1997) *The coming oil crisis*. Brentwood, Essex: Multi-science Publishing.

Columbia University Press (1998) Basic CGOS Style *About the Columbia Guide to Online Style*. http://www.columbia.edu/cu/cup/cgos/idx_basic.html

Commonwealth of Australia (2002) Australian way of studying, *Study in Australia*. http://studyinaustralia.gov.au/Contents/WhatToStudy/AustStudy.html (21 April 2002).

Cox, K (1994) 'Tertiary Level Writing by Magic—Presto! Nominalisation'. *EA Journal* 12/1, Autumn 1994.

Cox, K & Eyre, J (1999) 'A Question of Correction'. *English Teaching Professional* 12.

Cox, K (2000) *Changing Cultures, Changing English*. Paper presented at the 13th EA Educational Conference, Fremantle.

Crystal, D (1997) *English as a Global Language*. Cambridge: Cambridge University Press.

Crystal, D (2000) *Language Death*. Cambridge: Cambridge University Press.

Derewianka, B (1990) *Exploring How Texts Work*. Sydney: Primary English Teaching Association.

DETYA (2000) Australia Country Education Profile, 3rd Edition On-line. Canberra: DETYA. http://www.detya.gov.au/noosr/cep/australia/index.htm (21 April 2002).

Fairclough, N (1992) *Discourse and Social Change*. Cambridge: Polity Press.

Feez, S (1998) *Text Based Syllabus Design*. Sydney: Macquarie University (NCELTR).

Fischer, S (2001) Asia and the IMF: Remarks at the Institute of Policy Studies. *IMF News*. http://www.imf.org/external/np/speeches/2001/060101.htm

Fulbright Commission (2001) *School Education in the USA*. http://www.fullbright.com.uk/eas/school/school.htm (12 May 2002).

George, S. (1990) *A Fate Worse than Debt*. London: Penguin.

Ghuma, K (2001) 'It's Not Just Watcha Say'. *IATEFL Issues* 161: 11–12.

Gibran, K (1990) *Spiritual Sayings of Kahlil Gibran*. A Ferris (ed and translator), New York: Carol.

Halliday, MAK & Hasan R (1989) *Language, Context and Text: Aspects of Language in a Social-Semiotic Perspective*. Melbourne: Deakin University Press.

Halliday, MAK (1985) *An Introduction to Systemic Functional Grammar*. London: Edward Arnold.

Harmer, J (1991) *The Practice of English Language Teaching* (2nd ed). Essex: Longman.

Haycraft, J (1986) *An Introduction to English Language Teaching* (revised impression ed.). Harlow: Longman.

Hoey, M (1997) *How Can Text Analysis Help Us Teach Reading?* Paper presented at the IATEFL conference, Brighton, England April 1997.

Janks, H (1993) *Language, Identity and Power.* Johannesburg: Hodder & Stoughton.

Kaplan, RB (1966) 'Cultural Thought Patterns in Inter-Cultural Education'. *Language Learning* 16: 1–20.

Kaplan, RB (1993) 'TESOL and applied linguistics in North America'. In S Silberstein (ed) *State of the art TESOL essays*. Alexandria, VA: TESOL Inc.

Kenworthy, J (1987) *Teaching English Pronunciation*. Essex: Longman.

King, S (2000) *On Writing, A Memoir of the Craft*. London: Hodder and Stoughton.

Kramsch, C (1998) *Language and Culture*. Oxford: Oxford University Press.

Kress, G. (1993) Genre as social process in The powers of Literacy (eds) Cope, B and Kalantzis, M. Falmer Press, London p 36.

Lambert, T & Barreto, L (2001) *UTS Students' Association Postgraduate Handbook 2001*. Sydney: UTS Students' Association.

Larsen-Freeman, D (2000) *Techniques and Principles in Language Teaching*. Oxford: Oxford University Press.

Lewis, M (1993) *The Lexical Approach: The State of ELT and a Way Forward*. Hove: Language Teaching Publications.

Lewis, M (1997) *Implementing the Lexical Approach: Putting Theory into Practice*. Hove: Language Teaching Publications.

McCarthy, M (1990) *Vocabulary*. Oxford: Oxford University Press.

Macquarie Dictionary 2nd ed. (1991) Macquarie Library.

Malouf, D (2002). 'A great escape'. *The Age*, 31 August.

Martin, JR (1991) 'Nominalisation in science and humanities: Distilling knowledge and scaffolding text'. In Ventola E (ed), *Functional and systematic linguistics: approaches and uses*. Berlin; New York: Mouton de Gruyter.

Modjeska, D (2002) 'The fictional present', *The Age*, 31 August.

Moore, M (2001) *Stupid White Men … and other sorry excuses for the state of the nation*. New York: Harper Collins, p 204.

Nunan, D (1991) 'An Empirically Based Methodology for the Nineties'. In Arivan, S (ed) *Language Teaching Methodology for the Nineties*. RELC, p 78.

Nunan, D (1992) *Research Methods in Language Learning*. Cambridge: Cambridge University Press.

Oshima, A & Hogue A (1991) *Writing Academic English* (2nd ed). California: Addison-Wesley.

Oxford University Press (2000) *Oxford Advanced Learner's Dictionary* (6th ed). Oxford: Oxford University Press.

Phillipson, R (1992) Lingustic Imperialisation. Oxford: Oxford University Press.

Pilger, J (1989) *A Secret Country.* London: Vintage Press.

Powers, J (1997) *Ancient Greek Marriage.* MA thesis, Tufts University. http://www.pogodesigns.com/JP/weddings/greekwed.html (25th November 2002)

Rubin, J (1994) 'Review of Second Language Listening Comprehension Research', *The Modern Language Journal 78/ii*: 199–221.

Saunders, G (1988) *Bilingual Children: Guidance for the Family.* Clevedon: Multilingual Matters.

Schlosser, E (2001) *Fast Food Nation: What the All-American Meal is Doing to the World.* London: Penguin.

SIL International (2001) Languages of Vanuatu. *Ethnologue: Languages of the World (14th ed).* http://www.ethnologue.com/show_country.asp?name=Vanuatu (11 August 2002).

South Asian Voice (2000) Unrestricted globalisation—boon or hazard? *South Asian Voice: Views from South Asia.* http://members.tripod.com/~India_Resource/globalization.html (17 September, 2002)

Superville, D (2001) Many world languages on brink of extinction, UN says. Global Policy. www.globalpolicy.org/globaliz/cultural/2001/0619language.htm (11 August 2002).

Swan, M & Smith B (eds). (2001) *Learner English: A Teacher's Guide to Interference and Other Problems* (2nd ed). Cambridge: Cambridge University Press.

The US-UK Fulbright Commission (1999) School Education in the US. *The US-UK Fulbright Commission.* http://www.fulbright.co.uk/eas/school/school.html (12 May 2002).

Underhill, A (1994) *Sound Foundations.* Oxford: Heinemann.

UNEP (2000) *Global Environmental Outlook 2000: UNEP's Millennium Report on the Environment.* London: Earthscan Publications.

UTS Equity & Diversity Unit (no date given) Preventing discrimination and harassment. *UTS Equity & Diversity Unit.* http://www.uts.edu.au/div/eounit/unit/discrim.html (25 August 2002).

Weller, C Scott RE & Hersh A (2001) The unremarkable record of liberalised trade after 20 years of global economic deregulation, poverty and inequality are as pervasive as ever. *EPI Briefing Paper* (October 2001) http://epinet.org/briefingpapers/sept01inequality.html

Wolpert, E. (1984). *Understanding Research in Education - an introductory guide to critical reading.* USA: Kendall/Hunt, p 113.

index